WBI DEVELOPMENT STUDIES

Diaspora Networks and the International Migration of Skills

How Countries Can Draw on Their Talent Abroad

Edited by
Yevgeny Kuznetsov

The World Bank
Washington, DC

© 2006 The International Bank for Reconstruction and Development / The World Bank
1818 H Street NW
Washington DC 20433
Telephone: 202-473-1000
Internet: www.worldbank.org
E-mail: feedback@worldbank.org

1 2 3 4 5 09 08 07 06

This volume is a product of the staff of the International Bank for Reconstruction and Development / The World Bank. The findings, interpretations, and conclusions expressed in this volume do not necessarily reflect the views of the Executive Directors of The World Bank or the governments they represent.

The World Bank does not guarantee the accuracy of the data included in this work. The boundaries, colors, denominations, and other information shown on any map in this work do not imply any judgement on the part of The World Bank concerning the legal status of any territory or the endorsement or acceptance of such boundaries.

Rights and Permissions

The material in this publication is copyrighted. Copying and/or transmitting portions or all of this work without permission may be a violation of applicable law. The International Bank for Reconstruction and Development / The World Bank encourages dissemination of its work and will normally grant permission to reproduce portions of the work promptly.

For permission to photocopy or reprint any part of this work, please send a request with complete information to the Copyright Clearance Center Inc., 222 Rosewood Drive, Danvers, MA 01923, USA; telephone: 978-750-8400; fax: 978-750-4470; Internet: www.copyright.com.

All other queries on rights and licenses, including subsidiary rights, should be addressed to the Office of the Publisher, The World Bank, 1818 H Street NW, Washington, DC 20433, USA; fax: 202-522-2422; e-mail: pubrights@worldbank.org.

ISBN-10: 0-8213-6647-5
ISBN-13: 978-0-8213-6647-9
e-ISBN: 0-8213-6648-3
DOI: 10.1596/978-0-8213-6647-9

Library of Congress Cataloging-in-Publication Data

Diaspora networks and the international migration of skills : how countries can draw on their talent abroad / edited by Yevgeny Kuznetsov.
    p. cm. -- (WBI development studies)
 Includes bibliographical references and index.
 ISBN-13: 978-0-8213-6647-9
 ISBN-10: 0-8213-6647-5
 1. Alien labor. 2. Human capital. 3. Brain drain. 4. Employment in foreign countries. 5. Emigration and immigration--Economic aspects. I. Kuznetsov, Yevgeny (Yevgeny N.), 1964– II. Series.
 HD6300.D53 2006
 331.6'2--dc22
                          2006046424

Contents

Foreword

International migration is an increasingly important development issue. Transition to a knowledge-based economy creates a more integrated market for skills and puts a premium on talent. With talent and skills becoming the most precious assets of the world economy, the brain drain from the developing world is intensifying. The emergence of far-flung diasporas is a consequence of the global hunt for the best and brightest from the developing world. How to leverage the expertise and knowledge of diasporas for the benefit of sending countries is the main issue this book discusses.

For the World Bank Institute, publication of this book marks the beginning of a new agenda of promoting policy reform and institutional innovation in collaboration with diaspora members. Actors in diaspora networks can be crucial bridges between global state-of-the-art in policy, technological, and managerial expertise and local conditions in their home countries. Public sector reform, innovations in education and social services, and promotion of a knowledge-based private sector are just a few areas where diaspora members could team up with developing countries' governments and external funding agencies to promote a shared agenda of poverty reduction. This book describes emerging best practice of how this could be done.

Frannie A. Léautier
Vice President
World Bank Institute

Contributors

Alok Aggarwal is the co-founder and chair of Evalueserve. Prior to starting Evalueserve, he was the director of emerging business opportunities for IBM Research Division Worldwide. In July 1997, he set up the IBM India Research Laboratory inside the Indian Institute of Technology, Delhi.

Richard Devane, a graduate of Harvard Business School, is an investment and business consultant who has recently focused on projects in the area of diaspora mobilization. He is a former partner at the international consulting firm Bain & Company and is now developing a program with the Aspen Institute to support diaspora community leaders with homeland development.

David Ellerman spent 10 years at the World Bank highlighted by three years as adviser and speechwriter for Chief Economist Joseph Stiglitz. He is currently a visiting scholar at the University of California at Riverside, and in 2005 published a book, *Helping People Help Themselves*, that discusses an indirect and autonomy-respecting approach toward development assistance.

Lev M. Freinkman is a senior economist at the World Bank, where he has worked primarily on economies in transition since 1992. In 1998–2002 he was a country economist working on Armenia and led various Bank teams that were involved in developing several credits for the Armenian government, as well as in preparing reports on the country's reform policies.

Yevgeny Kuznetsov is a senior economist with the World Bank's Knowledge for Development Program. Trained as a mathematical economist, he is a specialist in innovation policies and institutions. For the past 10 years, he has held various operational positions at the World Bank. Prior to joining the Bank, he was with the Brookings Institution.

Mairi MacRae is currently country head for China with Scottish Development International, the International arm of Scotland's economic development agency. Previously she was responsible for developing and managing the globalscot initiative, an 850-strong network of Scots and those with an affinity for Scotland who are actively engaged in Scotland's economic development efforts.

Jonathan Marks, a South African national, teaches at the University of Cape Town's Graduate School of Business. His teaching and research interests include entrepreneurship, issues of international migration, and mechanisms for leveraging diaspora networks for the benefit of countries of origin.

Victoria Anahí Minoian, an Argentinean national, is a public information specialist at the World Bank. Born and raised in Buenos Aires, she considers herself a member of two diasporas: the Argentinean diaspora and the Armenian diaspora.

Adolfo Nemirovsky has been an independent consultant since 2002 working with early-stage technology companies and with business development organizations from Israel, the United States, and Latin American countries. Previously he launched two semiconductor companies, was a research associate at the University of Chicago, and taught in Brazil.

Abhishek Pandey, an Indian national, is a specialist in knowledge process outsourcing. At the time of writing the India chapter, he was working for the EvalueServe office in India.

Charles Sabel is a professor of law and social science at the Columbia Law School. After receiving his doctorate in government from Harvard University in 1978, he joined the faculty of the Massachusetts Institute of Technology, where he became the Ford international professor of social science in 1990. His recent research focuses on experimentalist regimes in the areas of education, labor, and environmental reform.

Federico Torres, at the time of writing the chapter on Mexico, was a consultant specializing in economic development and migration issues. He was involved in projects with the World Bank, the InterAmerican Development Bank, and the United Nations. He passed away in 2002.

Gabriel Yoguel is a professor of technology and innovation at General Sarmiento National University in Buenos Aires. He coordinates several major research programs on innovation and learning processes in firms and on production networks, innovation and employment, focusing on Argentina, Brazil, Mexico, and other Latin American countries.

Fernando Chaparro, a sociologist and economist, is director general of the Digital Colombia Foundation. From 1994 to 1998, he was director general of COLCIENCIAS, a Colombian government agency responsible for science and technology. Mr. Chaparro holds a Ph.D in industrial sociology from Princeton University.

Hernan Jaramilo is dean of economics and a faculty member at Rosario University in Bogota, Colombia. He is an economist who specializes in the economics of science and technology and industrial restructuring.

Vladimir Quintero is a specialist in technology policy and industrial restructuring. He has more than 30 years of professional experience and lives in Barranquilla, Colombia.

Martin Wight is the senior strategy manager with Scottish Enterprise, Scotland's national economic development agency. An economist by training, he joined Scottish Enterprise in 1998 after leading Edinburgh City Council's economic strategy team. His current policy and research interests include Scotland's economic geography, the role of cities, city regions and city collaboration and the factors influencing talent attraction.

Preface

International mobility of talent and its most visible manifestation, brain drain (usually defined as the migration of human capital from less to more developed economies), is an important and hotly debated development issue. This volume examines how expatriate talent can make a contribution to the development of their countries of origin. The focus is on self-organized groups of expatriates: diaspora networks. Rather than viewing a diaspora as a relatively homogeneous, all-inclusive group of people from a particular country, this book stresses the heterogeneity and diversity of such networks.

The defining characteristic of networks of expatriate professionals (diaspora networks) is that they pertain to talent, be it technical, managerial, or creative. Talent is an elusive category, but a powerful one. This book defines talent as individuals of high impact. That impact can be in science and technology, business, culture, and politics.

This book examines the interaction of expatriate talent and institutions in expatriates' countries of origin in an attempt to make the potential of diasporas and their knowledge a reality. The critical importance of institutions in the home country is a central theme. However large and entrepreneurial networks of diaspora professionals are, home country institutions that are interested in and capable of implementing joint projects with expatriates are critical. The quality of these institutions varies widely: some are extremely capable; others are not. Diaspora networks link better-performing segments of home country institutions with forward-looking segments of the diaspora. The latter have the potential to generate a virtuous cycle that develops both home country institutions and diaspora networks. The question of how to trigger and sustain such a virtuous cycle that generates benefits for all parties involved—sending countries, receiving countries, and expatriates themselves—is a central concern of this book.

This is a book for practitioners by practitioners. The main audience is policy makers in developing countries who are developing programs and interventions to design effective diaspora networks ands transform brain drain into brain gain. The focus is on the "how to" details of such interventions. The book will also be of interest to academics working on the migration of skills and development economics. Most of the chapters are written by individuals with direct knowledge of diaspora interventions or with diaspora experience. The wealth of such practical knowledge tends to remain tacit, therefore putting this knowledge in a coherent form is a major contribution of this book.

The book evolved as its editor and one of the co-authors, Lev Freinkman, became involved in practical projects to tap the potential of diasporas' talent. Starting with initial projects in El Salvador, they became involved in pilot projects and initiatives in countries as diverse as Argentina, Armenia, Chile, Mexico, and South Africa. In the process, they learned a good deal about how to leverage expatriate talent for the benefit of expatriates' countries of origin.

The analysis is structured in four parts. Part I, on analytical and policy issues, includes three chapters. Chapter 1, by Yevgeny Kuznetsov and Charles Sabel, provides an analytical overview of the main themes and introduces the book's key concepts. Decision makers pressed for time can read this chapter along with the concluding chapter, chapter 11, which summarizes policy recommendations.

Chapter 2, by David Ellerman, overviews the rapidly growing literature on the migration of skills, diasporas, and development and discusses virtuous and vicious cycles of development in the era of the global mobility of skills. It also explains why flows of remittances are unlikely to generate economic development, although they are certain to reduce poverty.

Chapter 3, by Richard Devane, surveys practical issues associated with mobilizing the expertise and financial resources of expatriates for the benefit of the home country. It highlights the role of diaspora networks in China, India, Israel, and Taiwan (China). The chapter shows how a few influential members of diasporas in decision-making positions in multinational companies can put their home countries on the map of major investment decisions of these firms.

Part II examines mature diaspora networks: large and sophisticated diasporas that have been in the making for decades. Chapter 4, by Abhishek Pandey, Alok Aggarwal, Richard Devane, and Yevgeny Kuznetsov, examines the evolution of the Indian diaspora and its contribution to India's development. It describes the evolution of diaspora networks and their members. The achievement of high professional status by a large number of Indian expatriates, which occurred in the 1980s and 1990s, seems to be have been a precondition for them to contribute to India's development.

Chapter 5, by Federico Torres and Yevgeny Kuznetsov, examines the contributions of low-skilled migrants from Mexico. The chapter discusses the evolution of collective action by the diaspora, an important theme of this book. Migrants' clubs in the United States initially emerged to protect the rights of Mexican migrants. Over time they developed significant social capital, which allowed them to develop innovative programs for collective remittances. This chapter on low-skilled migrants provides a contrast with the rest of the chapters, which all focus on diasporas of highly skilled migrants. Migrants' clubs and collective remittances are quite sophisticated institutions, but even these institutions seem to have a limited impact on local development in Mexico. This is a cautionary note for the current hype equating remittances with development. Sadly, Federico Torres passed away in 2002. Yevgeny Kuznetsov updated and added to this chapter.

Chapter 6, by Victoria Anahí Minoian and Lev M. Freinkman, focuses on the Armenian diaspora, whose wealth dwarfs that of Armenia itself. Although philanthropic contributions are massive, private investments by the diaspora are scant. The chapter describes diaspora investments and examines the conditions necessary to scale them up and make them demonstration cases for other investors.

Part III examines emerging networks of relatively small diasporas of highly skilled expatriates. Chapter 7, by Yevgeny Kuznetsov, Adolfo Nemirovsky, and Gabriel Yoguel, tells the fascinating story of Argentina's diaspora. It illustrates how the diaspora functions as a mirror of national development. Every one of Argentina's many political and economic crises resulted in the emigration of skills. The Argentine diaspora is relatively small, but it is highly entrepreneurial and highly motivated to help Argentina. This motivation has not translated into tangible projects, however, because Argentine institutions are weak. The individual ambitions of politicians and turf battles between government agencies have consistently blocked efforts to involve the diaspora in projects.

Chapter 8, by Jonathan Marks, on South Africa provides a contrasting story. South African institutions are relatively strong, but diaspora networks are too young to think seriously about investing in the home country (to say nothing about returning home). The chapter provides empirical evidence of diaspora motivation to get involved in the home country and describes innovative programs for transforming this motivation into tangible outcomes.

Chapter 9, by Fernando Chaparro, Hernán Jaramillo, and Vladimir Quintero, tells the story of the Network of Colombian Researchers Abroad, a network of Colombian graduate students abroad. The network showed promise because of the leadership of the head of the Colombian science and technology agency and support for scholarships abroad provided by a loan from the Inter-American Development Bank. Once the champion left his position and support for graduate scholarships dried up because of the budgetary crisis, the network ceased to be the vibrant network it once was. This is a story of institutional fragility. More robust institutional foundations are necessary to sustain this virtuous cycle. The chapter, written by the founders and advisers of the Network of Colombian Researchers Abroad, provides a critical assessment of the demise of the network and draws lessons for the future.

Part IV focuses on policy and institutional implications. Chapter 10, by Mairi MacRae, with Martin Wight, describes globalscot, a highly innovative and successful program to organize a brain circulation network of influential Scots abroad. It describes how a successful program can be constructed. The devil is said to be in the details, and the chapter provides those details with an engaging flow of argument and many telling examples.

The last chapter, by Yevgeny Kuznetsov, pulls the strands together by identifying the features of successful programs and interventions to organize effective diaspora networks. While home country institutions remain the key to success, key individuals in positions of influence can sometimes remedy institutional weaknesses. The chapter provides a taxonomy of different types of diaspora networks and relevant interventions for triggering such networks. It also touches on a broader issue of economic development by noting that diaspora networks are just one example of search networks. The "new industrial policy" is a new generation of interventions that addresses economic development problems without picking winners based on a diversity of search networks.

Yevgeny Kuznetsov

Acknowledgments

This book benefited from the talent of many individuals and diasporas in many countries. I would like to thank the U.K. Department for International Development's Knowledge and Skills Fund, and the World Bank President's Contingency Fund for generously supporting the preparation of the book and the pilot initiatives on which it is based.

I am most grateful to Elkyn Chaparro for his help in fermenting ideas about diasporas before such ideas were fashionable, and for providing inspiration at the embryonic stages of the book. Thanks also to Carl Dahlman, founder and former manager of the World Bank Institute's Knowledge for Development program and to Phil Karp for their advice and support. Finally, I would like to acknowledge Faythe Agnes Calandra, John Didier, and Alexey Volynets of the World Bank Institute for their help in the publishing process, and Alice Faintich for her able editorial assistance.

Part I
Analytical Framework
and Major Policy Issues

1

International Migration of Talent, Diaspora Networks, and Development: Overview of Main Issues

Yevgeny Kuznetsov and Charles Sabel

Actors in developing economies must have the capacity to acquire new knowledge—to learn new ways of doing things—if they are to compete in the world economy.[1] Learning, in turn, supposes and contributes to the ability to search out and usefully recombine scattered information about production methods, markets, and resources. Because development depends on learning and learning depends on searching, development almost invariably depends on linking the domestic economy to the larger, outside world, because even the strongest economies quickly rediscover (if they have ever forgotten) that they cannot generate all state-of-the-art ideas in isolation.

International mobility of talent and its most visible manifestation, brain drain (usually defined as the migration of human capital from less to more developed economies), is central for learning and development. This volume takes two key stylized facts about the international mobility of skills as given. First, it accepts that there are large stocks of highly skilled (university educated) expatriates from developing countries in developed countries. Among developing countries in 2000 (the latest year for which data are available), the Philippines had the highest emigration stocks of university-educated expatriates in high-income economies (1,126,260 people), followed by India (1,037,626), Mexico (922,964), and China (816,824) (Ozden and Schiff 2005, p.170).[2] Second, it assumes that the skilled expatriates could be a significant resource for the development of their home countries. As a well-known example, overseas Chinese contributed 70 percent of China's foreign direct investment during 1985–2000. By 1995, 59 percent of the accumulated foreign direct investment in China came from Hong Kong (China) and Macao, with a further 9 percent from Taiwan (China) (World Bank 2005, p. 67).

Expatriates do not need to be investors or make financial contributions to have an impact on their home countries. They can serve as "bridges" by providing access to markets, sources of investment, and expertise. Influential members of diasporas can shape public debate, articulate reform plans, and help implement reforms and new projects. Policy expertise and managerial and marketing knowledge are the most significant resources of diaspora networks. The overarching focus on the

---

[1] Part of this chapter was adapted from Kuznetsov and Sabel (forthcoming).

[2] Note that small countries suffer the most from emigration of highly skilled individuals. More than 85 percent of individuals with a tertiary-level education emigrate from such countries as Grenada, Guyana, and Trinidad and Tobago.

knowledge and policy contributions of expatriates and diaspora networks distinguishes this book from a rapidly growing literature on international migration.

The recent literature emphasizes remittances and their development impact (see World Bank 2005 for a summary of this view; for a perspective that is similar to this book's view and that stresses knowledge and institution building rather than financial flows, see Kapur and McHale 2005). In contrast, we are somewhat skeptical that remittances and other financial transfers by migrants can ever have a significant development impact, although they are certainly an important tool of poverty alleviation.

The Co-Evolution of Diasporas and Developing Economies

Historically, countries' contact with the outside world was often established through skilled migrants and the ethnic or religious communities they founded in the host country. Examples include the contribution of the Huguenots in France; the Jews in Monterrey, Mexico; the Chinese in Indonesia, Malaysia, and the Philippines; and the Indians in East Africa and later the United Kingdom. During much of the 20th century, multinational firms facilitated knowledge transfer by establishing facilities—usually for the manufacture or assembly of mature products—in developing countries, often with the assistance of local elites.

Viewed from this historical perspective, network diasporas are but the latest bridge institutions connecting developing economy insiders, with their risk-mitigating knowledge and connections, to outsiders in command of technical know-how and investment capital. At least for developing economies, the attraction of diaspora networks over immigrant communities and multinational firms is that networks promise to depoliticize the relationship between domestic actors and the foreign actors from whom they learn, transforming a volatile, often irrational, struggle for power into a mutually beneficial economic exchange. Economically powerful ethnic minorities have traditionally been suspected of having greater loyalty to their ethnic community than to the host country and of being tempted to exploit the latter to benefit the former. Powerfully autonomous and often footloose multinational firms are viewed as the agents, even the masters, of economic imperialism rather than as partners in development.

By contrast, the actors in diaspora networks are native sons and daughters. Even if they are wealthy or are connected to wealthy families or important multinationals, they seldom command the resources attributed to economically potent minorities (whose riches, though real enough, are often magnified by envy), and they are not manifestly at the command of the world's largest companies. They are, at least potentially, a connection to the indispensable world of foreign knowledge that can be domesticated and then used to discipline the behavior of ethnic communities and multinationals. That the members of network diasporas are likely to be suspected in their host countries of putting personal gain or ethnic ties above managerial professionalism makes them, from the point of view of the sending country, more pliant and more willing to cooperate on a truly equal footing. Diaspora networks seem to form spontaneously as a result of both the shortcomings and the successes of the meshing of individual and national strategies for economic advancement.

The reality of network diasporas is far more complex and unruly than this juxtaposition of suspicion and spontaneity suggests. Whether diasporas are seen as adjuncts to rather than adversaries of domestic elites depends on how the two groups have interacted historically. Whether, and in what way, diasporas connect domestic economies and the world economy depends on the interaction of changes in global production or supply chain patterns, changes in domestic growth opportunities, and changes in the economic activities and strategies of the diaspora members themselves. Thus diasporas are mirrors of national development, reflecting the migratory pushes of national crises and the pull of the global economy. Network diasporas are not a self-generating, context-free solution to the perennial problem of learning from abroad without being victimized by the foreign master; they co-evolve with the political and economic contexts within which they operate.

Facilitating Serendipity: Institutionalizing Nascent Diaspora Networks

In 1997, Ramón L. García, a Chilean applied geneticist and biotechnology entrepreneur with a doctorate from Iowa State University, contacted Foundation Chile. Foundation Chile is a private-public innovation organization that, among other missions, helps provide the technical infrastructure that allows Chilean agribusinesses to develop domestically viable variants of crops typical of California's Central Valley. García is the chief executive officer of InterLink Biotechnologies, a Princeton, New Jersey, company he co-founded in 1991. Interlink developed a way to identify novel chemical entities derived from microorganisms for use in new pharmaceuticals and enzyme additives for human food, animal feed, and biocontrol agents. It markets its technical expertise to other firms interested in transferring and licensing new biotechnologies.

After jointly reviewing their portfolios of initiatives, Interlink and Foundation Chile founded a new, co-owned company, Biogenetic S.A., to undertake the long-term research and development projects needed to transfer to Chile technologies key to the continuing competitiveness of its rapidly growing agribusiness sector. Without García's extensive knowledge of Chile, advanced U.S. education, exposure to U.S. managerial practices, and experience as an entrepreneur, the new company would have been inconceivable. Biogenetic has successfully developed a technology platform that uses biotechnology to improve grapes and stone fruits, two export crops that are important to the Chilean economy. The company genetically modified grapes to make them resistant to diseases and was instrumental in developing a program for developing pine trees resistant to an important insect pest. It is developing the technology to introduce important quality traits in stone fruits.

The fact that skilled expatriates can create enormous benefits for their countries of origin has been recognized in recent years through the conspicuous contributions that the large, highly skilled, and manifestly prosperous and well-organized Chinese and Indian diasporas have made to their home countries. But García's collaboration with Foundation Chile suggests that diasporas do not need to be large to have an impact: 10 Garcías could transform entire sectors of the economy in relatively small countries such as Armenia or Chile. Moreover, García's collaboration with Foundation Chile suggests that even the sparsely populated, informal diaspora networks linking small home countries with their talent abroad are not without some institutional resources and may prove capable of developing more.

García's collaboration with Foundation Chile was serendipitous. While the story tantalizes and inspires those who search for keys to economic development, it scarcely hints at how to proceed from the happy accidents of the Ramón Garcías in the emerging business diasporas of Chile and other countries to the robust and systematic diaspora involvement exemplified by China and India. Indeed, on closer inspection there seems to be a schism between the demonstrated success of mature diaspora networks in triggering knowledge-intensive activities in their home countries and the disappointing results in promoting diasporas' engagement in the development of their home countries.

This chapter seeks to bridge this divide. It presents a compact framework for understanding the large and related transformations in labor and product markets and in industrial organizations that are reflected in and furthered by the growing role of diasporas of both relatively low-skill workers as well as highly educated professionals. It then analyzes what has worked and what has not in facilitating diaspora networks and extracts some tentative and preliminary policy recommendations, addressed primarily to leaders of business communities and public organizations anxious to learn from and scale up the García case.

To illustrate this co-evolution of network diasporas with their environments and to identify potential obstacles, this chapter describes the development of the mature diasporas of Armenia, China, and India, described in more detail later in the book. All three are large, well organized, and centuries old. The first two have been enormously successful. The success of the Chinese diaspora grew out of—although it is no longer limited to—the traditional investment behavior of emigrant families that made their fortunes overseas. The success of the Indian diaspora is much more closely tied to recent changes in supply chain organization and the emergence of transnational innovation networks than to the investments of fixed capital of India diaspora members in India. Although a decade ago the success of the Armenian diaspora seemed nearly certain, it has failed to contribute substantially to domestic development (at least relative to its potential). The political divisions between the diaspora and the post-Soviet political class in Armenia, combined with the philanthropic generosity of overseas Armenians, thwarted development and buffered domestic actors from the costs of their actions. This experience suggests that the political context requires as much attention as the economic setting.

Following this review, the chapter looks at South Africa's efforts to institutionalize relations with its diaspora. Examination of South Africa's successes and failures suggests how policy makers can address the crucial problems involved in turning an emerging diaspora into a mature institution of economic development by bootstrapping (making a series of incremental steps, each suggested by the lessons learned in the preceding ones).

Diaspora Networks as Search Networks

The global circulation of high-skill and low-skill labor from poor economies to rich ones and back is opening new possibilities for economic development. The changes are most noticeable in the behavior of the most skilled workers. The brain drain pattern of migration long drew many of the most promising students from poor countries to lucrative and challenging careers in developed countries. Today this pattern shows signs of turning into a back and forth movement, or diaspora network, in which talented students still go abroad to continue their studies and work in the developed economies, but then use their own global networks, and especially those of their diasporas, to help build new establishments in their home countries.

There are also signs that emigrants with fewer skills, forced by poverty to go abroad but long confined to dead-end jobs in developed economies, are also finding new career possibilities. Increasingly, the entry-level jobs they take in factory production or the health care sector in host countries demand and teach problem-solving skills that blur the line between management and labor. Whether these new skills can be redeployed back home is an open question. But the changing nature of migrants' work suggests the possibility that these "birds of passage," traditionally in transit between a native land that cannot support them and a rich country that remains alien, may one day form distinctive, medium-skill diaspora networks that complement the diasporas of managers and entrepreneurs.

Behind these developments is the long-term, accelerating decentralization of decision-making responsibility from end-producers in the public and private sectors to their suppliers and the decentralization within public and private establishments from managers to frontline work teams. To take a frequently cited example, recognizing that they cannot possibly remain abreast of all the key technologies involved in making a car, automakers have largely divested themselves of their component-producing capacity. They co-design virtually every subassembly of the vehicle with independent suppliers. Facing analogous limits to their own managerial capacities, public administrations in developed countries routinely outsource the provision of new services to not-for-profit organizations and certain routine functions, such as servicing complaints, to for-profit call centers. This decentralization of production often allows firms to relocate activity in developing countries, creating many of the investment opportunities within reorganizing supply chains that members of the high-skill diaspora networks seize.

The managerial limits that propel the decentralization of production to suppliers also compel a shift from hierarchy to teamwork in end-producers and suppliers alike. As product life cycles shorten from years to months (in consumer electronics, cell phones, and computers, for instance) and quality expectations rise, it is impossible to shift from one production setup to another—and solve the inevitable start-up problems each changeover brings—without the active cooperation of the workers who will be doing the assembly. Organized as production and problem-solving teams, frontline workers are routinely asked to criticize and suggest improvements in the setup of their workplaces, the flow of production, and the provision of support services. They are asked to share in the quintessentially managerial task of co-designing the organization within which they are working. New training programs in problem solving and teamwork help equip them for this task. This entry-level exposure to problem solving and the new forms of training with which it is associated create a bridge between the traditional world of the immigrant worker and the knowledge economy. In doing so, this exposure may open the way to the formation of a medium-skill diaspora.

The decentralization of production to suppliers, as well as the shift from hierarchy to teamwork by end-producers and suppliers, can be viewed as part of a profound change in the principles of organizational design. In traditional organizations—the kind found in mass-production factories and large public bureaucracies—complex operations are accomplished by decomposing them into tasks sufficiently limited to be manageable by actors with "bounded rationality." Hierarchy is the result. But as a rapidly changing world has made the decomposition of tasks too time-consuming and costly to be practicable, organizations have stumbled on an alternative solution. Instead of responding to bounded rationality by simplifying the problems actors face, organizations create the infrastructure that allows actors charged with a task to find other actors—outside the organization as well as within—who are already solving (part of) the problem. Put another way, organizations shift from hierarchies in which subordinates execute their superiors' plans to search networks in which collaborators, through the very process of identifying one another, come to define the tasks they will jointly accomplish. In a world of search networks, changes in labor markets (who works with whom) can easily lead to changes in product markets (what businesses make), and even in industrial organization (how firms are structured internally and connected to one another).

From this point of view, modern diasporas networks, as the García and Foundation Chile anecdote suggests, are just an especially conspicuous (because they are publicly visible) variant of the search networks under rapid construction in firms worldwide. The shift from brain drain to brain circulation marks the shift from a world in which the function of long-range labor markets was to fill jobs with relatively fixed requirements to a world in which filling a job changes not only the definition of what needs to be done but also the setting in which future needs are defined.

The emergence of diasporas as a type of search network—a network that lets members find and collaborate with those who already know what they need to learn—poses new challenges for the articulation of coordinated training and economic development strategies within individual sending and receiving countries and for increased coordination between senders and receivers as distinct but increasingly intricately connected groups. Individual sending countries will presumably want to encourage the formation of diaspora networks by helping high-skill emigrants stay in touch with one another and the home country and by creating individual and corporate incentives for their re-engagement with the domestic economy. A key aspect of increasing the attractiveness of the domestic economy to potential investors will be introducing problem-solving skills in the public school curriculum and in continuing education programs to create a domestic workforce with the skills required by the new wave of decentralizing firms. Broad provision of these skills will also increase the chances that young job seekers who do not find work at home will be able to take advantage of new career possibilities afforded by entry-level jobs abroad.

Receiving countries have reasons of their own to encourage diaspora networks. Obstructing mobility in an epoch of decentralization imposes stay-or-go choices on energetic, ambitious, immigrant elite, potentially spurring the return en masse of high-skill expatriates. Promoting the circulation of high-skill labor from home country to adopted home and back reduces this risk and is therefore almost certainly in the long-term economic interests of the receiving countries. With their aging populations and low birth rates, traditional receiving countries will also likely find it useful to recruit immigrants for low-level jobs in the public service sector and manufacturing. But the blurring of managerial and executory tasks means that foreign entry-level workers—even those familiar with the new problem solving—will need complementary training in "soft" social skills relevant to the host country if they are to use their abilities to good effect.

Ideally, sending and receiving countries will develop these new, complementary programs in concert. The content of the problem-solving training in developing countries should profit from the extensive experience that global firms and host country training systems have already accumulated. Host countries' acculturation programs in soft skills will benefit from ongoing consultation with sending countries about the best ways to address cultural frictions that arise. By the same token, both sending and receiving countries can gain from meshing their efforts to support diaspora networks, and there is likely to be strong pressure from the high-skill members of such networks for them to do so. Both have interests in jointly regulating the working conditions and environmental responsibilities of decentralizing supply chains to prevent protectionist reactions to off-shore ventures by rich countries and local protests against multinational imperialism in poorer ones. Political realities will, of course, often obstruct the realization of potential gains, but an appreciation of the possibilities will help improve outcomes even when ideal solutions are beyond reach.

Juxtaposing High- and Low-Skill Immigration Streams

Global labor migration today can be divided into high-skill and low-skill streams. The superficial differences between the two conceal important common sources, features, and even consequences.

The high-skill stream is made up of diaspora networks. In the past decade, expatriates have come to play a critical and highly visible role in accelerating technology exchange and foreign direct investment in China, India, Israel, and the United States. Some expatriates became pioneer investors before the widespread decentralization of supply chains, and internal decentralization of authority assured major capital markets that these economies had rosy futures. Some of these pioneers had, and continue to have, nonfinancial motives for early-stage participation. Others had, and have, means of mitigating risk unavailable to other investors by virtue of their knowledge of their countries' language, culture, institutions, and counterparts.

The contribution of U.S.–based Indian managers to a spectacular surge in information technology and related services in India is an exemplary win-win situation, in which the migration of highly skilled professionals benefits both the sending and receiving countries. Other countries may be nearing the threshold of repeating the Chinese or Indian experience, in that they have both successful expatriate communities and high-risk economies that scare off mainstream investors, but provide the opportunities from which diaspora networks grow. Still other economies, such as the new members of the European Union and countries in Latin America, are struggling to move to more knowledge-intensive development despite significant foreign direct investment in recent decades. Their hope is that diaspora networks can overcome obstacles to deeper integration by serving as an entry point into new markets. Diaspora networks mesh so well with the architecture of the modern knowledge society that they are coming to be seen as one of its natural building blocks.

In contrast, workers in the low-skill migration stream have no advanced degrees and may not be able to show prospective employers any school-leaving certificate, or indeed any official documentation at all. They are not entrepreneurs, or at least not founders of high-tech firms. They often live in poor, high-crime neighborhoods, and their children are frequently not at home in their parents' culture or in their country of residence. Where diaspora networks seem to have emerged from nowhere to become part of a new, cosmopolitan elite, low-skill immigrants are frequently depicted as unchanging, indeed determined not to change, out of loyalty to the premodern cultures from which they come.

Official and public reaction to the two migratory streams underscores these differences: high-skill talent is welcomed in virtually every country, while most low-skill immigrants are illegal. High-skill professionals provide tangible benefits to the receiving country in terms of new business creation and human capital; unskilled immigrants are perceived as draining the budget for social expenditures and threatening solidarity.

Despite the apparent differences between the two streams, there are common features that do not figure in public discussion. First, the acquisition and development of skills is crucial to both streams. This is obvious in the case of the recent Indian with a doctorate who emigrates to the United States, but it is also true of the secondary school graduate from Mali who emigrates to take a cleaning job in a nursing home in France. Given the paucity of its current development possibilities, Mali is likely to have a comparative advantage in the production of such human capital, and as the health system crisis revealed by the European heat wave in the summer of 2003 showed, the need for the kinds of skills such workers offer is high in advanced countries. Put another way, many so-called low-skill migrants are low skilled only in comparison to certified professionals. They are far from unskilled compared with the bulk of the population in their country of origin, and they have skills that are in demand in the host country. Managerial skills are a case in point. After working for several years in Japan, Luis Miyashiro, a Peruvian national, came to Lima and founded Norkys, a chain of chicken restaurants. The chain, the first of its kind in an Andean country, combined Western standards of cleanliness and efficiency with the familiar corner food-stand concept common in Latin America. The idea, expertise, and initial capital needed to establish and manage the chain came from Japan.

Second, both migratory streams are being redirected and transformed by profound and pervasive economic restructuring that creates important opportunities and entry points. For skilled workers, the global restructuring of supply chains is turning brain drain into brain circulation, creating or strengthening diaspora networks in the process. In the case of the unskilled and illegal, the restructuring of public administrations that provide key social services, together with the restructuring of shop-floor work, is beginning to create career opportunities where earlier generations in similar positions faced dead ends. This is not to romanticize entry-level work in the new economy, but there is at least anecdotal evidence that even hamburger-flipping jobs now often lead somewhere and that public sector restructuring—just now coming to public notice—will accelerate this tendency.

Third, in both migration streams, social networks emerge as naturally occurring or spontaneous solutions to complex coordination problems—like manna, they fall from the sky—allowing emigrants to match themselves to jobs or entrepreneurial possibilities. In connecting emigrants to the world, these social networks create new possibilities for policy makers to learn from and with key social actors how to redirect institutions and incentives to meet emerging needs.

Much labor market theory in the late 20th century focused on industrial jobs. It was common, perhaps standard, to treat migration between countries as concerning low-skill workers and to treat skill acquisition as occurring through learning on the job within a large, hierarchically organized corporation. Given the organization of production in such firms, most learning was plant or firm specific. It followed from the decomposition of large projects, such as the design and production of a car, into small, linked tasks, and the fact that the machines needed for any step were highly specialized and tightly matched in specifications to the machines that produced their inputs and the machines that used their outputs. Machines designed to be used only with other machines in such a sequence are referred to as asset specific: they have no value for any other use. By the same logic, the skills needed to operate each machine consisted of the largely tacit knowledge of the peculiarities of each machine in relation to upstream and downstream operations. (The knowledge was almost sure to be largely tacit, because the machines were effectively unique. Formalization, at least in the then current view, was the statement of the general features of some process or situation.) Workers with little or no formal education learned these skills by progressing from machine to machine, acquiring the highly specialized knowledge they needed from more experienced colleagues, not from books. These job sequences are called job ladders.

It was a sign of the importance of tacit knowledge in these job ladders and the economy as a whole that returns to formal education were low. For many workers in the United States, for instance, there was little penalty, in terms of lifetime earnings, for quitting high school or skipping college, because in many cases the skills needed for high-paying jobs could be acquired by an industrial apprenticeship in a factory or firm.

In this world view, migration and skill acquisition were viewed as distinct phenomena. Migrants were presumed, correctly, to be seeking higher incomes and vastly increased possibilities for savings, not new skills, when they went abroad. Their goal was to remit as much as possible to their families at home while working in the receiving country and to return as soon as possible, with as much wealth as possible, to their home countries. They were not interested in investing in skill acquisition, because they were not planning to stay abroad long enough to reap the returns to their investment. Unattractive, low-skill jobs were acceptable, because they paid wages that were extraordinarily high by home country standards. Given these goals, these migrants were birds of passage, living in a no man's land between their home and temporary countries, often circulating back and forth between the two as economic and family circumstances dictated. The guest workers brought to Western European factories in the 1960s and 1970s fit this pattern perfectly, but they had many forbearers from the late 19th century on.

A central problem for these birds of passage was, and remains, the identification of plentiful, geographically concentrated supplies of low-skill jobs over long distances. The jobs had to be plentiful and close together, because being low skilled, and thus undifferentiated, there could be no guarantee than any particular job would prove stable. The potential instability of any one job was compensated for by the availability of others sufficiently close to each other that changing jobs did not require changing homes. Finding such jobs required scanning many possible destinations to determine whether jobs were available there for unskilled immigrants. An efficient way to scan was to rely on a network of relatives, friends, and acquaintances from one's home village who were looking for similar jobs themselves. Members or nodes in this network know little about each other—they have rarely worked or done business together—but they know all that migrants need to know, for the purposes of joint search, about labor market conditions. Links of this kind—rich in information about a particular, thin slice of the world, poor in information about the character and abilities of the network members—are called weak ties. The migration flows that result from a network of weak ties directing migrants from a given origin to follow the news of plentiful, low-skill jobs to a common destination is a migration chain.

A key consequence of the shift to networked, organization-based search networks rather than hierarchy is to "de-specify" machines and skills to make both more general-purpose. Assume that a firm knows in advance that it cannot be sure what products it will be making two years hence or how any of those products will be designed. In this case, it sacrifices some of the efficiency that comes with using a machine that can do only one thing and buys general-purpose machines that can easily be reprogrammed to do many different operations. There is less and less wholly unskilled work, and even the relatively unskilled work is no longer plant specific (think of the general teamworking skills needed by workers in just-in-time factories). A crude but revealing measure of this shift is the rapidly increasing returns to formal education and the corresponding increase in the gap between the lifetime wages of unskilled and skilled workers.

Potential migrants notice this shift. Those with good educational prospects at home go abroad to take advantage of still better opportunities, finding jobs that enable them to learn more than they could at home. Those with fewer opportunities at home start to think about improving their prospects by going abroad, fearing that their long-term employability depends on doing so. Instead of looking for destinations with plentiful unskilled jobs, migrants begin to look for destinations that offer many possibilities for skill acquisition at work or school. As job ladders are transformed into more open, interfirm, and formally skilled labor markets and weak ties among migrants begin to communicate information about learning possibilities, migration chains become open mobility networks, that is, means for discovering where to go to learn how to prosper in the reorganizing economy. High-skill diasporas are a conspicuous example of such networks.

The proliferation of professional associations of diaspora members is evidence of this transition from thin to thick search networks. Associations such as the Association of Doctors of Armenian Origin in the United States or the Association of Engineers from Latin America are thick networks that help members identify opportunities for professional advancement. Mentoring is a central feature of these associations. Perhaps the most successful organization of this kind, Indus Entrepreneurs, was started in 1992 as a conduit for experienced Indians to mentor others and provide a broad forum for networking and learning for its members. Indus Entrepreneurs is an institutionalized search network that helps its members move up their migration chains.

This change now extends beyond migrants with tertiary degrees. Hometown associations of migrants of Mexican origin (of which there are more than 70 in the United States) were started in the 1950s with the primary objective of defending the rights of often illegal labor migrants from Mexico, the vast majority of them unskilled. Hometown associations used to be paragons of institutionalized but thin search networks that identified job opportunities and provided mutual help, including practical ways to live and work as an illegal immigrant. Migrants from Zacatecas, a poor state in central-north Mexico, for instance, have a hometown association in almost every major U.S. city.

With time, and as many migrants became legal and progressed in their migration chains from hamburger flippers to supervisors of hamburger flippers, two things have started to happen. First, an acute shortage of native-speaking supervisors and shop-floor managers has emerged. Migrants from Mexico do not speak fluent English. For this reason alone, they prefer to work for Mexican managers. So significant is the shortage of Spanish-speaking immigrants in certain managerial positions that identifying and training such managers is now a central task of the Association of Latin American Professionals. Migrants' organizations such as Mexico's hometown associations, have contributed to this transformation by introducing mentoring also. For example, they direct their members to appropriate training programs and other job advancement opportunities.

Second, as migrants progress along their migration chain and acquire the self-confidence that comes with personal and professional success, they start thinking about giving to and helping not just their families, but their home communities. Hometown associations from Zacatecas, in collaboration with the state government of Zacatecas, designed and cofinanced a highly successful 3×1 program of investment in community infrastructure (secondary roads, schools, hospitals) in their home communities (see chapter 5). The program is called 3×1, because for every peso the hometown associations put in, state and federal governments each contribute another peso. Although the vast majority of members of hometown associations are not wealthy, the binding constraint for this program of collective remittances has always been contributions from the Mexico government, not the donations of the migrants.

Financial transfers are not the most important aspect of collective remittance; governance and monitoring are. Community infrastructure projects need to be identified, financed, and managed through a network of diverse stakeholders—municipal government, users of the infrastructure, migrants, and others—that previously had little trust in one another. As migrants are contributing their own money, they are highly motivated to make the project succeed, avoiding the decay that often characterizes public works projects. To make these projects work, migrants need to monitor them, both from abroad and through frequent visits to their hometowns.

Studying diaspora networks helps uncover the partial solutions that are working. It helps formalize the networks, rendering them more effective as incubators for new programs and as governance structures for new projects. It also reveals potential win-win dynamics benefiting both sending and receiving countries.

Mature Diasporas: China and India Compared with Armenia

The diasporas of China and India have had a highly beneficial impact on their home countries. In contrast, the wealthy Armenian diaspora has failed to help move the country up global value chains.

China

The story of the post–World War II Chinese diaspora is one of geographic mobility and economic diversification: the construction of a "bamboo network" linking Hong Kong (China), Indonesia, Malaysia, the Philippines, Singapore, Taiwan

(China), and Thailand to one another and to China through meshed webs of family firms operating first in traditional trading and manufacturing, then in high-tech and finance. For many refugees, the years following the Communist victory in 1949 were a time of testing relieved—some would say redeemed—by rags to riches stories. In the conventional telling, frugal, canny traders, often with nothing but the clothes on their back, worked their way up from factory floor to great wealth. Once they laid the foundations of their enterprises in one host country, they diversified and expanded geographically. Just as the House of Rothschild's *pater familias* sent his sons from Frankfurt to Paris, London, and Naples, the overseas Chinese internationalized their businesses, delegating family members to set up firms in other promising locations within what was becoming, from their vantage point, Greater China. The new firms drew on the founder's capital and the founder's rich social connections. But as the opportunities suggested by these connections were only accidentally connected to the founder's original business interests, internationalization typically went hand-in-hand with diversification across areas of business activity. In time, the family firms grew into dynasties, operating a myriad of small and medium firms in many sectors and countries, all under the direct but secretive control of the founding family.

In a vast geographic zone with underdeveloped financial markets and fragile legal institutions, the family and ethnic loyalties of the overseas Chinese—backed up by the credible threat to blacklist anyone who violated the community norms of fair dealing—reduced the cost to this group of organizing complex business transactions. The greater the reach of the bamboo network, the greater, in principle, the competitive advantage. Soon the overseas Chinese held key positions in real estate development, component manufacturing, and construction, sectors that put a premium on the ability to combine trading and productive skills. At the same time, Taiwan (China) was developing a distinctive style of business organization that fused elements of the traditional, small Chinese firm and the Silicon Valley start-up.

With the start of Deng Xiaping's open door policy, in 1978, China turned away from isolation and autarky and welcomed the successful overseas Chinese as investors. The influx from Hong Kong (China) and Taiwan (China) was particularly great because of proximity and historical ties. Multinational firms flocked to the mainland, partly to decentralize existing operations to a low-cost location, partly to participate in the widely anticipated growth of a huge market, and partly because partnering with key members of the Chinese diaspora was often regarded as indispensable to navigating an opaque political environment.

Today traditional lines of business are increasingly being abandoned in favor of the most modern sectors of the economy. Having helped transform China, the Chinese diaspora is now being transformed by the developments it encouraged.

India

The contribution of the Chinese network diaspora to Chinese development started, and was long sustained, by investments in manufacturing. In contrast, the contribution of the Indian diaspora to domestic development began by linking domestic and foreign firms in the service sector. The Chinese experience shows that certain traditional forms of risk-mitigating investment behavior are by no means limited to traditional industries. The Indian experience shows that new models of business organization emerging during the continuing reorganization of supply chains can give rise to new patterns of development, in which economic learning begins through service provision rather than industrial activity, and in which the key investments are in education and training rather than in equipment and plant.

The Indian software industry grew 40 percent a year in the 1990s. Revenues reached $10.2 billion in 2002, $7.7 billion of them from exports (see chapter 4). During the same period, employment grew from 56,000 to 360,000, absorbing most of the 75,000 new information technology graduates India produces every year. The number of software firms more than quadrupled, from 700 to more than 2,800, and the largest firms, such as Wipro and Infosys, are undertaking increasingly complex and valuable projects. India has demonstrated that success in outsourcing low-level business services can be a building block for higher value-added services.

The emergence of the Indian software industry was in some ways a fortunate accident that almost surely cannot be reproduced by other countries. But it was an accident waiting to happen, dependent on structural conditions that can indeed be influenced by policy. The Indian government's emphasis on higher education, especially scientific education, created a surplus of well-trained scientists, engineers, and technicians just when the Internet and telecommunications booms and the year 2000 problem produced a massive need for these professionals in the West. Still more providentially, excess U.S. demand for programmers developed just when a critical number of Indian expatriates who had emigrated to the United States in the 1970s and 1980s had become chief executive officers and senior executives at American technology companies. These executives played a critical role in giving their companies the confidence to outsource work to India. They were also patient sponsors as Indian firms gradually learned how to meet U.S. quality and delivery requirements.

Even with these propitious coincidences, however, Western firms could not have outsourced work extensively to India had the Indian government—unaware that software firms could become major employers and producers of tradable goods—not exempted the industry's largely white-collar workforce from much of the labor regulation that hampers India's traditional manufacturing. Even India's much criticized isolationist policy toward the computer industry proved fortuitous: by the early 1990s, when regulations were relaxed, isolation had weaned an entire generation of programmers from mainframes and forced them to master emerging client server and personal computer standards.

No other country or industry should expect to duplicate India's software luck. But India's experience demonstrates that outsourced business services can make a primary contribution to economic development in the 21st century and that diaspora networks can play a crucial role in establishing long-range collaboration in the supply chain. Growth based on business services eases the burden on developing countries in at least two important ways. First, unlike manufacturing, business services do not require much advanced infrastructure or large capital investments. The minimal requirements are educational: English-speaking workers with various technical proficiencies. Most developing countries have, or can be expected to develop, such human resources. Second, as a new industry in developing countries, business services face neither entrenched domestic competitors (with, perhaps, privileged access to government officials who set the rules of competition) nor trade unions (allied, perhaps, with ministries of labor). Traditional forms of regulation, however legitimate in the historical context in which they arose, are therefore unlikely to burden the development of business services in a novel and largely uncharted situation.

The emergence of the high-skill diaspora also reduces the burden on the developing country. The success of the diaspora equips its members with high-level, internationally current managerial skills of a kind that would, at best, be available to tiny elites at home. The apprenticeship that leads to the acquisition of such skills is long, even in the fast-paced sectors of the world economy: the average chief executive officer of a major U.S. corporation took office at age 48 (see chapter 4). Moreover, purely managerial training is complemented by a broader political education, which makes the successful members of the diaspora well suited to bridging the differences between home and host cultures. First-generation immigrants typically try to remain inconspicuous in their host countries. They know that their ethnicity can be a disadvantage, at best merely excluding them from the informal associations through which natives mentor their successors, at worst exposing them to outright discrimination. Reticence born of such concerns is noticeable in the Indian-American community. Individuals with the ambition and prospects of becoming the chief executive officer of a publicly traded company must face and overcome such obstacles. Their success makes them symbols and spokespersons of their community in the host country, and host country recognition gives new weight to their opinions at home.

Despite their different starting positions, the relationship of the Chinese and Indian diasporas to home country development seems to be converging. Recent surveys of their disposition to invest in the home country, discuss possible reforms and business opportunities with national officials, and consider returning permanently themselves do not suggest that the Chinese diaspora is more disposed to investment while the Indian diaspora focuses on relations among firms. Whether or not initial differences are being effaced by continuing development, the two diasporas continue to be alike in that both are manna solutions, win-win outcomes that fell from the sky.

Armenia

When home country elites see development as at least as great a threat as an opportunity, they may hesitate to cooperate with, let alone systematically enlarge, the role of a capable diaspora in the domestic economy. The case of Armenia illustrates the politics of the diaspora and how, perhaps, to mitigate such politics.

At the beginning of the 1990s, after the fall of the former Soviet Union, Armenia seemed well positioned for the transition to a developed, market economy. It was the most educated and most industrial of the Soviet republics. It was considered the Silicon Valley of the Soviet Union, with a major concentration of high-tech industries and developed infrastructure and a workforce known for its tenacity and ability. In addition, Armenia, which had about 3.5 million inhabitants in 1990, expected to be supported by its diaspora, which included more than 1.0 million Armenians living in the United States and at least 1.0 million living in Europe, the Middle East, and Latin America. This diaspora is successful both economically and professionally and is also well organized politically and socially. Another 1.5 million Russian Armenians, traditionally quite influential in the Kremlin, could be counted on as well. The territorial conflict in Karabakh mobilized Armenians worldwide, strengthening ethnic identity and advancing national consolidation. While Armenia also had serious economic disadvantages—its landlocked location, the impact of the 1988 earth-quake, and the loss of markets in the Soviet Union—on balance the country had great potential for development.

In the event, despite—indeed, partly because of—its diaspora, Armenia was unable to realize its potential for rapid growth. The chief obstacle to development was a domestic elite composed, like the elite of many contemporary stalled states, of communist bureaucrats, security service officers, and managers of large state-owned enterprises. This elite did, and does, push aggressively for economic liberal-ization and privatization, but in a way that allows its own members, especially enterprise managers, to capture the major benefits of reforms. While such elites in Armenia and elsewhere welcome economic and political support from the dias-pora, they do not want to see diaspora activists and investors perturb their own privileged position at home. They treat the diaspora primarily as a potential politi-cal and economic competitor.

The upshot is that the Armenian government has been interested largely in receiving humanitarian aid and long-term unrestricted loans, sources of funding it can control much more easily than direct investments. In addition, because state officials benefit so much from imports, which remain the most lucrative business, many oppose an influx of investments that could replace them with domestic pro-duction. Thus the hostility of insiders has thwarted most of the diaspora's attempts to invest.

Compounding the problem, major diaspora organizations have never systemat-ically tried to protect their members from the elite's abuse. The diaspora tends to limit its public criticism out of concern for the government's reputation. It has not attempted to rigorously evaluate the results of the massive assistance it has pro-vided in the past decade. For this diaspora, like others in similar situations, the act of giving seems more important than the actual effect. While the regime in Yerevan has been heavily dependent on the diaspora's support, the diaspora did not use this reliance to secure a more active role in Armenia's development process. Just the opposite: the diaspora gave unconditional financial and political support to a regime that has been blocking the diaspora's attempts to expand productive invest-ments. The diaspora's support relieves pressure on the domestic elite, thereby undermining demand for further reforms, especially for improvements in the busi-ness environment. The ruling elite gets additional resources for survival that pro-vide a breathing space for delaying necessary reforms despite extreme poverty and emigration of the most skilled.

The principal lesson of the Armenian experience is that absent extensive knowl-edge of the depth and direction of domestic reform, massive assistance by the dias-pora is not sustainable unless complemented by an active business support and investment program. By itself, assistance fuels emigration and the concentration of economic power and delays resolution of the most important challenges of devel-opment. This type of support is manna gone sour, even turned poisonous.

The Experience of an Emerging Diaspora: The Case of South Africa

Skilled South Africans began emigrating in large numbers before the end of apartheid and the turn to democracy in 1994. The data do not permit an accurate estimate of the skills lost, as the South African Department of Home Affairs and Sta-tistics South Africa take into account only emigrants who report themselves as such. The actual number of emigrants could be as much as three times official figures. Nonetheless, it is widely agreed that skilled workers continue to leave South Africa. Fully two-thirds of workers with the potential to emigrate have considered doing so, and the highly skilled—of all races—are most likely to be drawn abroad (see chapter 8).

As South Africa has struggled to integrate itself into the world economy while struggling with the AIDS/HIV pandemic, crime, and sharp fluctuations in the rand-dollar exchange rate, enhancing relations with the diaspora has become a salient concern. To that end, South Africa has initiated two diaspora networks, one encouraging direct collaboration and other transactions among members, the other encouraging the formation of mentoring relations between members already active in international markets and others aiming to become active. Together these networks suggest the range of activities that public–private partnerships of different sorts can use to explore the possibilities for directing diasporas in the direction of manna solutions.

The transaction-oriented South African Network of Skills Abroad (SANSA) was established in 1998 by the University of Cape Town's Science and Technology Policy Research Center and a leading French agency for scientific cooperation, the Institute of Research for Development. SANSA aims to promote collaboration between highly skilled expatriate scientists and technologists and their counterparts in South Africa. The target group is alumni of all major South African universities and technical institutes. The portal to the network describes SANSA's objectives and explains how to network with other members through electronic bulletin boards, discussion groups, and job postings. As of March 2002, SANSA had 2,259 members in more than 60 different countries, 58 percent of whom were South African citizens. In October 2000, the National Research Foundation, part of South Africa's National Department of Arts, Culture, Science, and Technology, took over responsibility for SANSA. After some initial fumbling, the National Research Foundation is managing, with some difficulty, to stabilize the network.

SANSA's strength—its ability to facilitate transactions by enabling partners to find one another directly—is connected with a serious limitation: the inability to track the outcome of exchanges and communications between network members. Because of the way the network is structured, there are no data on the successes and failures of the network, and those who operate it cannot learn from the successes and failures of the transactions they help generate.

The second mentoring network, the South African Diaspora Network, was developed by the University of Cape Town's Center for Innovation and Entrepreneurship through assistance from the World Bank Development Marketplace. Founded in 2001, this network focuses on developing knowledge and entrepreneurial connections between local South African firms and well-connected individuals in the United Kingdom. Drawing on expatriate organizations such as university alumni associations and the South African Business Club, an organization with members in the United Kingdom and the United States, the South African Diaspora Network aims to facilitate continuing collaboration between respected and influential business people from South Africa in key overseas markets and young, high-potential start-up ventures based in South Africa. Local clients were recruited through extensive media coverage in South Africa. More than 60 South African companies applied to be part of the project, some of which were selected to participate. About 40 overseas members, most of them well-connected South Africans living in Greater London, were recruited through presentations held at the South African Business Club in London and a meeting of the London chapter of the University of Cape Town's Graduate School of Business Alumni Association.

So far the mentoring model of the network has resulted in some promising connections between growing firms and capable expatriates. But it is clear that the model will take time to yield results and that the network will have to develop the equivalent of a strategic plan to increase the number and improve the quality of the connections it encourages. A network that facilitates direct contacts between members cannot be self-organizing. Determining which tools and additional infrastructure can make mentoring and transactional networks more effective is a major problem confronting policy makers aiming to make emerging diaspora networks mature as quickly as possible.

References

Kapur, Devesh, and John McHale. 2005. *Give Us Your Best and Brightest. The Global Hunt for Talent and Its Impact on the Developing World.* Washington, DC: Center for Global Development.

Kuznetsov, Yevgeny, and Charles Sabel. Forthcoming. "Work Globally, Develop Locally: Diaspora Networks as Springboards of Knowledge-Based Development." *Innovation: Management, Policy, and Practice* 8 (1–2).

Ozden, Caglar, and Maurice Schiff, eds. 2005. *International Migration, Remittances, and the Brain Drain.* New York: Palgrave Macmillan.

World Bank. 2005. *Global Economic Prospects 2006. Economic Implications of Migration and Remittances.* Washington, DC.

2

The Dynamics of Migration of the Highly Skilled: A Survey of the Literature

David Ellerman

This chapter focuses on South-to-North skilled labor migration, considering the policy problems from the viewpoint of the sending country. The field is not without controversy. Policy discussions often seem imbued with a Panglossian optimism that all voluntary labor migration will ultimately work out for the best for all. Natural sympathy for those who seek a better life for themselves and their families by migrating makes some researchers and policy makers reluctant to recognize the adverse consequences of migration. The dynamics of migration are implicitly assumed to be benign and equalizing rather than adverse and divergent. Self-reinforcing processes are taken to be virtuous rather than vicious circles.

The basic decision facing a potential migrant can be stated in terms of Hirschman's (1970) contrast between the logic of exit and the logic of commitment to making a better home. The literature often reflects the implicit assumption that all social institutions should operate, like the market, on the logic of exit, so that any public policy to increase commitment is seen only as an impediment to exit.

This chapter looks at a broader class of dynamic models and reviews a number of policy options from the perspective of those models. Understanding the underlying dynamics leads to two types of policy suggestions. The first is to critically review some policies that may make matters worse in view of the actual dynamics. The second is to try some new policies based on a better assessment of the dynamics. These include policies that reinforce the logic of commitment, in order to reduce the brain drain in the first place, and policies that help involve emigrants in developing their country of origin.

Opening Match: Harry Johnson Versus Don Patinkin

In an early anthology of papers, two prominent economists, Harry Johnson and Don Patinkin, debate the brain drain (Adams 1968).

Harry Johnson's "Internationalist" Model

Johnson begins with one of the basic policy questions in the field: better or worse for whom? Is the relevant group the people of the home country or region (excluding those who have left or might leave) or the people of the world as a whole? Is the policy commitment to a specific place or nation or to an identifiable set of people?

Johnson, a Canadian who taught at the University of Chicago and the London School of Economics, stakes out what he called the "cosmopolitan liberal position," noting that he expects "many educated international migrants would share this position" (Johnson 1968, p. 70). The basic assumption in this position is that the international flow of human capital is a beneficial process, because "it reflects the free choices of the individuals who choose to migrate."

According to this view, the policy reference group is the world as a whole. Most people have a culturally conditioned attachment to their home country, but, in a sense, that is an artificial path-dependent phenomenon. Had the individual been born and grown up in another country, a similar attachment would have developed to that country. With such "artificial barriers to migration" in operation, less migration from low- to high-income countries occurs than is economically optimal, according to Johnson. Hence when such migration does occur, he puts the burden of proof squarely on any argument against it being economically beneficial.

"Like any profit-motivated international movement of factors of production [voluntary migration] may be expected to raise total world output . . . [except] when the migrant's private calculation of gain from migration excludes certain social costs that his migration entails," according to Johnson (1968, p. 75). Externalities that are not taken into account in private calculations may or may not outweigh the benefits of the migration. As the externalities associated with the brain drain may include positive ones in the receiving country as well as negative ones in the sending country, Johnson argues that the externalities will, to some extent, cancel each other out and will not, on the whole, outweigh the direct benefits to the migrants.

Even if in theory the benefits of migration outweigh the costs in the sense that winners could more than compensate losers, there is, in practice, no system for doing so. (The discussion of compensation assumes that citizens are "owned" by their home country and that the home country is therefore due compensation when they migrate.) Migrants send back remittances and sometimes return themselves, but there is no systematic mechanism for compensating the home country for their departure.

Johnson recognizes one case in which compensation could be justified. Home countries often finance the higher education of citizens under at least an implicit expectation that they will contribute to the country. Johnson suggests that providing university loans might be a better policy than providing grants. Some alternatives, such as a required service or a tax or bounty paid by the receiving country or employer, would be less in the liberal spirit and would be difficult to enforce internationally. Johnson argues that it is up to home countries to make it attractive for their educated citizens to stay (or to get the diaspora productively involved in their home country) rather than to expect host countries to pay subsidies or compensation for people who freely choose to emigrate.

There are two weaknesses in Johnson's powerful statement of the cosmopolitan liberal position. One is his implicit assumption that local value-increasing actions (for example, factor movements) will yield global improvements. Today externalities in the form of interdependencies are seen as ubiquitous. Game theory is the theory of interdependent decision making. In the coordination problems popularized by the prisoners' dilemma game, the individually preferred strategies lead to an outcome that is Pareto dominated by the cooperative option.

If economic development in a developing country or region is modeled as a multiperson prisoners' dilemma in which many people who are more socialized into the home country or less mobile opt to "cooperate" (commit to make home better), less socialized and more mobile people would be encouraged to "defect" (exit to find a better home), which would benefit them individually (Schelling 1978, chapter 7; annex 1 to this chapter). But these gains would not accrue if everyone defected and tried to emigrate, because the doors of potential host countries would close, vastly raising the costs of migration and dissipating the benefits. A new, lower equilibrium would be reached, with the benefits of neither migration nor development. In these we're-all-in-this-together situations, cosmopolitan liberalism does not seem justified in urging defection on the grounds that it benefits the defectors as long as most others do not defect.

The other major weakness in the cosmopolitan liberal argument is that in practice it is used to defend the right of out-migration more than the right of inmigration. It is used to attack countries trying to limit who leaves; it is less often used to attack countries trying to limit who comes in, which is taken as the "proper" exercise of national sovereignty.

How can cosmopolitan liberalism in developed countries push for two-way openness in goods and capital but not in people? According to Rodrik (2001, p. 3), "The short answer . . . is that developed countries cannot have it both ways. Either they put their money where their mouth is, and include labor flows in the agenda of liberalization, or they recognize the need for national autonomy and space, in which case they must extend to the developing countries the same privileges in the areas of trade and capital flows."

But if cosmopolitan liberalism is not applied across the board, what is the second-best policy? Today we are much more attuned to the subtleties in second-best arguments. We cannot simply assume that liberal policies applied to everything but labor are automatically second best to 100 percent liberal policies.

Don Patinkin's "Nationalist" Model

Don Patinkin of the Hebrew University, Jerusalem, took the point of view of a middle-income developing country concerned with possible brain drain, a concern that is "implicitly a rejection of the viewpoint that the 'world' should be considered as a single aggregate from the welfare viewpoint—and that the welfare of this unit is maximized by the free flow of resources between countries" (Patinkin 1968, p. 93). Patinkin pointedly notes that developed countries do not adopt this viewpoint about the "free flow of resources" when the resources are the "population masses of (say) Far Eastern Asia." Developing countries do not take this viewpoint when the resources are their own skilled members of the population. Both developed and developing countries take into account the distribution effects among nations; neither group of countries adopts the free flow view across the board.

While adopting a nationalist viewpoint without apology, Patinkin nevertheless starts with the liberal assumption of free emigration and asks what developing countries can do to limit the brain drain. One approach would be to ask the more advanced countries to limit immigration of highly skilled people. Patinkin rejects this as being impractical, if not quixotic, as the firms and scientific institutions of the developed world would lobby for such immigration and governments would tend to support it. Rather than ask the developed countries not to compete for this talent, he suggests what developing countries can do to retain it: encourage trained scientific personnel to identify with the development of the country, show that these people can indeed fulfill a vital role in that development, and provide at least the minimal conditions that allow them to fulfill their scientific aspirations.

Patinkin provides some concrete guidelines. When training abroad is necessary, two years is probably a minimum period to get acclimatized and four years is a maximum period, after which there is likely to be much attrition or readjustment problems upon return. Study should be at the graduate level, preferably at the doctoral level or above. If there is an adequate doctoral program at home, specialized training should be postdoctoral. Greater advantages would flow from sending more mature, already employed, and preferably married people abroad, that is, those who might already be committed to making home better. Upon return from abroad, students could train others in what they had learned abroad. These guidelines would give the learner who goes abroad a "higher degree of identification with his home society and home institution" (Patinkin 1968, p. 97). In Patinkin's opinion, losing more than 10–15 percent of nationals who study abroad is cause for alarm. But, he adds, if there were no brain drain at all, the country would be underutilizing the opportunities for training abroad.

As to fellowships offered by developed countries, Patinkin notes that it would be better to fund instructors and professors to come to the developing countries, so that more students could be reached. In a similar manner, U.S. firms might establish subsidiary research and development plants abroad to employ scientists in their home countries, probably at much lower cost than in the United States.

One form of exit-voice reasoning is the safety valve idea of migration. If jobs are not available in the home country, some static efficiency is achieved and some pressure is released through the safety valve of migration (exit). This may be dynamically inefficient, however, by relieving some of the pressure (voice) to make the domestic reforms necessary for business development that would create jobs at home. Brain drain exit opportunities show the government that the scientific community has other options and should not be taken for granted. The possibility and exercise of some exit alerts the government that it needs to improve conditions at home for the domestic scientific community.

Patinkin added an appendix to the published paper to reflect some of the discussion at the original conference at which the paper was presented. It reflects his annoyance at Johnson's argument that the free flow of resources increases world welfare and that opposition to that flow reflects an illiberal, nationalistic anachronism. Patinkin notes that welfare economics had not been able to produce a "world social welfare function." Moreover, the "free flow of resources" reflects the effective demand created by very nationalistic forces in the developed countries. He wonders how the U.S. government defense and space programs and the "nationalistic war in Vietnam" would be reflected in a "world social welfare function."

In his appendix, Patinkin argues for the sort of intellectual diversity that would result from having at least one good university with a developed educational and cultural life in every developing country. He notes that the dynamics of agglomeration are at work in the formation or de-formation of intellectual centers. There needs to be a critical mass of good people. Even within a developed country, "brain raids" by one university on another can lead to a process of decline that is hard to reverse. The same dynamics are even stronger between developed and developing countries. As soon as a scientist establishes some prominence in a developing country, hard to resist offers come in from developed countries, making it difficult to maintain a top-flight university even in a mid-level developing country. The people who may be a few more small jewels in the crown at a Harvard or a Cambridge may make all the difference to the critical mass in their home country.

The Effect of Critical Mass on Migration

The critical mass argument used by Patinkin is ubiquitous in the brain drain and broader development literature, so it may be worthwhile to present a simple statement of the idea for later reference.[1] One type of critical mass dynamics is driven by expectations. Suppose that each scientist in a home country reference group will make plans to stay or leave depending on his or her expectation about how many others will stay or leave. These expectations are summarized in a reaction function. Given the information that X percent of the scientists in a group are staying, Y percent will consider that sufficient for them to stay. If given that 40 percent are staying, only 35 percent consider that sufficient for them to stay, then 40 percent would not be an equilibrium (where expectations match reality). The numbers would spiral downward to some low-level equilibrium. If given that 75 percent would stay, at least 80 percent consider that sufficient to stay, the dynamics would work the other way. The number of scientists staying would spiral upward to a high-level equilibrium. In between there would be a critical mass number that would separate the downward and upward dynamics. At each point, the dynamics are indicated by comparing the reaction function to the upward-sloping 45 degree line (figure 2.1).

Above the critical mass C, the "more the merrier" dynamics of agglomeration set in to drive toward the high-level equilibrium at B. Below the critical mass, the dynamics of disagglomeration work to ghettoize the scientific community, until the low-level equilibrium is reached at A. Starting at B, if a few key people are cherry-picked or poached by the developed countries, the system may be pushed down below the critical mass at C, which would trigger the self-reinforcing downward spiral to A.

The downward dynamics below the critical mass are not a self-equilibrating process between the sending (home) and receiving (host) countries. The more people who leave the home country, the greater the push to leave and the greater the pull of the receiving countries. The situation snowballs to divergent outcomes rather than equilibrating to a benign one.

Expectational dynamics need not work in this manner to drive toward an upper or lower equilibrium with a critical mass in between. Instead, a "room for more"

---

[1] See Schelling (1978) for an extensive treatment. The reaction function model presented here is a reinterpretation of the faculty meeting model he presents in chapter 3 of his book. The dynamics of divergence can operate between two populations or within one population to divide it into upper and lower strata. For instance, a virtuous circle of city growth might have a positive "spread effect" in a suburban neighborhood but a negative "backwash effect" in a nearby rural area. This effect is sometimes called the Matthew principle, after the Biblical reference "for to every one who has will more be given, and he will have abundance; but from him who has not, even what he has will be taken away" (Matthew 25: 29). Myrdal (1957) did the most to popularize these dynamics in the economic development literature, particularly to account for persistent and increasing national and international inequality.

Figure 2.1 *Critical Mass Dynamics of Emigration*

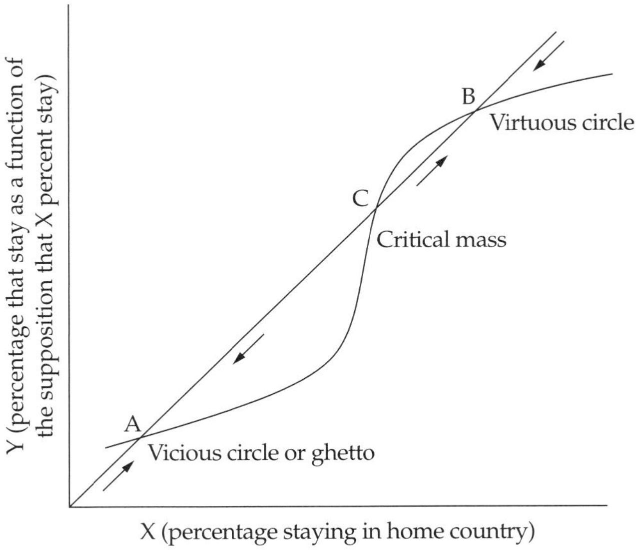

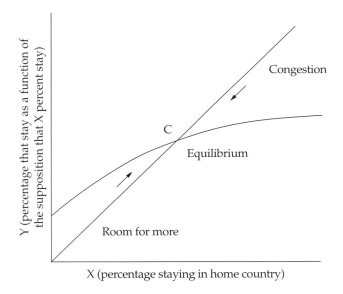

Source: Author.

dynamic could dominate at low levels and a dynamic of overcrowding and conges-
tion could dominate at higher levels, so that a single stable equilibrium is reached
in between at C (figure 2.2).

Many people would go to a restaurant that has room for more without getting
crowded but would avoid a crowded one. That would lead to the single equilibrium dynamics shown in figure 2.2. In contrast, in the case of a nightclub, people

Figure 2.2 *Equalizing the Dynamics of Emigration*

Source: Author.

might prefer to be where the action is, which would lead to the critical mass dynamics shown in figure 2.1.

Many discussions in the migration literature are based on neoclassical models that picture migration induced by wage differentials as equalizing the differentials between countries or regions of origin and destination. But this is tantamount to assuming that the equalizing dynamics are in operation (for example, diminishing returns to labor within a static production function in each country), when the question of the dynamics may be precisely the point at issue. In terms of the restaurant and nightclub example, a group of people leaving the waiting line at restaurant A to go to less crowded restaurant B may help equalize conditions between the two establishments, but a group of people leaving one nightclub to go to another may induce even more migrations in the same direction. (The dynamics between the two groups are treated in a reaction square diagram in annex 2.)

Clarity in migration policy research starts with understanding these two dynamics. Are the migration flows part of a critical mass dynamic driving one region away from a high equilibrium toward a low equilibrium, and perhaps doing the reverse for another region? Or are the flows part of an equilibrating dynamic reducing the push and pull factors between two countries or regions?

North-To-North Migration

These equilibrating dynamics are often assumed in policy discussions. The historical North-to-North migrations from a crowded Europe to a sparsely populated North America might be represented by the equilibrating dynamics (Hatton and Williamson 1998; O'Rourke and Williamson 2000). The flow of the "tired and huddled masses" from the "teeming shores" of Europe to North America in the 19th century may have relieved the crowding in Europe, reducing the push factor. The "empty spaces" of North America became less empty, and may have reduced the pull factor, causing migration to equilibrate the pressures on both ends as shown in figure 2.3.

In North-to-North migration, the sending country or region is relatively developed, so the question of the migration being detrimental to the sending region tends not to arise. Migration equilibrates pressures (like water flowing between two containers) and does not start a disequilibrating downward spiral to a low-level equilibrium "trap." If all migration was of this type, it would be much less of a development issue.

South-To-North Migration

South-to-North migration is migration from a relatively undeveloped region or country (South) to a relatively developed one (North). The economic differential between the sending and receiving ends is the main determinant of South-to-North migration. It should not be assumed that push factors, such as a lack of local jobs, are predominant; it is the differential that counts.[2] The label South-to-North is

---

[2] A manager of a tire factory in Ecuador reports, "We don't have a labour market here any more . . . They finish their education and they go" (*Economist* 2002a, p. 42). He now requires neither prior experience nor a high school diploma and he has had to double the salary he offers new workers.

Figure 2.3 *Equilibrating Migration*

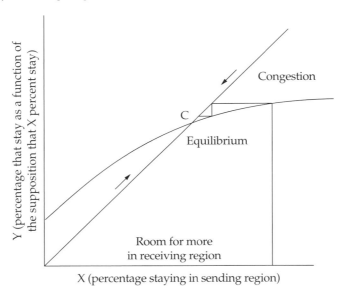

Source: Author.

applied to migrations in which there is a presumption that the development of the South is still a policy goal of the national government or international development agencies. There is no presumption that any detrimental effect on the sending region is an intended goal or an acceptable by-product of other policy goals.

South-to-North migration causes many of the migration-related problems in the world today in both the sending and receiving areas. The focus here is on the developmental impact in the sending areas. Powerful economic forces drive South-to-North migration. The communication and transportation revolutions that are part of globalization have accelerated the pace and expanded the flows. The interaction, and perhaps collision, of these globalizing forces with the policy goal of developing the sending area has generated much commentary and speculation about the long-run effects. Is the out-migration part of an equalizing dynamic that will improve conditions (by relieving "overpopulation," for example) in the sending region? Is the out-migration a temporary negative factor that might be more than compensated for by the flow of remittances and skills that, together with other developmental forces, will drive the area from a low to a high equilibrium and thus eventually reduce out-migration? Or does the out-migration largely feed and sustain a low-level equilibrium, notwithstanding the flow of remittances and returnees? Perhaps a happy face should be put on the whole question by seeing the production and export of unskilled and skilled labor as a comparative advantage of the sending area that might be promoted as an export industry? These are some of the basic policy questions and perspectives that run through the current policy literature on South-to-North migration.

"Temporary" Labor Migration as a Permanent Way of Life

Migrants from Turkey and the Balkans who came to Germany as guest workers (*Gastarbeiters*) after World War II were originally seen as potential drivers of development for the sending regions. Workers would learn industrial skills and new technologies that could then drive development in their home countries. They would observe societies with more economic development and different laws, institutions, and habits.[3] Remittances and the savings of returnees would provide the capital for a developmental liftoff in the less developed regions.

None of this was impossible. Yet the guest worker phenomenon has not, on the whole, driven development in the sending regions. It may be useful to explore some of the reasons for its failure to do so.

Historically, temporary work elsewhere was a way to acquire a capital stake. During the Gold Rush in the United States in the mid-19th century, people from across the country rushed to the West Coast to try to make quick money. Some made money directly from gold and silver, many others made money from selling provisions. But diminishing returns soon set in, as the rich veins of gold and silver were exploited. Many of the miners and provisioners returned home with their capital stake, to the benefit of the sending regions. One of the key elements was the time limit on the Gold Rush. Staying on in a Gold Rush town was not a permanent way of life.

Temporary work abroad can also be a means of technology transfer. When the Axis powers occupied the former Yugoslavia during World War II, a sizable number of technically trained workers and engineers—particularly from the most Germanized part of the country, Slovenia—were taken to Germany to work in advanced industries. When the forced migrants returned after the war, Slovenia drew on their knowledge to build a group of electrical and electronics companies, the Iskra (Spark) Group. Iskra laid the foundation for modern high-tech industry in Slovenia. Here again, the labor migration was temporary.

A similar story can be told for some internal rural to urban migration and return. During the Chinese civil war, some peasants moved to the industrial cities, such as Shanghai, to escape the chaos in the countryside. After the revolution, they returned home with enough industrial skills to begin some off-farm rural industrial workshops. These workshops laid the foundations for the success of the township and village enterprises founded many years later.

Thus it is not impossible for temporary labor migration to provide the capital stake and technological knowledge to drive development in the sending region. But is that an accurate description of the temporary labor migrations between the less developed and more developed parts of the world today? So far, it would seem the answer is no. As a number of observers have quipped, there is nothing more permanent than temporary migration. Some family members go abroad to work not as a temporary measure to acquire capital or knowledge, but as a career choice that will increase and diversify the income of the whole family.

Some researchers have promoted the idea of migrants returning home during the economically active part of their lives, that is, before retirement, and then using their capital and knowledge for economic development. However, this proposed development strategy may conflict with the psychology of the migrant worker (Bovenkerk 1974, 1982). Coming home to work before retirement may be seen as a sign of failure, an indication that the worker was not good enough to keep his or

---

[3] As John Stuart Mill noted, "It is hardly possible to overrate the value, in the present low state of human improvement, of placing human beings in contact with persons dissimilar to themselves, and with modes of thought and action unlike those with which they are familiar . . . Such communication has always been, and is peculiarly in the present age, one of the primary sources of progress" (1899, pp. 99–100).

her job abroad. It is hard to build a development strategy on people doing what they, their families, and their peers perceive as failure. Many of the speculations about the potential developmental role of remittances and returnees fail to take into account the perceptions of temporary labor migrants about their careers.

It is compatible with the self-perceptions of guest workers to successfully complete their "careers," return home, and ease into semiretirement by starting a small life-style business, such as a shop, café, or small boarding house. But that is far from being an engine of development.

Any rethinking might start with the idea that temporary should mean limited to a fixed time period of at most several years. Migrants from Asia to the Gulf States are called temporary because each episode is limited in time and workers are not permitted to immigrate. But this temporary migration is a permanent way of life. There is no sum-of-episodes limit on the number of years one can work in the Gulf. Making this migration temporary would require setting a limit on the total number of years foreigners can work in the Gulf (like term limits for politicians). Such a limit would change workers' expectations. Like a student who receives some education abroad and then returns home for a career at home, a worker would see the time-limited migration as the chance to receive an on-the-job education abroad and build up a capital stake in order to then return home to make a career.

The Deleterious Effects of Migration of the Best and the Brightest

Temporary labor migration is usually not temporary. Migrants usually have some entrepreneurial drive toward self-betterment (of which their migration is testimony), some skills, and some resources to finance their travel. Remittances may lead to more migration, because they show that migration works; finance other family members' trips; and show what the neighbors have to do to "keep up with the Jones's."

This highlights another way in which labor migration can be detrimental to development. Many of the best and the brightest blue-collar workers and college-educated "brain workers" leave their home region. Their talents and capabilities are not brought to bear on overcoming the barriers to development at home.[4] This migration facilitates the meritocratic rise of the best and brightest in a transnational world.

But this is also a variation on the old theme about how a meritocracy works to perpetuate a stratified society.[5] For the sake of simplicity, consider a society divided into two strata, an upper stratum and a lower stratum.[6] The "smart" way to organize such a stratified society is as a meritocracy, in which the best and the brightest from the lower stratum can be recruited without prejudice into the upper stratum.[7] Moving into the upper stratum should be the very definition of success for someone born into the lower stratum. Such individual cases of ascent into the upper stratum should be celebrated as examples to which any ambitious young person born

---

[4] Using a production function such as $Y = AK^aL^b$, there are two effects: the reduction in L and the retardation in the processes to increase the residual coefficient A (which represents the influences aside from capital K and labor L). The second effect is the more important one from the developmental viewpoint.

[5] The classic satire about such a society is Young's *The Rise of the Meritocracy* (1962).

[6] The stratification can also be spatialized, with the lower stratum identified with a ghetto.

[7] There may also be some social mobility the other way, as in the notion captured in quips about rags to riches and back to rags in three generations.

into the lower stratum might aspire, and with every success story, those in the upper stratum might pat themselves on the back for sponsoring a society that allows such social mobility that is based on merit and is blind to the accidents of birth. In this manner, the talents devoted to maintaining the stratification and privileges of the upper stratum are constantly renewed by meritocratic recruitment from below. The Mandarin-dominated structure of ancient China was both static and long-lived, in part, because it operated on such a meritocratic basis.

The problem is that such a dynamic may well be at work in the South-to-North migration of the unskilled as well as skilled migration in today's globalized world. The development divide may be perpetuated by the successes of the best and the brightest from the South making their careers in the North. This is a broad-brush argument; there are individual Moses-like exceptions, such as Gandhi or Martin Luther King, who return to help organize structural change, but the typical case is unfortunately rather different.

Migration as a Safety Valve

The flip side of increased exit is that there is decreased voice, or, in more general terms, decreased pressure, to break through the barriers to structural change. Hirschman's (1970) example of exit-voice dynamics started with the conventional wisdom that increased competition to the Nigerian railroads from trucking would bring pressure on the railroads to reform. In fact, it had the opposite effect, because the best and brightest of the client base (the discriminating customers, who needed to get their goods to a given place at a given time) exited the railroad system and switched their business to trucking. As the railroads could not be just shut down, the state continued to subsidize them. Thus there was even less pressure to break through the barriers required for difficult reforms in the railroad system.[8]

The pressure of problems that demand social change can be relieved without being resolved in many ways. One is to discover oil or gas deposits in one's backyard and then to soften the rough edge of pressing problems with the natural resource rents. Another is to misuse external aid or loans to buy time and postpone real changes: to pay the costs of not changing rather than paying the costs of change (Stern 2001).[9]

Migration often seems to work in a similar way as a safety valve to relieve the pressure of a pressing problem rather than to resolve it. When yesterday's elites use their power to lock in their position and thereby stifle innovation, which can always be threatening, the economy will stagnate and young people will not be able to find jobs that utilize their skills and match their ambitions. Migration provides the ambitious and skilled with individual exits. It helps export the unemployment problem for both skilled and unskilled workers. Overall, it relieves the pressure to change the structural barriers to improving the business climate. History is ripe with examples of stagnant societies in which the elites have found ways to constantly suppress or bleed off the pressure for change.

---

[8] Hirschman (1970) notes other examples in which exit undercuts voice. Latin American powerholders have long encouraged the voluntary exile of political opponents, which takes the pressure off internal reforms. Another example is the tendency of Indian industrial companies to generate their own electricity where the public supply is unreliable. This takes the pressure off the public suppliers to reform the old system, so the situation is self-reinforcing.
[9] Both examples are discussed in World Bank (2003, chapter 7).

In the context of the safety valve argument, remittances amplify the deleterious effect of migration by relieving the pressure of pressing problems. Many governments in developing countries have now discovered the "oil well" of remittances, which help them paper over problems and pay the costs of not changing.

All this does not deny the fact (which Hirschman also noted) that exit itself can be a form of voice. National pride cannot be sustained for long if young people seek to obtain degrees largely as exit visas. This is why the deleterious effects of migration (the exit of the best and brightest, the relief of pressures for change) operate with greatest force where the collective self-image is of a ghetto. Out-migration is a key part of the self-perpetuating ghettoization mechanism, that is, the self-reinforcing low equilibrium in the critical mass dynamics. A ghetto will never be successful as long as the internalized definition of success is individual exit.

Remittances: Streamlining Transmission and Increasing Developmental Impact

Remittances from North-to-South labor migration have received great attention in the migration literature (see, for example, Athukorala 1993; Massey and others 1998; Woodruff and Zenteno 2001). There is much concern about the developmental impact of aid transfers from the North to the South, and yet, on the whole, remittances are even larger than all aid transfers. Thus the potential developmental role of remittances should be an important topic for policy research and experimentation.

The volume of remittances is growing rapidly, so that the market for remittance transfers is attracting more for-profit and nonprofit competition. Costs now seem to be falling as a result of these market forces, thus the expenditure of scarce government attention and resources may not be necessary to reduce transmission costs.

Perhaps public policy attention should focus on increasing the developmental impact of remittances. There is an old stylized fact that most remittances are spent on consumption, health care, education, land, and the like, but that there is little expenditure or investment in direct productive uses. Many authors have argued that even if remittances are spent nonproductively, there is still a pro-development multiplier effect, particularly if the expenditures are used locally instead of on imports. There are two problems in this multiplier argument, at least if it is used to argue that further policy initiatives are unnecessary.

The first problem in the multiplier argument is that the multiplier is a double-edged sword. As is evident in a recession, reductions in expenditure have a downward multiplier effect. Thus any volatility in remittances will be amplified through the multiplier effect in the home economy. Businesses depending not just for their start, but for their continuation, on remittances will create a vested interest in the economy for continued migration and remittances as a way of life.

The second problem in the multiplier argument is a more subtle distinction between expenditures that are essentially sterile for development and expenditures that bring forth development that is soon independent of reliance on remittances.[10] Jacobs (1969, 1984) has forcefully developed this distinction (box 2.1).

---

[10] Many argue that the education of the young financed by remittances is a merit good (an end in itself). But that is quite different than arguing that remittances are used for education so that the next generation does not have to migrate. Indeed, there is considerable evidence to the contrary. Where migration has become a way of life, education is seen as the road to a better migratory outcome (perhaps with permanence) rather than local development without migration.

Box 2.1 *Jacobs on Regions That Workers Abandon*

Jacobs (1984) considers the problems of rural settlements or regions that workers abandon to migrate to jobs in cities. After World War II, workers from Turkey, the former Yugoslavia, and a number of other countries in southern Europe and North Africa were welcomed into northern Europe, particularly the Federal Republic of Germany. The remittances sent back were sizable, and in some countries were the single largest source of foreign exchange. Yet when unemployment rose abruptly in northern Europe, for example, in 1974 and 1980, hundreds of thousands of guest workers lost their jobs and returned to "the same unemployment and underemployment they had left" (Jacobs 1984, p. 74). The remittances, in the mean time, had not put their home regions on the road to development. According to Jacobs (1984, p. 75): "Remittances, while they last, do alleviate poverty in abandoned regions, just as any forms of transfer payments from rich to poor regions alleviate poverty while they last. The money buys imports for people and institutions which they would otherwise have to go without, but that is all it does."

Jacobs (1984, p. 75) tells the story of a small Mexican village, Napizaro, that for 40 years has been dependent on remittances largely from migrant workers in the Los Angeles area. "Today Napizaro is as prosperous a settlement as can be found in its entire region. The village's twelve hundred people live, for the most part, in comfortable brick houses with pretty patios and TV antennas. The community has street lights, a modern infirmary, a community center, and a new bull ring named The North Hollywood in honor of the industrial section of Los Angeles, some fifteen hundred miles away, from which this prosperity comes."

The road between Napizaro and North Hollywood is now well-trodden; it has become a way of life. When boys get to working age, they are trained by retired returnees about what to expect in the American factories, and other villagers working in Los Angeles help to find them jobs. Over the years, it seems that many men have considered starting their own companies at home because they had acquired most of the skills necessary, but they have abandoned the idea, as it seemed that their village was too isolated. As Jacobs (1984, p. 76) notes: "The skills and experience the men have acquired in Los Angeles are usable only in the context of a city economy with its symbiotic nests of suppliers and its markets, not in this economically barren region. One and the same lack—a vigorous city right in the region—forces the men to find work far away and also makes it impossible for them to start an industrial plant of their own, at home."

Commentary on the Remittances Literature

INCREASING INCOME IS NOT INCREASED DEVELOPMENT. Overall, the remittance literature seems too sanguine about the expenditure of remittances. Much of the expenditure is sterile for development purposes, for example, nonlocal expenditures on conspicuous consumption.[11] Abella (2002), the head of the International Labour Organisation's Migration Program, voiced some of the skepticism at a recent World Bank conference:

> There is general agreement among observers that by itself labour migration is unlikely to significantly improve the development potential of a sending country. While individual migrants and their families tend to gain from

---

[11] Some researchers have even noted that conspicuous consumption by some migrant families may spur other families to send out migrants: "Migration may represent an effort to 'keep up with the neighbors'—if migrant families have better homes and TVs, then nonmigrant families may be motivated to send a migrant abroad to earn money to overcome their relative deprivation" (Martin and Straubhaar 2001, p. 3; see also Stark 1991).

migration (in terms of greater economic security), the same cannot be claimed for the countries, as a whole. There is little evidence to indicate that labour migration and flows of remittances have generated sustained growth . . .

Take a look at the variation in recent development performance of major labour-sending countries—Mexico, Turkey, the Philippines, Pakistan, Yemen, Egypt, Morocco, Lesotho, Burkina Faso, Jamaica, etc. Which countries have managed to sustain high rates of economic growth?

In a community now largely dependent on income from migrant remittances, development would mean building local enterprises that would not live off remittances directly or indirectly (via the multiplier), so that local jobs could be sustained without continuing migration and remittances. While the initial investment funds, or even initial sales of the products, might come from remittances (a pump-priming effect), the idea is that the products should be largely exported from the community to satisfy demand unrelated to the community's remittances. Remittances could jump-start the local engines of development, but should not supply the ongoing fuel.

CHANGING THE PSYCHOLOGY OF LABOR MIGRATION. Today there is increasing policy interest in the development impact of labor migration on the home region, yet much of the policy discussion takes as a given that the labor migration is essentially a way of life for the local communities. Instead of seeing the temporary export of labor as a means to acquire a capital stake or as a learning experience, the export of labor, no matter that it is nominally called "temporary," is the way of life of the communities (box 2.2).

The project of local development is probably lost if this labor migration continues as a way of life. There are two related arguments here. One argument is that the static-efficiency option of increased earnings through semipermanent labor migration is dynamically inefficient in the sense of foreclosing on the option of local development. Martin and Straubhaar (2001, p. 18) note this when commenting on studies such as Abadan-Unat (1976) about the Turkish experience with guest workers:

These studies concluded that Turkish areas of origin were not primed for an economic take-off before emigration began, and that remittances and returning migrants reinforced trends that prevented a take-off rather than fueling the take-off for reasons that included . . . :

- nonproductive use of remittances, e.g., to speculate on real estate or to imitate a successful service such as a delivery service, taxi, or a shop
- the retirement of many migrants, so that skills acquired abroad are not used to promote development
- some distortion of local incentives, as when children do not stay in school because the wage for unskilled work abroad is several times the wage for skilled work at home.

In sum, the conclusion of the leading study of the 1970s was that labor emigration is "cumulative and self-perpetuating" (Abadan-Unat 1976, p. 384)—migrants leave an area because it is less developed, and remittances and returns reinforce the dependence of the areas on an external labor market.

In depressed and underdeveloped regions, if the pressures of local unemployment and poverty are routinely relieved by labor migration, then the various barriers

> **Box 2.2** *Ahmeti's Village*
>
> A detailed case study (European Stability Initiative 2002) of Zajas, an ethnic Albanian village in Macedonia, provides an example of a community where living off remittances has become a way of life. The local Albanian economy runs almost entirely on remittances.
>
> > There are 184 shops crammed into the Albanian end of Aleksandar Makedonski Street, selling carpets, furniture, jewellery and wedding gowns. The shops make most of their annual turnover during the summer months, when thousands of Albanian migrants return to get married or build houses in their villages. In this period, the Albanian quarter bustles with activity, and Cadillacs and other impressive cars with Chicago and Alaska license plates are parked along the sidewalks. Many of Kicevo's 300 private taxi drivers make a living shuttling the diaspora to and from Skopje airport. The heart of the Albanian economy is made up of traders, restaurateurs, construction workers, money changers, tradesmen and a few lawyers and private doctors (European Stability Initiative 2002, p. 4).
>
> The social expenditures of the Albanian diaspora tend to be unrelated to local development, for example, a hall for social functions such as weddings, and even a new soccer stadium. The researchers illustrated the social structure and expectations by looking at the entering 1989 class in a high school in the neighboring ethnically mixed town of Kicevo and then seeing what they were doing a decade later. Of the ethnic Albanians, all except one were working abroad and the latter's father was working in Germany. Of the ethnic Macedonians, all continued to live in the immediate region. This illustrates the self-reinforcing, critical mass dynamics of the labor migration for the ethnic Albanians and the lack of migration for the ethnic Macedonians. According to the European Stability Initiative (2002, p. 21): "Emigration tends to be a cumulative process. Its incidence is a positive function of the number of earlier emigrants who provide money, information and support for newcomers. If Kicevo's ethnic Macedonians have relatives abroad, they usually emigrated for Australia in the 1950s and no longer maintain close links with family who remained. There is no equivalent of the dense networks which Albanians have constructed between Kicevo and the outside world over the past two decades."
>
> There was one interesting exception to the rule of nonproductive expenditure of the remittances from the Albanian diaspora (concerning Albania itself, see Martin, Martin, and Pastore 2002; Nicholson 2002). An ethnic Albanian with a clothing company in France set up a cut-and-sew subcontracting company in Kicevo with about 100 workers (ironically, all but two of them are ethnic Macedonians who had worked for a Yugoslav textile company). Cloth is trucked in from France and the finished product is sent back, with the company in France acting as the contractor. While this is not an example of a migrant returning permanently to run a business at home, it is a case reminiscent of the small garment factories (*maquiladoras*) in Guanajuato, Mexico, where the company is a labor-intensive part of a value chain based in the North.

to development will probably not be surmounted and the regions' lack of development will be perpetuated.

The second argument is that the psychology of labor migration as a way of life does not bode well for local development. As noted previously, returning home to make one's living there before retirement is seen as a failure to sustain one's "career" as a labor migrant.

Brain Drain Effects of Migration

In the immediate post–World War II period, the brain drain was seen as a problem (see, for example, the Johnson-Patinkin debate and the other papers in Adams

1968), a bad cold that might hinder the activities of developing countries. Today, with the quickening of international processes that is referred to as globalization, the brain drain has become more like a pneumonia, crippling the activities of some countries, such as those in Sub-Saharan Africa, and particularly South Africa. Some policy ideas suggested in the past, such as legal restrictions on exit or a departure tax paid by receiving countries to sending countries,[12] are now seen as archaic and unimplementable. Other ideas, such as the creation of a transnational community of scientists and engineers helping both receiving and sending countries, may be more feasible because of globalization. Thus while globalization may exacerbate some old problems, it may also entrain some new solutions.

TREATING SKILLED LABOR AS AN EXPORT. When a young doctor goes abroad to work, does he or she do so to acquire first-hand knowledge of medical practices in industrial countries in order to improve practices at home and perhaps obtain enough capital to open up a practice upon his or her return? Or is the purpose to find long-term employment in the North? The evidence suggests that the bulk of cases fit the second profile.

One policy response is to make the best of it by treating the training of skilled people as essentially an export industry for which payment is made in the form of remittances. The training of medical personnel in the Caribbean, the Philippines, and a number of other countries would seem to fit this model. If this training take places at privately financed institutions, public policy would have little purchase. If the training is at public expense, it would seem, at least at first glance, that this is a waste of public expenditure. There is a multiple loss: the human capital, the public monies that funded the training, and the later fiscal loss. As the *Economist* notes (2002b, p. 25):

> To the loss of productive potential, add the fiscal loss from migration. Taxpayers in developing countries have paid to educate many of those who leave (and who may well end up working in jobs below the level their qualifications would justify at home). And emigration leaves behind fewer workers to pay the cost of looking after the old . . . A recent study of the fiscal effects of the Indian brain drain, by Mihir Desai of Harvard University and two colleagues (Desai, Kapur, and McHale 2001), points out that the 1 million Indians in the United States accounted for a mere 0.1 percent of India's population but earned the equivalent of a staggering 10 percent of India's national income.

Any remittances received in return for this exported human capital go privately to the families of the skilled migrants, which would hardly justify public expenditure.

One way of preventing the loss of investment in public education is to treat it as a loan (secured in some fashion) unless the graduate satisfies certain minimal

---

[12] Until 1824, the United Kingdom had restrictions on the out-migration of skilled artisans. The restrictions were imposed not out of fear of brain drain in the United Kingdom, but out of fear of brain gain to competing countries in Europe. The effect was less to prevent out-migration as to discourage return migration: "Restriction on emigration of artisans failed to prevent their departure, but did inhibit their return" (Kindleberger 1978, p. 47). A similar perverse side effect has been noted for tightened restrictions on unskilled in-migration. As Cornelius (2002, p. 6) notes: "The current strategy of border enforcement is keeping more unauthorised migrants *in* the United States than it is keeping *out*."

requirements of public service after graduation. This policy seems fair, but it may be difficult to implement. Travel abroad would have a broadening effect, and further study abroad might greatly enhance the value of the graduate's education. "Hard" requirements to enforce the education loans, such as exit bonds or liens against family assets,[13] might reduce the graduate's intrinsic commitment to and identification with the country, and thus lead to perverse consequences. If one's obligation to one's home country was thus represented simply as the need to pay off a bank loan, then once paid in full, the graduate would have little compunction in seeking opportunities elsewhere. Public service obligations might have some of this crowding out effect, but they would probably be much smaller than a monetized obligation.

A counterargument against seeing public grant funding of education for export as a clear loss is that if students see higher education as a means to out-migrate, many more students may be attracted into these professions. The country will have a net increase in supply, even after the migrants leave. Due to the ease of immigrating to the United States as a doctor, Jamaica loses four out of every five doctors trained, but it still retains one out of five.

Where a professional degree is seen as an exit visa, the demand for such degrees will increase. After the financial collapse in the Russian Federation in 1998, enrollment in science and technology rose. The initial delight of educators was somewhat tempered when interviews showed that since the getting rich exit door had closed, many students saw a science and technology education as the next best road out of Russia. The net result of this natural experiment may well be that Russia will end up with more trained scientists and engineers than would otherwise have been the case.

While this mechanism may operate on its own, the idea of promoting it as policy seems bizarre. Even leaving aside the substantial waste of national education resources, how could any country that takes pride in its scientific, engineering, or medical professions urge students to become educated in those professions as a means to exit the country? If that were officially promoted as the goal of science education, a country's national academy of science would soon be seen as a ghettoized national academy of second- and third-rate science, made up of nationals who were not good enough to get jobs in the advanced industrial countries.[14] But at least this policy idea has the virtue that if accepted by the developing countries, the developed countries could continue their poaching of the best and brightest of the trained scientists and professionals with a clear conscience.[15]

ORGANIZING THE DIASPORA. The interplay (or dialectic) of exit and voice (or commitment) is subtle. Sometimes exit can function as a kind of voice to spur reforms; sometimes it exacerbates a downward spiral. For those who leave, exit could mean the abandonment of voice, or it could lead to new, and perhaps even

---

[13] In establishing the University of Naples in 1224, Frederick II tried to entice students by arranging for creditors to supply loans. The students could not leave the city unless the loans were paid back or markers were left with the creditor.

[14] In countries such as India, which have significant emigration of scientists, scientists who remain home for whatever reason may be viewed as second-rate. Programs to top up the salaries or extend other enticements to professionals who return are resented by professionals who never emigrated or who returned without "bribes."

[15] In biological terms, the poaching would have advanced from a form of parasitism to a form of symbiosis.

more effective, kinds of voice. Emigrants have exercised the logic of exit, but that does not mean that they have forsaken any commitment to making home better. The entrenched authorities in the home country might be accustomed to ignoring domestic voices for reform, particularly if those voices have no real alternative. But calls for reforms coming from the diaspora might find a different reception. The diaspora could bring new knowledge and capital to the home country, but its members have alternatives. Indeed, the emigrants have a new home in addition to their old home. Their exit may have increased the effectiveness of their voice at home.

While emigrants may have left for economic reasons, there is no reason to think that mobilization of the diaspora is solely an economic proposition. Intrinsic motivation taps into the roots of identity, and an emigrant's home country is likely to be part of that emigrant's identity (Deci and Ryan 1985; Lane 1991). The social rewards of working with other successful emigrants to help the home country may also play an important role, but the economic rationale cannot be ignored. At best, the intrinsic and the more extrinsic motivations should be aligned, like arrows pointing in roughly the same direction.[16] Intrinsic motivation can take the lead, but its energy will eventually flag if sound economics does not soon follow behind.[17]

One meta-principle of development assistance is to look at what spontaneous, unassisted, or self-organized social processes have helped development and to then figure out how to catalyze those processes in other countries or regions. Development practitioners look at where water flows naturally and where it is flowing in the right direction, then deepen the channel so that a stream might swell to a river.[18]

The reinvolvement of the diaspora in the home country through investment and integration in networks is an historical process that many countries and agencies are now trying to catalyze. The policy idea of organizing the diaspora complements efforts within home countries to increase the retention of scientists, engineers, and professionals. The point is not to treat emigrants as being irreparably lost to the home country, but to view them as potentially playing a positive, transnational role.[19] Bhagwati (2003) argues that such a diaspora model is much more likely to succeed today than a retention strategy.

One major historical model of diaspora-assisted development is the role of the 50 million overseas Chinese in China (Weidenbaum and Hughes 1996). The overseas Chinese have been remarkably successful in business and can bring considerable experience, network connections, and capital back to benefit investment in

---

[16] McGregor's (1960) theory Y is based on the principle of integration and self-control, in the sense that work and tasks are designed so that the intrinsic motivation of staff is aligned with the objectives of the organization.

[17] See Hirschman (1977) for more on the interplay of the passions (intrinsic motivations) and the interests (extrinsic motivations).

[18] Where the water is flowing in the wrong direction, instead of trying to build a dam, it is better to try to rechannel the water into acceptable nearby channels. A related "pave the paths" metaphor is used by Williams (1981). Rather than pave paths on a campus of new buildings at the time the buildings are constructed, let grass grow between them, see where footpaths develop, and then pave the paths. The question development assistance organizations face is how to pave the paths worn in the diaspora's self-organized reinvolvement in its old country.

[19] "Transnational" connotes more globalization-enhanced betweeness, circularity, back-and-forthness, and toing-and-froing than old-fashioned terms like "international" (Portes 1999).

China. Their common language, culture, and family networks gave them connections (*guanxi*) that non-Chinese investors did not have.[20]

Indian governments at the state and national level and various expatriate groups have now become active in involving the extensive Indian scientific and business diaspora in India (Kapur 2001; Saxenian 2000). The year 2000 (Y2K) problem in the late 1990s provided the sudden need for much reprogramming in "archaic" computer languages, which created opportunities for companies in Bangalore. The experience and trust built up from that episode, aided by the temporary migration of many Indian software engineers and programmers to the West, spilled over into substantive business deals during the dot.com boom. In addition to this trade in services, the Indian high-tech diaspora in Silicon Valley and other technology centers in the United States has become organized, forming a transnational community that brings experience, connections, capital, and deals to India.[21]

Governments and expatriate groups have tried to form mutually beneficial transnational communities in countries with sizable diasporas, including Argentina, Armenia, Israel, Pakistan, and South Africa. In addition, many Internet-based networks specialize in science and engineering. These networks build on the experience of the United Nations Development Programme's Transfer of Knowledge through Expatriate Nationals Program. The South African Network of Skills Abroad has identified some 40 networks, such as the Arab Scientists and Technologists Abroad, the Network of Colombian Researchers Abroad, the Iranian Scientific Information Network, the Global Korean Network, the Philippines Brain Gain Network, the Polish Scientists Abroad group, the Association of Thai Professionals in North America and Canada, and the Tunisian Scientific Consortium (Brown 2000; Solimano 2002).

A menu of policy options is associated with catalyzing the organization of skilled and professional diasporas, starting with supporting the use of the Internet by expatriates to build organized groups and by agencies in the home countries to build relationships with the centers of expatriate activity. The transnational relationship might start with discussion and information exchange. The challenge is to develop transactions and business deals that lead to the investment of diaspora expertise and capital in the development of the home country. Emigrant groups and ministries in the home country can collaborate on investment fairs in developed countries and tours of investors in the home country. Business incubators may play a role in both countries: home-country exporters may need a base in a developed country, and fledgling businesses in the home country could be sponsored or mentored by successful emigrants.

REDUCING BRAIN DRAIN THROUGH EDUCATIONAL POLICIES. If a company upgrades a worker's skills (which are always to some extent transferable), another

---

[20] Some have argued that the bulk of the Chinese diaspora investment into China was by the Hong Kong (China) Chinese, who, in the face of Hong Kong's reabsorption into China had special incentives to gain favor from the Chinese authorities (Naughton 1999).

[21] One part of the transnational diaspora community idea is to downplay the role of return migration to obtain these outcomes. Various programs to facilitate permanent return migration for highly skilled professionals have become notorious for their meager outcomes, and that seems unlikely to change in the countries that need help the most.

company can offer a higher wage to try to poach the trained worker.[22] To prevent poaching, firms could privatize worker training by having workers pay for their own training. This is analogous to a country privatizing its higher education system so that no public resources are expended on those who exit. In both cases, this policy would restrict training to those who already have the required resources if loans were not provided. If loans are provided, however, the firm or country faces the problem of collecting from those who exit.

Another corporate strategy is to provide for worker education, but to build a corporate culture that increases worker identification with the company and reduces exit. "Identification becomes an important means for removing or reducing those inefficiencies that are labeled by the terms *moral hazard* and *opportunism*," writes Simon (1991, p. 41). This is one of the keystones of human resource policies in Japanese firms and firms using Japanese-style policies (Kagono and Kobayashi 1994). As each firm develops its own routines and procedures in a path-dependent manner, an increasing proportion of worker training may be firm specific, so that retention becomes self-reinforcing over time.

How might migration lead to the dynamics of North-South divergence rather than convergence? Can migration be viewed as the exit or defect option in a multi-person prisoners' dilemma game? Such models are abstract and barren of pointers to alternative policies. But the adverse dynamics of migration are based on the logic of exit (find a better home), and Hirschman's (1970) development of the interplay between the logic of exit and the logic of commitment (commit to making home better) seems to suggest alternative policies.

The contrast between the logic of exit and the logic of commitment is well developed in the case of work organizations, for example, in the contrast between models of Japanese-style and Anglo-American-style firms (table 2.1). Applying the logic of commitment to a country as a whole, particularly to the tertiary education system, can help combat brain drain in source countries.

Can the ideas of Japanese-style human resource management be applied to reforming higher public education in a developing country to reduce the incidence of brain drain? Dore (1976, 1997), an economic sociologist who specializes in the Japanese economy, has proposed education reforms based on these principles. Although he was concerned with education reform for its own sake, his suggestions have the indirect effect of helping reduce the brain drain in developing countries. They therefore overlap with Patinkin's suggestions.

Dore's diploma disease critique focuses on the effects of the obsession with credentials and with the escalation of the credentials required for jobs. In developing countries, where there are more graduates than jobs, the level of credentials is used as a filter for job applicants. Students thus strive to obtain even more credentials, and employers escalate their requirements. The original purpose of education—the learning needed to perform a job—has been crowded out by the need to obtain the credentials needed to obtain a job. The content of education systems is often based

---

[22] Williams (2000) notes the analogy between the brain drain problem and training by firms that may result in the loss of trained people. Fear of losing employees would lead to an underinvestment in non-firm-specific, firm-sponsored training. Vocational education subsidies in the United Kingdom try to overcome this underinvestment problem.

Table 2.1 *Organization of Work Based on Logic of Exit and Logic of Commitment*

Item	Logic of exit	Logic of commitment
Efficiency	Resources are allocated to highest value use. Allocative efficiency is enhanced by mobility.	Greatest value is reaped from resources allocated to given use. X-efficiency (effort) is enhanced by immobility (Leibenstein 1984).
Results of education	Universal certification is provided to maximize mobility, and thus the efficiency of allocation.	Knowledge is local, embedded, partly tacit, and shown in practice, not in certificates.
Identity	Mobility is enhanced by identifying with a profession or other universal category.	Individuals identify with and are motivated to improve their social group, village, company, or institution.
Labor mobility	Mobility is high, so changes take place primarily by replacing old workers with new workers embodying new knowledge.	Mobility is low, so changes take place primarily by workers acquiring new knowledge.
Process improvement	Work is reduced to standard repetitive tasks, so that workers are replaceable. Skills change exogenously. Expertise is exogenous or located in management, so that workers are replaceable. Staff do not identify with a firm or institution.	The plan-do-study-act cycle of continuous improvement is applied. Learning takes place as the scientific method is applied. Expertise develops as embedded local and tacit knowledge of staff involved in continuous improvement grows. The system encourages staff identification with the firm.
Payment system	Employees are paid the going rate for certified skills. Workers receive equal pay for equal work. Payment is associated with the work performed and the results achieved.	Employees are paid according to seniority and skills demonstrated in firm-specific jobs. Payment is associated with individuals (usually under the going rate at the beginning and over it at the end, as incentive to stay).
Motivation	Employees are expected to be motivated by individual material self-interest.	Employees are expected to identify with the organization and have shared group interests.
Stability and trust in relationships	Low-trust relationships imply explicit contracts and competitive, arm's length, exit-oriented relationships. The lack of investment in building trust or loyalty leads to low-trust relationships. Individuals pay for learning.	High-trust relationships imply incomplete relational contracts. Voice-oriented relationships requiring investment in building trust and loyalty lead to high-trust relationships. The company pays for learning.
Entry into firm	Entry is at all levels.	Entry is at lower levels. Promotion is from within.
Style of interpersonal relationships	Standardized, professional behavior is used as a means of coordinating people. Low interpersonal knowledge is associated with high turnover.	Familiarity and intimacy in long-term relationships is used as a means of coordinating people. High interpersonal knowledge is associated with low turnover.
Application to migration	Nationals exit to find a better home.	Nationals commit to making home better.

Source: Based on Ellerman (2005b).

on standards from the former colonial center or on today's globalized standards and has little relevance to local jobs. Moreover, even that content is sacrificed in the rat race of the diploma disease.

Dore's proposals call for coordinated transformation in the tertiary education system and in the organizations providing jobs. Under his proposal, individuals begin work at an earlier age. Learning (at tertiary educational institutions as well as on the job) becomes a life-long process guided by the requirements and opportunities of the work.[23] The work organization pays for continuing tertiary education. Filtering is based on the demonstrated ability to continue to learn and to perform a job, not on the acquisition of universal certificates. Under this system,

> the civil service, for instance, would no longer recruit graduates. There would, instead, be a single major entry port for all grades at the age of 16 (or whatever was fixed as the school leaving age) and everyone would start as a clerk; some, on the results of internal tests, or on the basis of work performance, would be promoted fairly quickly to the executive grades and given such further training as was necessary, and some of those would similarly be selected—and educated/trained—for administrative posts. The same pattern could apply to other professions. Future engineers could train first as craftsmen; some of the craftsmen could be trained as technicians, and the ablest of those sent off for full training as engineers. Doctors could begin as medical assistants; teachers as pupil-teachers; university teachers as research assistants or secretaries or schoolteachers; architects and accountants and quantity surveyors could begin as clerks and be selected for professional training (Dore 1976, p. 143).

Cooperative education programs (which alternate semesters studying and working in a company) are a step in this direction. When study abroad is appropriate, it would be financed by the company and would probably take place at an older age, when the individual not only had a job waiting upon return, but had a family and other roots in the home country. A national system of education and work designed along Dore's lines would maximize the retention of the best and brightest, just as Japanese-style human resource management policies have done within firms.

Perhaps in order to keep more brains at home, the tertiary education system has to be improved so that its centers of excellence have higher international ranking and better recognition. The value of the credentials these institutions provide must be improved, perhaps with help from independent international certification, to relieve some of the pressure for the best students to get degrees abroad. Independent certification of graduates would also increase job prospects for graduates. This argument can be cast in the terms of information economics. Certification would help overcome the informational asymmetry faced by the work organizations (domestic or international) that might provide jobs for graduates.

What is wrong with this argument? How could anyone be against focusing, say, African tertiary education systems on centers of excellence with better international certification of their graduates? Dore's diploma disease argument opposes just such

---

[23] This is similar to the Japanese-style firm, where entry occurs at an early age and continuing education is promoted by the firm. With changing technologies, workers "require formal training at regular intervals in a quasi-school environment that complements the informal training they receive on the job in order to systematize their experiences on the job" (Aoki 1988, p. 52).

an effort. The certification argument is an example of an argument based entirely on the logic of exit, without recognizing that there is an alternative way to address the problem. Organizations based on the logic of commitment address the information asymmetry problem by taking people on board at an earlier age and slowly learning about their attributes and capabilities through direct interaction.

For example, the Japanese-style firm "can identify slow learning, low productivity, low motivation, and uncooperative workers by actual observation and differentiate them in pay and status over the long run, while attempting to lock in fast-learning, highly productive, highly motivated, cooperative workers by discouraging them from quitting in midcareer" (Aoki 1988, p. 50). Hence this system emphasizes the X-efficiency of retaining and developing the best and brightest as opposed to a system designed to equip people with universal credentials so that they have the greatest mobility to seek the highest-paid opportunities available in an allocatively efficient global labor market.

Thus the certification approach is not the only way to address the information asymmetry problem. Moreover it will tend to aggravate rather than alleviate the brain drain. Many of the homilies about the globalization of educational standards make this clear. "The proportion of foreign students studying for professional degrees or doctorates in the university systems of the major industrialized countries, in particular the United States, is large, and more than two-thirds simply stay on. The situation is similar in Europe, albeit on a smaller scale. At the same time, centres of excellence in higher education in labour-exporting developing countries are increasingly adopting curricula that conform to international patterns and standards. Given the facility of language, such people are employable almost anywhere" (Nayyar 2002, p. 164).

There is also a more subtle problem in the certification argument. One consequence of focusing on international certification with universal standards is that the type of knowledge that is internationally certifiable—that will have currency in Paris, London, or New York, for example—is emphasized. This redirects the focus away from the types of local knowledge important for a developing region. For instance, instead of training physicians in local tropical diseases, knowledge of little use in the North, doctors would receive universal training that would be as applicable in Alberta as in Angola. Policy makers should not be surprised when doctors with such training emigrate to Alberta rather than stay in Angola.

Summary of Conceptual Issues

The field of migration and development is unsettled and unresolved for good reason. The dilemmas are basic and fundamental. Seemingly good arguments can be made on both sides of major issues; intelligent people (like Johnson and Patinkin) can disagree. Some issues in the sphere of migration studies reflect larger issues that rend the field of development studies. Some of those basic issues are summarized here.

The Dynamics of Convergence or Divergence

One basic issue is the question of the underlying dynamic mechanisms. The contrast is between negative feedback, self-limiting mechanisms (equalizing dynamics) and positive feedback, self-reinforcing mechanisms (critical mass dynamics). Almost all neoclassical economics is based on the assumption of diminishing returns. As factors move from low-return uses to higher-return uses, the high return falls and the low return rises, eliminating the discrepancy. But the opposite case of positive feedback (increasing returns) is now receiving increasing attention in the literature of economics (Myrdal 1957 was an early example) and the sciences. Increasing returns lead to multiple equilibriums, perhaps of a high and low variety (the twin peaks dynamics of divergence).

The North-to-North migration from Europe to North America during the 18th and 19th centuries was, for the most part, an equalizing dynamics mechanism.[24] Part of the controversy today is about whether South-to-North migration is part of an equalizing dynamics of convergence or a critical mass dynamics of divergence. Time and again, one finds unguarded and unstated assumptions in the literature that a factor movement from a low to a high return will equalize rather than increase the discrepancy in returns, as if the flight of human and financial capital out of a country could be expected to improve its development prospects.

This argument can also be stated in terms of Hirschmanian inducement or pressure mechanisms and exit and voice dynamics. Suppose there are two groups, A and B. If problems and bottlenecks appear in group B, then the migration of some members from B to A could have either a positive or negative effect on B. The exit or defection of some members of B might alert the other members or their leaders that changes needed to be made to resolve problems and overcome bottlenecks, leading to equalizing dynamics between A and B. But it might work the other way. The members exiting from B might be the most articulate or capable members, whose exit makes it even less likely that vested interests will be overcome to resolve the problems. This would lead to the dynamics of divergence.

When the entrenched elites in a developing country see highly educated young people emigrating, does that steel their resolve to make the changes necessary to staunch the brain drain? Or does it reduce the pressure on them to give up the privileges that are barriers to development and that lead to the brain drain in the first place? This is not a question that can be settled a priori. But there should be no a priori assumption that exit (switch rather than fight) rather than nonexit (fight rather than switch) is the best way to induce reforms; no assumption should be made that exit will equalize rather than increase the difference.

A number of social mechanisms are designed to mitigate, if not defeat, the dynamics of divergence of the Matthew principle. Antitrust policy tries to break the size begets size dynamics in the merger market, so that companies maintain some parity and rivalry. Separation of powers, term limits,[25] and other constitutional limitations are designed to mitigate the power begets power dynamics in the political sphere. In an economy in which wealth begets wealth independently of effort and innovation, the breakdown of primogeniture and the enactment of progressive income taxes and inheritance taxes help mitigate those dynamics. In professional sports, the practice of having the worst teams get first choice in the draft of new players is aimed at defeating the dynamics of divergence and maintaining some competitive parity.

---

[24] An argument could be made that migration out of some regions, such as southern Italy and Sicily, contributed and continues to contribute to the poverty of those regions.

[25] For similar reasons, term limits were suggested earlier for temporary labor migration schemes to defeat the self-reinforcing, rut-deepening tendencies of such schemes.

Box 2.3 *The Logic of Exit and the Logic of Commitment in Other Contexts*

Situations in which decision makers must choose between the logic of exit and the logic of commitment appear in many contexts, for example:

- A hiker seeking to climb the highest peak in a mountain range in which visibility is poor can adopt either the logic of commitment by continuing to climb the peak he or she is on (fight rather than switch), or the logic of exit by switching to another peak, which might be higher (switch rather than fight).
- The process of selection in evolution (including its mathematical versions in genetic algorithms), starts with the commitment to the existing set of genetic possibilities and then exploits or refines them to determine the fittest. In addition, there is the process of variation (for example, mutation and crossover or sexual reproduction), which works to exit the given hill on the fitness landscape and explore other possibilities. This is the evolutionary version of the previous example: commit to climbing farther up a given hill or search for another, possibly higher, hill.
- A detective must decide when investigating a crime whether to spend time following up on a given clue or searching for more clues.
- A manager must decide whether to make a commitment to a given team and focus on developing its capabilities or to take those characteristics as given and focus on shuffling team members to get a better combination.

Every potential migrant faces a similar situation: to make a commitment to staying home and trying to improve it or to take its characteristics as given and search elsewhere for a new and better home. Economic models tend to model only the exit option, ignoring the possible logic of commitment, with its inherent uncertainties about the possibilities of transformation.

Universal public schooling aims to disrupt the dynamics of educational divergence across generations. Proposals for school vouchers are often criticized as attempts to reintroduce the logic of exit and individual visions of success as getting one's child into a better school instead of the collective action logic of working to make the child's school better. Proponents of voucher plans assume that the underlying dynamics are equalizing and convergent. If the primary sources of pressure for betterment were the articulate and concerned parents who would also be the first to exit under a voucher plan, then the underlying dynamics are those of divergence and ghettoization.[26]

The Logic of Exit Versus the Logic of Commitment

If the characteristics of resources and structures (or uses) are taken as fixed, then efficiency is seen through the logic of exit. Resources should exit or be replaced if there are feasible higher-valued allocations for them. If, however, the location of the resources in a use is taken as essentially fixed but the characteristics of the resources and structures are taken as variable, then efficiency is seen through the logic of commitment. How can a given set of resources and surrounding structures be transformed to reach a higher-value outcome (box 2.3)? That is the domain of X-efficiency. In some formulations, the

---

[26] New Zealand adopted a voucher-like program, Tomorrow's Schools, in the early 1990s. The better schools soon filled with hand-picked students and turned away the hard to teach poor or minority students, who had no alternative but to return to their now more depleted old schools. The dynamics of divergence left the schools even more stratified along socioeconomic and ethnic lines than they had been (Wylie 1998).

contrast between allocative and X-efficiency might be rendered as static efficiency (fixed characteristics of resources and uses but variable allocation of resources to uses) versus dynamic efficiency. The two logics are elaborations of Hirschman's (1970) treatment of exit versus voice. He analyzes the choice of taking characteristics as fixed or variable as "trait-taking" or "trait-making" (Hirschman 1967).

The stylized models of the American versus the Japanese firm—such as Aoki's (1988) distinction between the A-firm and the J-firm—are based on these two logics (Ellerman 2005b). The manager in the A-firm sees the organizational problem in terms of the market logic of exit and replacement: how to find the best resources on the market, buying and selling or hiring and firing as necessary, to obtain the highest-value allocation of resources. Management in the J-firm sees the organizational problem in terms of a community model (Dore 1987) of commitment to an essentially given set of people: how to develop and transform their skills and capabilities and those of the surrounding organizational structures to obtain the highest-value outcome.

What the exit logic views as inflexibility or rigidity (for example, taking the allocation of people to an organization as a given), the commitment logic views as commitment and loyalty. Some organizational mechanisms, such as barriers to exit (Kagono and Kobayashi 1994), are seen as irrational by one logic and rational by the other. For instance, the organizational norm of expecting the captain to go down with the ship or the failed manager to fall on his sword is designed to close off the logic of exit and to promote the logic of commitment and transformation. As Chinese township and village enterprises faced a hard budget constraint (that is, they were like a ship that could sink), the relative immobility of labor (the lack of lifeboats on the ship) was viewed by the logic of exit as allocative inefficiency. The commitment logic viewed it as promoting the commitment, voice, and effort (that is, X-efficiency) of the workers and managers to make sure that the enterprise stayed afloat.

These two logics cut across the analysis of migration and development. If a worker in a developing country takes the characteristics of the place as fixed, he or she will view advancement through the logic of exit. Commitment and voice are pointless if transformation is seen as impossible, at least within the relevant future. These workers are looking for the best exit in search of a higher-value use of their human resources. This is the market-based logic exemplified in Johnson's cosmopolitan liberalism.

Others, such as Patinkin, take the people as essentially given. Starting with that commitment, they face the task of finding out how the skills and capabilities of the people and the surrounding structures can best be transformed and developed. This logic of commitment and transformation is behind policies at Japanese-style firms, Dore's educational reforms, and the thinking of development-oriented policy makers in developing countries.

Individual Versus Collective Visions of Success

In the prisoners' dilemma game, the individual strategy for success is not the best collective strategy for success. An individual vision of success comports well with the logic of exit (defection), while a collective, group, or community vision of success evokes the logic of commitment.[27]

---

[27] See the related ego-focused and group-focused visions of change in Hirschman (1958, chapter 1), as well Hirschman's (1982) analysis of individual versus collective action.

Consider a situation in which there are two companies, countries, or groups, A and B, and that group A is much better than group B. An individual in group B with an individual vision of success might well use the logic of exit to find a way to migrate from B to A. An individual in group B with a collective vision of success might well use the logic of commitment to find a way to transform B so that it becomes better than, or at least comparable to, group A.

The dynamics of migration by the best and brightest from B to A might well be the dynamics of divergence. Group A might be able to sustain and increase its advantage over B by poaching the most capable people from B. One subtle way for group A to promote that outcome would be to promote the universal adoption of the objective meritocratic standard, in which success on the basis of one's merits means joining the currently best group, not working to make one's own group best. As Young's *The Rise of the Meritocracy* (1962) forcefully shows, such a meritocratic structure would tend to perpetuate the supremacy of group A.

Increased Income Versus Increased Development: The Three D's Deal

Debates about migration and development may reveal basic differences about the goals of development assistance. Some view the goal of development assistance as putting resources in the hands of the poor—a certain kind of poverty reduction. They view increased income and increased living standards as development. Others view increased income for the poor as a worthy goal, but not in itself as development. Indeed, depending on how it is achieved, poverty reduction (in the form of long-term charitable relief, for example) may even be inimical to development. These observers view development in a country or region as based on developing and diversifying the skills and capabilities of the people in the country so that they can increase their incomes by adding value (as opposed to merely extracting natural resources) in an autonomous and sustainable way.

A question helps frame the issue. Suppose a poor and undeveloped country discovers a large deposit of oil and gas, so that the average income is substantially increased and living standards are improved. Is that by itself development?[28]

Now reframe the question so that the large deposit of oil and gas is replaced by long-term South-to-North migration, with the ensuing flow of remittances to the sending country. These remittances reduce poverty, increase incomes, and improve living standards. Are they not, then, a form of successful development? In today's world of globalized transportation and communication, must nationals work in their home countries? No one says that a suburban bedroom community is underdeveloped because it contains no internal sources of income. Why should the judgment be different when the bedroom community is hundreds or thousands of miles away?

A deal—some would say a devil's deal—has been struck between the North and the South. In the developed North, many dirty, difficult, and dangerous jobs (the three D's) are not being filled by native workers. For unskilled migrants, these jobs may pay four times what they could earn at home. Hence a deal is struck. The North will be the primary site of development in the sense of jobs, including the

---

[28] The aggregate growth models of development economics provide remarkably little insight into such questions. Some of the best and most accessible thinking on this topic is in the works of Jacobs (1969, 1984).

low-end jobs that native workers will not fill. The South will be a kind of long-distance bedroom community furnishing workers for these jobs. This arrangement will satisfy many of the conventional criteria for development in the South: increasing income, reducing poverty, and improving living standards.

There seems to be a fault line running under the field of migration and development concerning this three D's deal between the North and the South. The deal is usually not stated in such bald terms; euphemisms, blinkered vision, and Pollyanna scenarios abound. Some supporters of the three D's deal emphasize the benefits to governments in the South, which can export their unemployment problems and import the hard currency they need to relieve their balance of payments problems. Some keep their eyes riveted on the improved living standards of the temporary migrants and their families and ignore the lock-in to a pattern of economically sterile bedroom communities in the South. Some ignore decades of disappointed hopes for development led by guest worker remittances in order to embellish the lingering hope that these patterns could lead to real development in the South. Others cut that Gordian knot and in effect redefine development in terms of poverty reduction and improvements in living standards. The debate, implicit or explicit, over the three D's deal is fundamental to policy questions in migration and development.

Complicating the Discourse on Migration and Globalization

Globalization is often praised as being unambiguously positive on the grounds of the market-driven logic of exit, the equalizing dynamics of convergence, and the individual visions of success. The conceptual framework used here complicates the discourse by showing that the usual approach to globalization is one–sided (for more analysis, see Ellerman 2003, 2005a). The logic of commitment and transformation that embodies a group-focused or collective action vision of success has an equal claim as a strategy for social improvement. Moreover, to the extent that the underlying mechanism for South-to-North interaction is the dynamics of divergence, the logic of exit to obtain individual success will perpetuate and aggravate the North-South divide.

Annex 1. Multiperson Prisoners' Dilemma Games

The standard two-person prisoners' dilemma game illustrates a symmetrical situation in which each player has a choice of cooperating or defecting. In this game, regardless of what the other player does, each player's best strategy is to defect, but the outcome of both defecting is worse for players than the outcome of both cooperating (table A1.1.1).

Table A1.1.1 *Payoffs in a Two-Person Prisoners' Dilemma Game (amount of payoff)*

		Player 1			
		Cooperate		Defect	
Player 2	Cooperate	1	1	-1	3
	Defect	3	-1	0	0

Source: Author.

The two-person game can be graphed in a way that can then be generalized to a multiperson game (figure A1.1.1). The two sloping lines "I defect" and "I cooperate" show the results for each player depending on what the other player does. The other player is either at the left end (defect) or at the right end (cooperate) of the horizontal line. The fact that no matter what the other player does, it is better for a player to defect is indicated by the fact that the "I defect" curve is always above the "I cooperate" curve. If both players defect, each gets a payoff of 0; if the players cooperate, each gets a payoff of 1.

In figure A1.1.2 which represents a multiperson game with $n + 1$ players, the length of the horizontal line is n. A point such as m along the line represents the players who cooperate, so that $n - m$ represents the number of defectors. The two sloping lines give the payoffs to any player given the assumed number of other players who defect or cooperate. (The payoff curves need not be straight lines. They are shown as such here for simplicity.) Thus the vertical line at m intersects the "I cooperate" and "I defect" lines at the points giving the payoffs to the marginal player (which could be any player). As the "I defect" curve dominates the "I cooperate" curve no matter what the other m players do, it is still in the interest of each player to defect. The payoff to each is then 0, whereas universal cooperation gives each a payoff of 1.

Figure A1.1.1 *Payoffs in a Two-Person Prisoners' Dilemma Game*

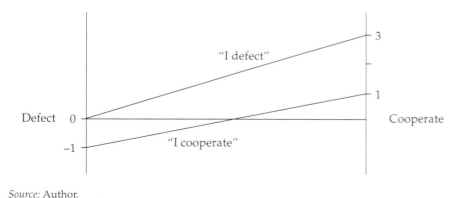

Source: Author.

Figure A1.1.2 *Payoffs in a Multiperson Prisoners' Dilemma Game*

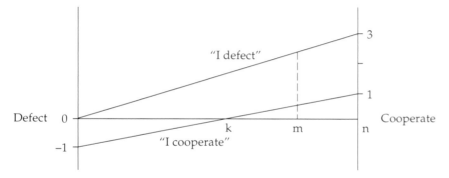

Source: Author.

Figure A1.1.3 *Migration as a Multiperson Prisoners' Dilemma Game*

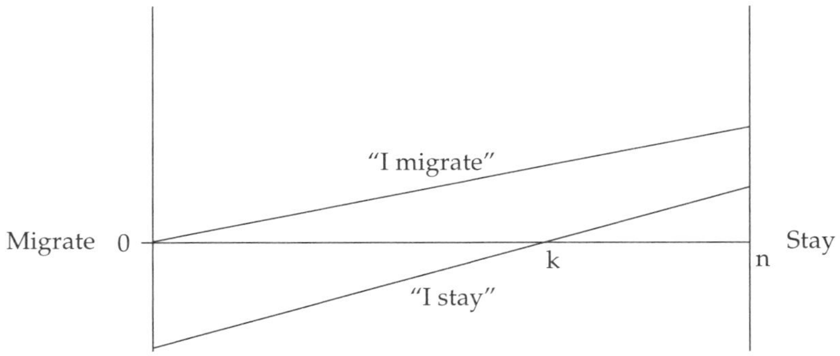

Source: Author.

The universal defection point is arbitrarily taken as the origin. The point k is the minimum "coalition of the cooperating" needed for the payoff to exceed the universal defection payoff no matter what the other players do.

The "dilemma" is in the game as long as the "I defect" curve is always above the "I cooperate" curve.

In figure A1.1.3 the migration decision is interpreted as a multiperson prisoners' dilemma game. This model is about a simple stay or leave decision. There are no remittances or return migrations. The payoff curves give a simple economic return to individuals (or families).

This model assumes diminishing returns to migration. As more people migrate, the payoff to each is reduced. This could be interpreted as a tightening of controls at the receiving end, which raises the cost of migration. The payoff to each player when all migrate is taken as the zero point. The point k represents the minimum number of stayers needed so that each stayer receives at least the universal migration payoff. At every combination of stayers and migrants, it is always in the individual interests of the marginal player to migrate, but the result of all migrating is dominated by the outcome in which all stay.

These prisoners' dilemma models of collective action situations typically do not represent the whole situation, as collective action does take place (Hirschman 1982). The game might represent the situation absent a law to require cooperation (such as paying taxes), absent some social sanction against defection, or absent some social preference for cooperative action. The migration example might represent the individual economic payoffs absent any social disapprobation against leaving. Accounting for such factors complicates the analysis, because different individuals have different susceptibilities to social sanctions.

The migration version of the multiperson prisoners' dilemma game illustrates an important point: the cosmopolitan liberal position that each individual should choose the option that improves his or her own position is not good policy advice in a prisoners' dilemma situation.

Annex 2. The Dynamics of Convergence and Divergence

Picturing the Dynamics of Convergence

The equalizing dynamics between two regions (rich and poor) that are driven by wage differentials can be illustrated by drawing two labor demand curves (figure

Figure A2.2.1 *Effect of Migration on Poverty Reduction*

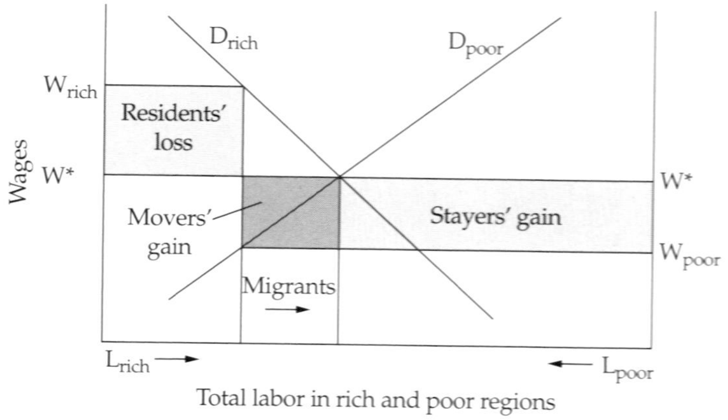

Total labor in rich and poor regions

Source: Williamson (2003).

A2.2.1). The vertical axis on the right is the wage scale in the poor country; the quantity of labor supplied in the poor country, L_{poor}, is represented on the horizontal axis as increasing from right to left. Thus the demand curve for labor, D_{poor}, in the poor country is represented as backward sloping, right to left. The total combined labor of the two countries is the length of the horizontal axis. At the initial, premigration equilibrium, the wage is W_{rich} in the rich country and W_{poor} in the poor country. When the gate between the two labor reservoirs is opened, the equalizing flow of labor from the poor country to the rich country is the migration that equalizes the wage rate in both countries at W^*. By comparing the equilibrium wages before and after the migration, we can compute the residents' loss for the original workers in the rich country, the movers' gain for the migrants, and the stayers' gain for the workers who remain in the poor country.

This illustration of the dynamics of convergence is a comparative statics diagram that represents two equilibriums and not the dynamics in between. The key assumption is that there are no economies of agglomeration or disagglomeration in either country, an assumption embodied in the partial equilibrium representation of the demand for labor curves being the same despite a significant medium-term shift in population from one country to the other. The alternative assumption is considered in the next section.

A different dynamics of convergence is given by the reaction curve model. Consider a world with just groups A and B. Each of a fixed number of individuals is in one group or the other. The reaction function shows what percentage (Y) of people are willing to be in group B given that X percent are in group B. But in a two-group world, the reaction function can also be read as saying given (100 – X) percent in A, (100 – Y) percent are willing to be in group A. Then the reaction function dynamics between the two groups can be represented by a square diagram reminiscent of the Edgeworth box (figure A2.2.2). The reaction curve for group A has its origin at the northeastern corner of the square.

Whether looked at from the viewpoint of group A or group B, there is a unique and stable equilibrium where the reaction curve crosses the 45 degree line. Given an exogenous shock that moves it away from the equilibrium, the dynamics will restore it.

Figure A2.2.2 *Reaction Square with Dynamics of Convergence*

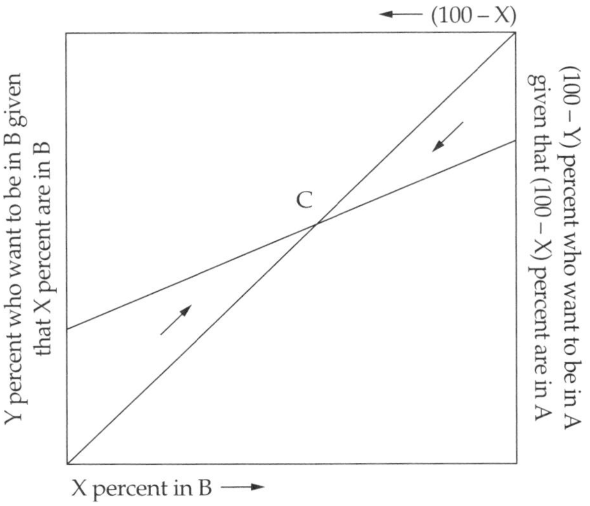

Source: Author.

Picturing the Dynamics of Divergence

The comparative statics model shown in figure A2.2.2 assumes no economies of agglomeration or disagglomeration as labor moves from one country to the other. These economies and diseconomies go beyond the general equilibrium multiplier effects, which are usually ignored in the partial equilibrium comparative statics approach. Cities (or Alfred Marshall's industrial districts) may exhibit such economies. As labor comes in to satisfy demand, other medium-term dynamics are set in motion. As firms expand, they may diversify into new product lines, which would shift the demand for labor. Some operations may spin off from expanding large firms, and the vigor of the spin-offs may shift the demand for labor upward.[29] Some "resident" workers, as well as some migrants, may decide to go into business for themselves, which also shifts demand for labor.

On the sending side, there may also be medium-term dynamic effects. Some firms may collapse in the face of rising costs or the loss of key personnel to the North, which, in turn, may have a knock-on effect on the viability of related firms (suppliers or customers). In fact, some migrants may themselves have been propri- etors of microenterprises. These effects would shift labor demand downward in the sending country, part of the dynamics of disagglomeration or ghettoization. Remit- tances would have an opposing multiplier effect, increasing labor demand (at least where the money is spent). But that demand would collapse if workers returned to take remittance-funded jobs unless the remittances were used to create jobs that did not depend on remittances. Remittances might also have the negative effect of inspiring and funding the migration of additional family members. In the absence of positive developmental changes, one would expect remittances to only mitigate and not reverse the downward shift.

---

[29] Nature thrives by having old growth constantly seeding new growth rather than just expanding old growth.

Figure A2.2.3 *Effect of South-to-North Migration on the South-North Divide*

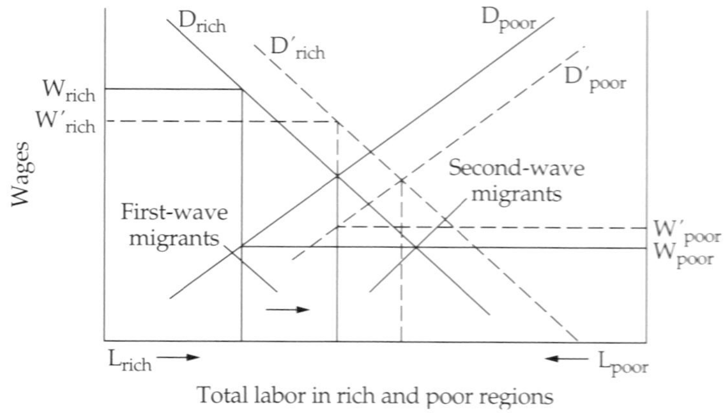

Source: Author.

Figure A2.2.3 shows three equilibriums. When the labor gates are opened, the separate equilibriums given by W_{rich} and W_{poor} create the first wave of migrants from the poor to the rich country. But the dynamic agglomerative effects of the migration shift the labor demand curve D_{rich} outward to D'_{rich} in the rich country, and the ghettoizing effect in the poor country shifts the labor demand curve D_{poor} downward to D'_{poor}. This still leaves a wage differential between W'_{rich} and W'_{poor}. Additional waves of migrants will come until the differential is eliminated. The size of the shifts is drawn so that after the first wave of migration, the wage in the poor country, W'_{poor}, is still higher than the original wage W_{poor}. The ghettoizing effect in the South is shown by the lower level of labor demand at each wage level, that is, the overall drop in economic activity, even though the remaining workers may earn higher wages.[30] Long before this dynamics of divergence worked its way out, however, the rich country would probably close its gates. The net effect of the intervening migration episodes would be agglomeration in the rich country and ghettoization in the poor country, increasing the South-to-North divide and contributing to "divergence, big time" (Pritchett 1997).

The reaction function model also illustrates the dynamics of divergence (figure A2.2.4). There are two stable equilibriums: A, in which almost everyone is in group A, and B, in which the groups are more evenly split but most people are in B. If the system is at B, then a large enough exogenous shock, such as massive poaching by group A, would increase the percentage in group A (and decrease it in group B) to beyond the critical mass point C, so that mass migration would be started, which would push the system to the new equilibrium at A. Almost everyone would be in group A, and group B would be ghettoized to a small remnant of diehards.

---

[30] For a dramatic example, suppose that a group of doctors in a hospital is attracted away to hospitals in the North in a package deal. Although the hospital would nearly collapse, the immobile wealthy would be willing to pay more to obtain the services of the remaining doctors.

Figure A2.2.4 *Reaction Square with Dynamics of Divergence*

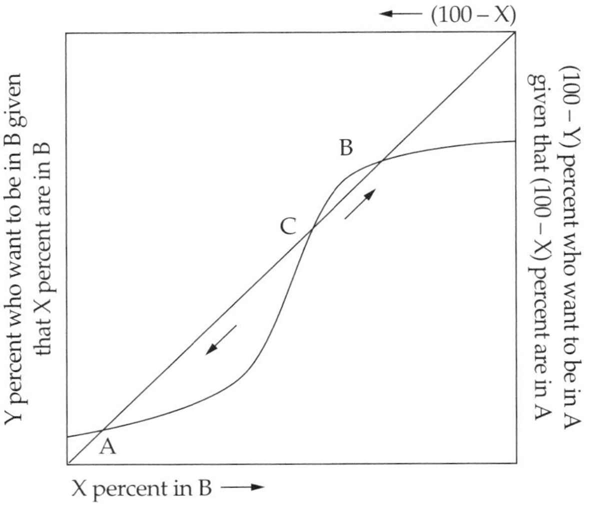

Source: Author.

References

Abadan-Unat, Nermin, ed. 1976. *Turkish Workers in Europe (1960–1975)*. Leiden, Netherlands: E. J. Brill.

Abella, Manolo. 2002. "International Migration Development Impacts on Sending Countries: Experience and Potential." Remarks at World Bank Environmentally and Socially Sustainable Development Week, Washington, DC, April 10.

Adams, Walter, ed. 1968. *The Brain Drain*. New York: Macmillan.

Aoki, Masahiko. 1988. *Information, Incentives, and Bargaining in the Japanese Economy*. New York: Cambridge University Press.

Athukorala, P. 1993. *Enhancing Developmental Impact of Migrant Remittances: A Review of Asian Experiences*. New Delhi: Asian Regional Programme on International Labour Migration.

Bhagwati, Jagdish. 2003. "Borders Beyond Control." *Foreign Affairs* 82 (1): 98–104.

Bovenkerk, F. 1974. "The Sociology of Return Migration: A Bibliographic Essay." *Publications of the Research Group on European Migration Problems 20.* The Hague: Martinus Nijhoff.

———. 1982. "Why Returnees Generally Do Not Turn Out to Be 'Agents of Change.'" In *Return Migration and Remittances: Developing a Caribbean Perspective*, ed. W. F. Stinner, K. de Albuquerque, and R. Bryce-Laporte. Washington, DC: Smithsonian Institution.

Brown, Mercy. 2000. "Using the Intellectual Diaspora to Reverse the Brain Drain: Some Useful Examples." University of Cape Town, South Africa. http://sansa.nrf.ac.za/interface/Publications.htm.

Cornelius, Wayne. 2002. "Outward Bound." *The Economist,* September 28.

Deci, Edward, and Richard Ryan. 1985. *Intrinsic Motivation and Self-Determination in Human Behavior.* New York: Plenum Press.

Desai, Mihir, Devesh Kapur, and John McHale. 2001. "The Fiscal Impact of the Brain Drain: Indian Emigration to the U.S." Paper prepared for the Third Annual NBER-NCAER Conference, Neemrana, India, December 17–18.

Dore, Ronald. 1976. *The Diploma Disease: Education, Qualification, and Development.* Berkeley, CA: University of California Press.

———. 1987. *Taking Japan Seriously.* Stanford, CA.: Stanford University Press.

———. 1997. *The Diploma Disease: Education, Qualification, and Development,* 2nd ed. London: University of London, Institute of Education.

The Economist. 2002a. "Emigration from Latin America: Making the Most of an Exodus." February 23.

———. 2002b. "The Longest Journey: A Survey on Migration." November 2.
Ellerman, David. 2003. "Policy Research on Migration and Development." Policy Research Working Paper 3117, World Bank, Washington, DC.

———. 2005a. "Labour Migration: A Developmental Path or a Low-Level Trap?" *Development in Practice* 15 (5): 617–30.

———. 2005b. "The Two Institutional Logics: Exit-Oriented Versus Commitment-Oriented Institutional Designs. " *International Economic Journal* 19 (June 2): 147–68.

European Stability Initiative. 2002. *Ahmeti's Village: The Political Economy of Interethnic Relations in Macedonia.* Berlin: European Stability Initiative. http://www.esiweb.org/pdf/esi_document_id_36.pdf.

Hatton, Timothy, and Jeffrey Williamson. 1998. *The Age of Mass Migration: Causes and Economic Analysis.* New York: Oxford University Press.

Hirschman, Albert O. 1958. *The Strategy of Economic Development.* New Haven, CT: Yale University Press.

———. 1967. *Development Projects Observed.* Washington, DC: Brookings Institution.

———. 1970. *Exit, Voice, and Loyalty.* Cambridge, MA: Harvard University Press.

———. 1977. *The Passions and the Interests.* Princeton, NJ: Princeton University Press.

———. 1982. *Shifting Involvements: Private Interests and Public Action.* Princeton, NJ: Princeton University Press.

Jacobs, Jane 1969. *The Economy of Cities.* New York: Random House.

———. 1984. *Cities and the Wealth of Nations: Principles of Economic Life.* New York: Random House.

Johnson, Harry. 1968. "An 'Internationalist' Model." In *The Brain Drain,* ed. W. Adams. New York: Macmillan.

Kagono, Tadao, and Takao Kobayashi. 1994. "The Provision of Resources and Barriers to Exit." In *Business Enterprise in Japan,* ed. K. Imai and R. Komiya, 89–102. Cambridge, MA: MIT Press.

Kapur, Devesh. 2001. "Diasporas and Technology Transfer." *Journal of Human Development* 2 (2): 265–86.

Kindleberger, Charles. 1978. *Economic Response: Comparative Studies in Trade, Finance, and Growth.* Cambridge, MA: Harvard University Press.

Lane, Robert. 1991. *The Market Experience.* New York: Cambridge University Press.

Leibenstein, Harvey. 1984. "The Japanese Management System: An X-Efficiency Game Theory Analysis." In *The Economic Analysis of the Japanese Firm,* ed. M. Aoki, 331–57. Amsterdam: Elsevier.

Martin, Philip, Susan Martin, and Ferruccio Pastore. 2002. "CEME Best Practices to Manage Migration: Italy-Albania." University of California, Davis. http://migration.ucdavis.edu/ceme/italy_albania.html.

Martin, Philip, and Thomas Straubhaar 2001. "Best Practices to Foster Economic Growth." *Cooperative Efforts to Manage Emigration (CEME).* University of California, Davis. http://migration.ucdavis.edu/ceme/index.html.

Massey, M., J. Arango, G. Hugo, A. Kouaouci, A. Pellegrino, and J. Taylor. 1998. *Worlds in Motion: Understanding International Migration at the End of the Millennium.* Oxford, U.K.: Clarendon Press.

McGregor, Douglas. 1960. *The Human Side of Enterprise.* New York: McGraw-Hill.

Mill, John Stuart. 1899. *Principles of Political Economy.* New York: Colonial Press.

Myrdal, Gunnar. 1957. *Economic Theory and Underdeveloped Regions.* New York: Harper Torchbooks.

Naughton, Barry. 1999. "Between China and the World." In *Cosmopolitan Capitalists: Hong Kong and the Chinese Diaspora at the End of the Twentieth Century,* ed. G. G. Hamilton. Seattle: University of Washington Press.

Nayyar, Deepak 2002. "Cross-Border Movements of People." In *Governing Globalization: Issues and Institutions,* ed. D. Nayyared. Oxford, U.K.: Oxford University Press.

Nicholson, Beryl 2002. "The Wrong End of the Telescope: Economic Migrants, Immigration Policy, and How It Looks from Albania. " *Political Quarterly* 73 (4): 436–44.

O'Rourke, K., and J. Williamson. 2000. *Globalization and History. The Evolution of a Nineteenth-Century Economy.* Cambridge, MA: MIT Press.

Patinkin, Don. 1968. "A 'Nationalist' Model." In *The Brain Drain,* ed. W. Adams. New York: Macmillan.

Portes, Alejandro. 1999. "Globalization from Below: The Rise of Transnational Communities." In *The Ends of Globalization: Bringing Society Back In,* ed. D. Kalb. Boulder, CO: Rowman and Littlefield.

Pritchett, Lant. 1997. "Divergence, Big Time." *Journal of Economic Perspectives* 11 (3): 3–17.

Rodrik, Dani. 2001. "Comments at a Conference on Immigration Policy and the Welfare State." July. http://ksghome.harvard.edu/~.drodrik.academic.ksg/papers.html.

Saxenian, Anna Lee. 2000. "The Bangalore Boom: From Brain Drain to Brain Circulation?" In *Bridging the Digital Divide: Lessons from India*, ed. K. Kennistan and D. Kumar. Bangalore, India: National Institute of Advanced Study.

Schelling, Thomas C. 1978. *Micromotives and Macrobehavior.* New York: W. W. Norton.

Simon, Herbert. 1991. "Organizations and Markets." *Journal of Economic Perspectives* 5 (2): 25–44.

Solimano, Andrés. 2002. "Globalizing Talent and Human Capital: Implications for Developing Countries." Paper presented at the Annual Bank Conference on Development Economics, Oslo, June 24–26.

Stark, Oded. 1991. *The Migration of Labor.* Oxford, U.K.: Basil Blackwell.

Stern, Nicholas. 2001. *A Strategy for Development.* Washington, DC: World Bank.

Weidenbaum, Murray, and Samuel Hughes. 1996. *The Bamboo Network.* New York: Free Press.

Williams, Christopher. 1981. *Origins of Form.* New York: Architectural Book Publishing Company.

Williams, Peter. 2000. "Brain Drain." DFID Imfundo Knowledge Bank. http://imfundo.digitalbrain.com/imfundo/web/plan/kb21/.

Williamson, Jeffrey. 2003. "Migration and Development: Policy Issues." Paper prepared for the International Bank for Reconstruction and Development/ Immigration, Développement, Démocratie workshop on Migration and Development: The Research Agenda. Paris, May 19.

Woodruff, Christopher, and Rene Zenteno. 2001. "Remittances and Microenterprises in Mexico." University of California, San Diego, and Instituto Tecnológico y de Estudios Superiores de Monterrey, Monterrey, Mexico.

World Bank. 2003. *World Development Report 2003: Sustainable Development in a Dynamic World.* New York: Oxford University Press.

Wylie, Cathy. 1998. *Can Vouchers Deliver Better Education? A Review of the Literature, with Special Reference to New Zealand.* Wellington: New Zealand Council for Educational Research. http://www.nzcer.org.nz/publications/reports/ vouchers.htm.

Young, Michael D. 1962. *The Rise of the Meritocracy.* London: Pelican.

3

The Dynamics of Diaspora Networks: Lessons of Experience

Richard Devane

Skilled emigration (defined as emigration after the completion of tertiary education) is a substantial phenomenon in most developing countries, with annual emigration rates for countries with populations of more than 20 million ranging from 0.6 percent in Brazil to 15.0 percent in Uganda (Carrington and Detragiache 1998). Skilled emigration is increasing, and most attempts to control and manage it by prohibition and taxation have failed (Lowell 2001).

The United States is the major destination for skilled workers: 40 percent of its foreign-born adult population have a tertiary-level education (Cervantes and Guellec 2002). Since the early 1990s, some 900,000 highly skilled professionals, mainly information technology workers from China; India; the Russian Federation; and a few countries of the Organisation for Economic Co-operation and Development (OECD), including Canada, Germany, and the United Kingdom, have migrated to the United States under the H-1B temporary visa program. The United States also takes in 32 percent of all foreign students studying in OECD countries. Indeed, higher education is an important channel for U.S. firms recruiting highly skilled migrants: some 25 percent of H-1B visa holders in 1999 had studied at U.S. universities.

Saxenian's (1999) study of 11,443 high-tech start-up companies in Silicon Valley between 1980 and 1998 shows that one-fourth had ethnic Chinese and Indian immigrants as senior executives. Taiwan (China) was a major beneficiary of this business success. Forty percent of the companies started in Taiwan's (China) science-based industrial park in Hschinchu were led by returned emigrants. Saxenian's study highlights the role of international, ethnic professional networks in facilitating this process of repatriation and "brain circulation." The typical role of immigrant associations in mutual aid and trust building was extended internationally to facilitate access to capital, marketing skills, and markets for Taiwanese start-ups.

Saxenian's study was one of the first to identify the potential for mitigating brain drain through brain exchange (or brain circulation). Devan and Tewari (2001), reviewing China's and India's apparent success in mobilizing diaspora resources, recommend this approach for all developing countries. They note that most developing countries have done little to leverage their expatriate talent and recommend a development strategy for mitigating the effects of brain drain by encouraging emigrants to participate in the economic development of their home countries.

In their study of the Chinese diaspora, Weidenbaum and Hughes (1996) conclude that the overseas Chinese are logical pioneer investors. The diaspora was well positioned to do business with China because of its widespread entrepreneurial experience, specialized knowledge, and relationships, which allow it to overcome the language, cultural, and legal barriers that frustrate non-Chinese investors. The nonfinancial motivation of overseas Chinese to reconnect with their homeland is also seen as an important stimulus for early-stage investment. They are certainly experienced investors. Chinese entrepreneurs were the first or second most significant source of foreign investment in the Philippines, Thailand, and Vietnam (Kao 1993). Their ethnic networks were strong: 39 percent of Kao's sample report that their international working relationships are with other Chinese.

These international networks seem to exist for many nations. Portes, Haller, and Guarnizo (2001) describe how declining communications and transportation costs stimulated the emergence of small-scale transnational entrepreneurs (individuals conducting business in their native countries while residing in the United States) among skilled expatriates from the Dominican Republic, Ecuador, and El Salvador. Brown (2000) identifies 41 expatriate organizations with Internet sites that could be developed as channels for identifying and motivating native country assistance and investment.

There seems to be widespread interest in using these networks. A survey by Saxenian (1999) of more than 1,500 first-generation Chinese and Indian migrants reveals that 50 percent go back to their home country on business at least once a year and 5 percent return at least five times a year. Even more telling, 74 percent of Indian respondents and 53 percent of Chinese said they hoped to start a business back home (*Economist* 2002).

Gillespie and others (1999) surveyed 572 U.S.–based first- and second-generation immigrants from the investment-deficient economies of Armenia, Cuba, the Islamic Republic of Iran, and the West Bank and Gaza. They report substantial interest by migrants in investing in their native countries in situations where their ethnicity would confer an advantage either in understanding opportunities or conducting business. The major obstacles to conducting business successfully were not seen as deterrents. This interest has not yet produced any significant expatriate investment in these economies.

Investment Booms and Expatriate Leadership

China, India, and Israel enjoyed investment or technology booms over the past decade, and these booms are linked (though not necessarily caused by) expatriate leadership in all three countries. The uniqueness of the circumstances each country faced, however, suggests that their experiences may not be easy to reproduce elsewhere.

China

China has experienced one of the most remarkable investment booms in history over the past two decades, making it a model for many developing countries. The Chinese diaspora has been prominent in this development, providing an estimated 70 percent of recent foreign investment (Devan and Tewari 2001).

Naughton (1999) shows that diaspora investors in China were not the 50 million with connections (*guanxi*), but the 6 million Hong Kong Chinese who had unique motivations for investing in China. Labor costs made manufacturing in Hong Kong (China) increasingly uncompetitive: between 1985 and 1995, manufacturing employment decreased by two-thirds, or 700,000 jobs. The need to move manufacturing to lower-wage countries occurred just as China was opening up. Thus it may have limited the significance of international economic development, particularly for distant expatriates. Naughton indicates that the choice of China was influenced by anxiety about China's policy intentions toward its soon to be reabsorbed territory. Investment in China was a way to earn favor with the new government and buy protection for Hong Kong assets.

According to Naughton, trade volumes in Hong Kong (China) should have decreased as production moved to mainland China. In fact, they increased during this period. His explanation is that Hong Kong was a convenient vehicle for "property rights arbitrage," where officials' control of public goods could be converted into private assets. He claims that a substantial part of Hong Kong trade and investment represented this process. These conditions do not exist for any other diaspora community.

As extensive as it was, diaspora investment in China was limited largely to low-wage manufacturing operations. Huang (2002) shows that investment was unusually diversified and small scale, with expatriates investing an average of $2.4 million in 1997 in a wide variety of manufacturing sectors. The average Hong Kong–based corporate investor was itself quite small, averaging 81 employees at headquarters.

Expatriate investment has not yet been a force for high-tech business development in China. In part, this may be due to the relatively recent arrival of large numbers of Chinese science and engineering graduate students in the United States (National Science Board 2002). If, as occurred in India and Taiwan (China), these graduates become high-tech executives and entrepreneurs, an expatriate-led technology boom may occur in China in the next decade or two.

India

India is the only country in which distant expatriates played a significant role in high-tech development, almost entirely in the software industry. India may be of great relevance to other developing countries, because its software industry grew at a time when its infrastructure was poor, its regulatory and legal environment was murky, and there was no government policy for high-tech investment and diaspora participation.

Information technology develops quickly. By 2000, Saxenian (2000b) acknowledged that rather than being a dead end, low-end software development had been a building block for high-end software development.

Dhume (2002) and Saxenian (2000a) criticize the "meager" investment by Indian expatriates, who prefer to act as middlemen brokering deals between Indian companies and U.S. partners. Dhume estimates that the Indian diaspora has provided only 3 percent of India's foreign direct investment. Though this may have more to do with the economics of the software industry than with the motivation of Indian expatriates. Software services, especially for export, are highly profitable and have good cash flows. Fixed asset investment is typically less than 25 percent of revenues (Ghemawat 1999). Most firms have been funded without external capital (Arora, Gambardella, and Torrisi 2001), but the expatriate role has been critical. According to Alok Aggarwal, cofounder and chair of Evalueserve and former vice president of emerging research at IBM, in an interview with the author:

> Expatriates provided valuable links with foreign markets, helped Indian . . .
> firms to absorb technical and managerial practices and establish contacts

with foreign customers. For instance, some Indians who had emigrated to work for U.S. firms in the 1980s have helped U.S. buyers find suppliers in India. Field interviews with U.S. customers revealed that in a couple of cases, the initial impetus for outsourcing to India came from employees of Indian origin . . . Most, if not all, U.S. subsidiaries in India are headed or staffed by employees of Indian origin.

It does not seem to matter if the process starts with the establishment of a U.S. subsidiary or a start-up with a U.S. outsourcing contract. Both generate jobs and support virtuous cycles of improved capabilities and valued added.

Israel

Israel experienced remarkable growth in its high-tech industries in the 1990s (Nitzan and Bichler 2002). From a negligible base in 1990, venture capital investment increased to nearly $3 billion by 2000. Foreign direct investment increased from less than $100 million in 1990 to $9 billion at its peak in 2000. Thousands of high-tech companies were started and hundreds went public. Large-scale immigration of Jewish scientists from Russia gave Israel the largest per capita concentration of engineers in the world. The complete absorption of this largely one-time immigration sets a limit on Israel's potential for technology growth.

Jewish diasporas were not the leaders of this phenomenon. Even though the Jewish diaspora, particularly in the United States, has been famously generous to Israel and critical to its foundation and success, diaspora Jews have never been major business investors in Israel. Direct diaspora investment and stock purchases averaged only 6 percent of domestic gross capital formation between 1948 and 1995 (Kleiman 1996). Kleiman speculates that the reasons for this lack of investment include security fears; regulations that are complex but corruptible, that is, avoidable; the need to employ unproductive, political employees; and even the desire to avoid tainting one's philanthropy with profit-seeking activity.

The stimulus for Israel's technology growth was defense research and development and government support. Zuckerman (2001) indicates that the boom was initiated with the commercialization of Israeli defense technology, financed by the U.S. and Israeli governments. The Israeli Defense Force's capabilities in communications network security and management proved central to the development and support of the Internet. Many technology pioneers were veterans of the elite intelligence services.

The Yozma Program is regarded as the critical first step in the Israeli venture capital industry (de Fontenay and Carmel 2000). A $100 million fund of funds begun in 1993 and operated by the Office of the Chief Scientist, it stimulated 10 private venture capital funds with $200 million in capital by 1996. While the diaspora was represented as investors and managers in these funds, they also attracted many nondiaspora investors, such as Daimler Benz of Germany and Kyocera of Japan.

Traditional venture capital did not arrive until 1995, when the boom was well under way. The diaspora community did support the remarkable acceleration of the technology industry. Israeli venture capital and technology were closely integrated with the U.S. technology community, but it was government research and development and government venture capital that got the Israeli technology industry under way.

The Silicon Valley Model

The belief persists that many countries should duplicate the culture and conditions of Silicon Valley to produce successful high-tech industries. But the emergence of high-tech start-ups in Silicon Valley and Wadi Valley (in Israel), which so many countries seek to emulate, are a feature of mature technology industries, not incipient ones. The primary driver is the commercialization of decades of government-funded research and development.

The first formal venture capital fund, ARD, founded by Georges Doriot in the 1950s, had as its explicit objective the commercialization of U.S. defense technology developed during World War II. The U.S. technology boom of the late 20th century was directly stimulated by the Bayh-Dole Bill, which relaxed patent controls on government-funded research. Israel's boom was built on government-funded defense technology. Thus it is not surprising that Silicon Valley cannot be duplicated where there is not a rich research base as the stimulus for innovation.

Even if it were possible to reproduce the Silicon Valley and venture capital system, it might not be appropriate for emerging market economies to do so. Despite their recent prominence, start-ups are not a substantial part of high-tech investment. Even in the United States, technology companies account for only 0.46 percent of small businesses start-ups (Martin 2002). Most high-tech start-ups fail, and the majority of the remainder are acquired by larger corporations. In Israel, for example, many of the start-ups of the 1990s have become U.S. subsidiaries. Even the independent survivors may not stay.

Venture capital is also a mirage for most emerging market countries. Formal venture capital is a lagging indicator of investment growth; it focuses on later-stage investments to suit the institutional investors who provide most of the funds (Gompers 1994). This is especially true of venture capital investment in emerging market countries, where most funds look for investments in companies with revenues of $50 million or more. With a fixed investment horizon of five years or less, funds face large, unmanageable exchange rate risks in most emerging market countries that further discourage investment (Stein 1997). A better model may be to imitate and adapt established technologies.

The Outsourcing Model

Bresnahan and others (2001) identify several successful, nascent clusters of technology-based innovative activity around the world—in India, Ireland, Israel, Scandinavia, and Taiwan (China)—which they call young Silicon Valleys. In the case of India and Ireland, this appellation seems inappropriate. Arora, Gambardella, and Torrisi (2001) emphasizes the differences between the Indian and Irish clusters and Silicon Valley, noting that much software-related work in India and Ireland is noninnovative and involves activities such as offshore development and testing, "localization," and online technical support. These firms are essentially outsourcing centers rather than centers of innovation. Their success represents a hopeful sign for other countries hoping to duplicate the success of India or Ireland. India has demonstrated that investing in low-end technology niches can be a building block for the development of higher-value services and products.

This may be true generally. In a study of 50 developing countries, Zheng and Zou (1995) find that imitation and regional adaptation rather than primary innovation can be the best development strategy. Productivity growth depends on imports of foreign machinery and borrowing of foreign technology rather than innovation.

Technology development that begins with low-end outsourcing has several benefits. It begins a cycle of low-risk trust building with the outsourcing partner that can result in an improved reputation for quality and higher-end outsourcing assignments.

Services Enabled by Information Technology

India's success may be helpful to other emerging market economies in other ways as well. No country can duplicate the depth of India's engineering and computer science labor resources, which powered its software industry. But India's success as an information technology outsourcing center has stimulated the emergence of a services industry enabled by information technology with substantially lower technological requirements. These are services that can be provided over telecommunications or data networks. India has proven the viability of Indian-based third-party provision of services as varied as accounts receivable processing, medical transcription, and airline ticket processing. This sector is growing at 40 percent a year and is expected to generate $142 billion in revenue and to employ 1.1 million people in India in 2008 (Kennedy 2002).

These services do not require extensive engineering and science skills. The requirements are a critical mass of educated English speakers and a reliable telecommunications infrastructure, which many emerging market countries possess. This sector has the same building block potential as the software industry. The process can start with low-risk outsourcing of routine back office processes and move up to expert services such as research and data analysis.

The Role of Diasporas

Diaspora members are not likely to be pioneer investors in the high-tech industries of their native countries. Even in the highly developed U.S. angel investment community (a major source of early-stage investment), most investors prefer investments located within five hours of their home so that they can easily supervise their progress (Roberts 2000). Only about 5 percent of investors seriously contemplate investing in an emerging market (Stein 1997).

Foreign direct investment is very much a big company game. U.S. foreign investors tend to be the largest firms in their industries (Huang 2002). Their technology, proprietary assets, scale economies, and managerial skills allow them to succeed in unfamiliar environments. Their investment horizons have no necessary limit, so they can make the long-term commitments often necessary for success.

The Indian experience shows that expatriates may have advantages as facilitators, accelerating and leveraging the international success of domestic entrepreneurs and companies. They can be crucial in building awareness of and confidence in investment opportunities among OECD corporations, the usual providers of foreign direct investment, partnerships, and outsourcing contracts. Kapur (2001) notes that "this points to the cognitive effects arising from the projection of a coherent, appealing, and progressive identity on the part of the diaspora, which signals an image of prosperity and progress to potential investors and consumers."

This finding suggests that expatriate mobilization efforts for investment might best be focused not on mass mobilization (the alumni model), or even on politically active or wealthy philanthropic members of the diaspora community. The key players are expatriates who have become senior executives in relevant companies. Because most major corporations are now considering international outsourcing of Internet-enabled business services, the key role for these well-placed expatriates is in building awareness in their corporations of their native countries as outsourcing candidates.

This channel of influence is both an opportunity and problem. On the one hand, the process is much more efficient than the mass diaspora mobilization networks that several countries are attempting, as potential facilitators can be easily identified and contacted (Lowell 2001). On the other hand, many countries with educated diasporas have few candidates. Expatriates who are doctors, lawyers, or scientists, however sympathetic they may be to their native countries, are not likely to be able to influence corporate investment or outsourcing decisions. Of course, these professionals can contribute in many other ways. The large Indian-American medical community is beginning to take part in improving the quality of Indian hospitals (through sabbatical residencies) and developing an Indian medical testing industry.

However, major business investment is likely to come through the efforts of a small number of well-placed expatriate executives. To the extent possible, developing countries should encourage their skilled emigrants to pursue these strategically important careers.

References

Arora, Ashish, Alfonso Gambardella, and Salvatore Torrisi. 2001. "Cloning the Silicon Valley: A Case Study of the Indian and Irish Software Industries." Paper prepared for the conference on India: Ten Years after Liberalization, University of Michigan, Ann Arbor, September 22–23.

Bresnahan, Timothy, Alfonso Gambardella, AnnaLee Saxenian, and Scott Wallsten. 2001. "'Old Economy' Inputs for 'New Economy' Outcomes: Cluster Formation in the New Silicon Valleys." Policy Paper 00-43, Stanford Institute for Economic Policy Research, Stanford, CA.

Brown, Mercy. 2000. "Using the Intellectual Diaspora to Reverse Brain Drain: Some Useful Examples." University of Cape Town, School of Economics, Cape Town, South Africa.

Carrington, William J., and Erica Detragiache. 1998. "How Big Is the Brain Drain?" Working Paper, International Monetary Fund, Washington, DC.

Cervantes, Mario, and Dominique Guellec. 2002. "The Brain Drain: Old Myths, New Realities." *OECD Observer,* May 7.

de Fontenay, Catherine, and Erran Carmel. 2000. "Israel's Silicon Wadi: The Forces behind Cluster Formation." Policy Paper 00-40, Stanford Institute for Economic Policy Research, Stanford, CA.

Devan, Janamitra, and Parth Tewari. 2001. "When the Best Brains Go Abroad." *McKinsey Quarterly* 38 (September).

Dhume, Sadanaud. 2002. "Bangalore to Silicon Valley and Back." In *India Briefing: Quickening the Pace of Change,* ed. Alyssa Ayres and Philip Oldenbur. Armonk, NY: M. E. Sharpe.

The Economist. 2002. "The View from Afar: Emigration Also Affects Those Left Behind." October 23.

Ghemawat, Pankaj. 1999. *The Indian Software Industry in 2002.* Harvard Business School Note, Harvard University, Cambridge, MA.

Gillespie, Kate, Liesl Riddle, Edward Sayre, and David Sturges. 1999. "Diaspora Interest in Homeland Investment." *Journal of International Business Studies* 30 (3): 623–34.

Gompers, Paul A. 1994. "A Note on the Venture Capital Industry." Harvard Business School Note, Harvard University, Cambridge, MA.

Huang, Yasheng. 2002. "FDI in China." Harvard Business School Note, Harvard University, Cambridge, MA.

Kao, John. 1993. "The Worldwide Web of Chinese Business." *Harvard Business Review* (March–April).

Kapur, Devesh. 2001. "Diasporas and Technology Transfer." *Journal of Human Development* 2 (2): 265–86.

Kennedy, Robert E. 2002. "Exporting IT–Enabled Services from Developing Countries." Harvard Business School Note, Harvard University, Cambridge, MA.

Kleiman, Ephraim. 1996. *Jewish and Palestinian Diaspora Attitudes to Philanthropy and Investment.* Tel Aviv: Hebrew University Press.

Lowell, Lindsay B. 2001. "Policy Responses to the International Mobility of Skilled Labour." International Migration Paper 45, International Labour Office, Geneva.

Martin, Justin. 2002. *Fortune Small Business,* December 1.

National Science Board. 2002. *Science and Engineering Indicators 2002.* Washington, DC: National Science Board.

Naughton, Barry. 1999. "Between China and the World." In *Cosmopolitan Capitalists,* ed. Gary G. Hamilton. Seattle: University of Washington Press.

Nitzan, Jonathan, and Shimshon Bichler. 2002. *The Global Political Economy of Israel.* London: Pluto Press.

Portes, Alejandro, William Haller, and Luis E. Guarnizo. 2001. "Transnational Entrepreneur: The Emergence and Determinants of an Alternative Form of Immigrant Economic Adaptation." Working Paper WPTC01-05, University of Oxford, Institute of Social and Cultural Anthropology, Transnational Communities Program, Oxford, U.K.

Roberts, Michael J. 2000. "Angel Investing." Harvard Business School Note, Harvard University, Cambridge, MA.

Saxenian, AnnaLee. 1999. "Silicon Valley's New Immigrant Entrepreneurs." Public Policy Institute of California, San Francisco.

———. 2000a. "Back to India." *Wall Street Journal,* Technology Journal Asia, January 24.

———. 2000b. "The Bangalore Boom: From Brain Drain to Brain Circulation?" In *Bridging the Digital Divide: Lessons from India*, ed. Kenneth Kennistan and Deepak Kumar. Bangalore, India: National Institute of Advanced Study.

Stein, Elizabeth. 1997. "The Advent of Venture Capital in Latin America." Harvard Business School Note, Harvard University, Cambridge, MA.

Weidenbaum, Murray, and Samuel Hughes. 1996. *The Bamboo Network.* New York: Free Press.

Zheng, Xiaoming, and Heng-Fu Zou. 1995. "Foreign Technology Imports and Economic Growth in Developing Countries" Policy Research Working Paper 1412, World Bank, Washington, DC.

Zuckerman, Ezra W. 2001. "Venture Capital in Israel: Emergence and Globalization." Harvard Business School Note, Harvard University, Cambridge, MA.

Part II
Expatriate Talent and Home Country Development: Lessons of Mature Diaspora Networks

4

The Indian Diaspora: A Unique Case?

Abhishek Pandey, Alok Aggarwal, Richard Devane,
and Yevgeny Kuznetsov

This chapter analyzes the increasingly important role of the Indian diaspora in the United Kingdom and the United States in facilitating growth and improving process management within the knowledge-intensive industries in India. It identifies and analyzes future opportunities for these sectors in the global economy.

The Importance of India's Diaspora

The Indian diaspora constitutes an important and unique force in the world economy. As a result of centuries of migration, more than 20 million people of Indian origin live in 70 countries (table 4.1). They represent more than 40 percent of the population in Fiji, Guyana, Mauritius, and Surinam and account for prominent minority communities in Australia, Canada, Malaysia, South Africa, Sri Lanka, Uganda, the United Kingdom, and the United States (figures 4.1, 4.2, and 4.3). The earnings of the 20 million-strong Indian diaspora are equivalent to about two-thirds of the gross domestic product (GDP) of India, with a population of more than 1 billion people (Agrawal).

Some Indian emigrants have had a significant impact on the economies of both India and their new countries. Gujarati migrants, for example, many of whom migrated to East Africa in the early 20th century, dominate some of the key old economy sectors, such as trade in diamonds.

In the post–World War II period, Indians and other South Asians provided the labor that helped rebuild war-torn Europe, particularly the Netherlands and the United Kingdom. The Indian diaspora in the United Kingdom, which numbers more than 1.2 million, has become prominent, with a significant presence in various businesses and high-skill professions, such as information technology (IT) and medicine. Medical professionals from India are in great demand by the British National Health Service, 6 percent of whose doctors are of Indian origin (Center for Immigration Studies). Of the 18,250 expatriate IT professionals who entered the United Kingdom in 2000, 11,474 were from India (Ministry of External Affairs, India [b]). In 2000, there were more than 300 influential, nonresident Indian businesspeople and 150 other very rich and prominent Indians in the United Kingdom. These include Gulu Lalvani (electronics industry), Manubhai Madhvani (sugar industry), Lakshmi Mittal (iron and steel industry), Lord Swaraj Paul (manufacturing and supply of steel and engineering products), and Jasminder Singh (hotel industry).

The Indian community has also been active on the political front in the United Kingdom. In 2000, it had four members of parliament in the House of Commons and 11 lords in the House of Lords (U.K. Department for Education and Skills).

Table 4.1 *Indian Emigration in the 19th and 20th Centuries*

Destination	Period	Reasons for emigration and profile of emigrants
British, Dutch and French colonies	1834–1920	Migration of unskilled, mostly indentured, Indian laborers to Burma, Canada, Ceylon, Fiji, Guyana, Hong Kong (China), Jamaica, Japan, Malaya, Mauritius, New Zealand, Nigeria, Surinam, Trinidad and Tobago, Thailand, Uganda, and elsewhere was prompted by demand for labor by new plantations, industrial enterprises, and commercial ventures in European colonies. The abolition of slavery in the British (1834), French (1846), and Dutch (1873) colonies caused severe shortages of laborers on sugar, tea, coffee, cocoa, rice, and rubber plantations. China and India provided alternative sources of labor.
	Late 19th and first half of the 20th centuries	Most unskilled migrant laborers settled overseas, although the system of indenture was abolished in 1917. Indian traders, skilled artisans, bankers, petty contractors, clerks, professionals, and entrepreneurs migrated to Burma, East Africa, Fiji, Natal, Malaya, and Mauritius to tap new opportunities, booming trade, and thriving industry.
Industrial countries	Post–World War II	Although some Indians migrated to the United Kingdom during the period of British rule, the major influx of Indians took place after 1947, when large numbers of educated Indians migrated to Australia, Canada, New Zealand, the United Kingdom, and the United States. Some people of Indian origin from Africa and the Caribbean also migrated to the Netherlands and the United Kingdom. In contrast to the indentured populations, these migrants have maintained close ties to India, particularly through remittances and investments. Large-scale migration of Indians to the United States occurred after the repeal of the Immigration and Nationality Act in 1965. By 2001, about 1.5 million Indians were living in the United States. They belong primarily to the educated and professional elite class and include engineers (primarily information technology engineers), scientists, teachers, accountants, doctors, managers, hoteliers, and businesspeople.
Gulf countries	Mid-1970s–2004	Most skilled and unskilled migrants to the Gulf countries have been working on a contract basis, hired to build, manage, and operate the infrastructure needed by the oil export industry. Their major impact has been the flow of large remittances to India.

Source: University of Hyderabad.

Figure 4.1 *Distribution of the Indian Diaspora in Countries of the Organisation for Economic Co-operation and Development as of December 2001*

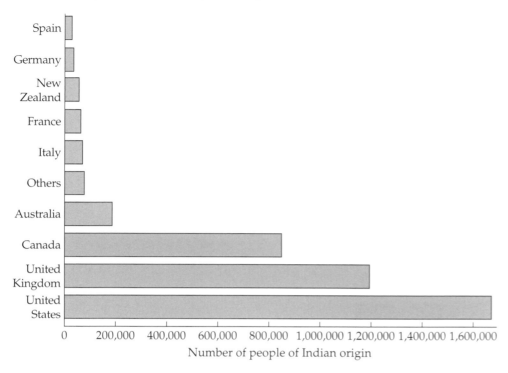

Number of people of Indian origin

Source: Ministry of External Affairs 2001[a]; Evalueserve data and analysis.

In recent years, unskilled workers from India—along with some skilled ones—have been the main force in transforming the physical landscape of the Gulf countries. These contract workers have repatriated most of their earnings to India, contributing significantly to the Indian economy.

In other developed countries—particularly Canada and the United States—Indians have been very successful in most knowledge-intensive professions, including engineering, IT, medicine, finance, business administration, and accounting.

The Success of the Indian Diaspora in the Knowledge-Intensive Sectors of the United States

Indians may belong to the most successful immigrant community in U.S. history. Even during the recent economic slump, Indians in the United States not only retained their wealth, but also added to it (Economic Times [b]). As of May 2004, 1.7 million members of the Indian diaspora were living in the United States. Some 200,000 of these families were headed by millionaires, and the median annual income of people of Indian origin was $60,093, substantially higher than the median U.S. income of $38,885 (Ministry of External Affairs, India [a]). Two-thirds of foreign-born Indian-Americans have university degrees, three times the figure for the United States as a whole. About 44 percent of these immigrants hold managerial or professional positions.

Figure 4.2 *Distribution of the Indian Diaspora in Selected African and Middle Eastern Countries and Localities as of December 2001*

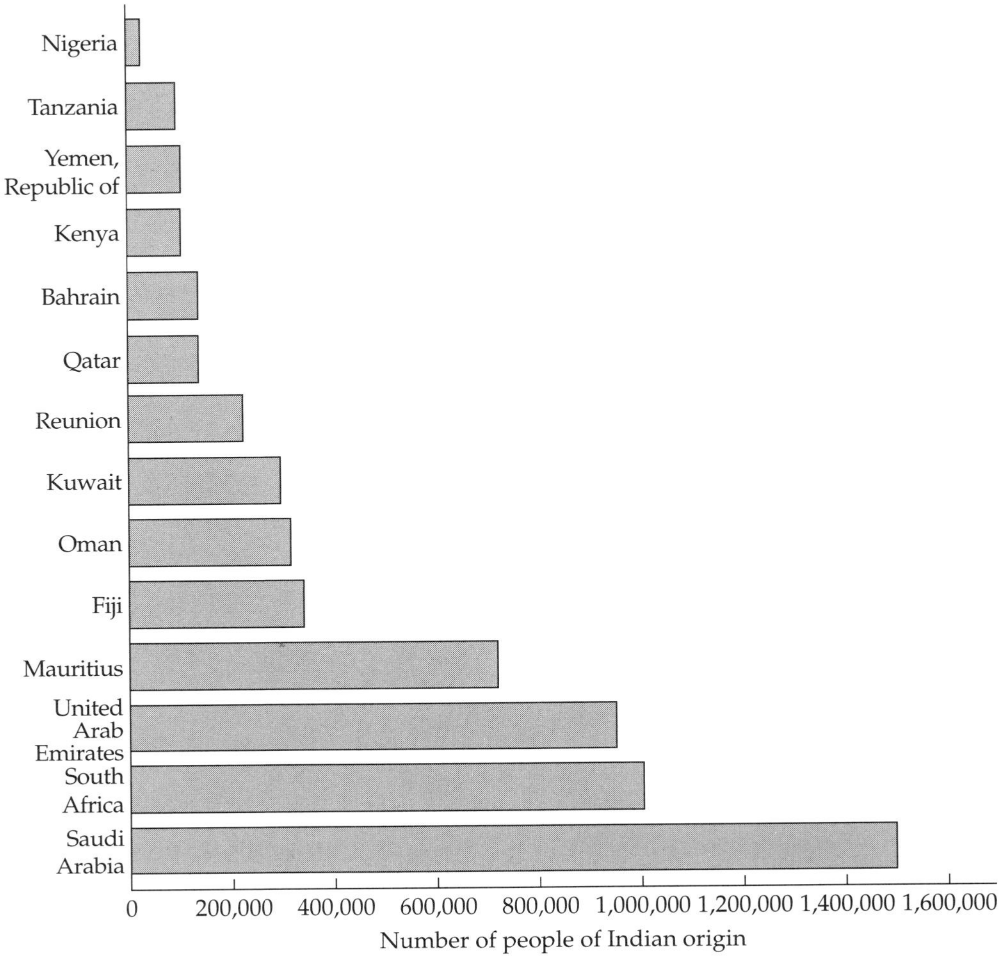

Source: Ministry of External Affairs 2001[a]; Evalueserve data and analysis.

Most people of Indian origin in the United States work in medicine, engineering, management, or business. During the 1960s and 1970s, a majority of Indians who migrated to United States were engineers, doctors, and lawyers. After moving to the United States, many earned doctorates, masters' degrees, or masters in business administration and started working on critical projects in government or private research laboratories, such as those run by IBM, Boeing, Bell Labs, and DuPont.

More than 300,000 people of Indian origin work in the IT sector in the United States. Although this number represents only 3 percent of the total IT workforce, it includes a substantial number of executives in midsize and large companies, and at least 15 percent of IT start-ups were created by Indians (Economic Times [b]). Prominent Indians in the IT sector include Gujuraj Deshpande, the chief executive officer (CEO) of Sycamore and Arun Netravali, the former president of Bell Labs. In addition, several people of Indian origin are professors at prominent engineering

Figure 4.3 *Distribution of the Indian Diaspora in Selected Countries and Localities in Asia and Latin America and the Caribbean as of December 2001*

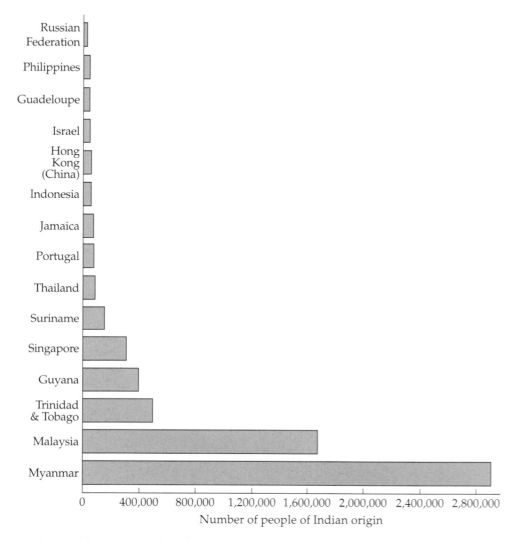

Number of people of Indian origin

Source: Ministry of External Affairs 2001[a]; Evalueserve data and analysis.

and technology institutes, such as the Massachusetts Institute of Technology, Stanford University, and Carnegie Mellon University.

Several Indians have climbed up the corporate ladder in U.S. businesses. Some prominent Indian executives include Ramani Ayer, CEO, Hartford Insurance & Financial Group; Rono Dutta, former CEO, United Airlines; Rakesh Gangwal, former CEO, U.S. Airways; Vijay Goradia, CEO, Vinmar International, Limited; Rajat Gupta, former managing director, McKinsey and Company; Shailesh Mehta, former CEO, Providian; Victor Menezes, former senior vice-president, Citigroup; Vikram Pandit, former chief operating officer, Morgan Stanley; and James Wadia, former managing director, Arthur Anderson & Company.

There are more than 38,000 physicians of Indian origin in the United States, about 5 percent of the total. About 12,000 Indians and people of Indian origin are medical students and residents, constituting about 10 percent of the total in the United States. Indians represent the largest non-Caucasian segment of the U.S. medical community.

The Indian diaspora has done extremely well in owning and running small businesses. People of Indian origin own about 77,000 of the 135,000 convenience stores in the United States, providing employment to more than 300,000 people. Total convenience store sales in the United States reached $337 billion in 2003, with pretax profits of $4.04 billion. Stores owned by people of Indian origin had estimated sales of about $195 billion and pretax profits of about $2.2 billion. Indians recently started an American Asian Convenience Stores' Association (http://www.aacsa.org and www.nacsonline.com).

The Indian diaspora owns about 17,000 of the 47,040 hotels in the United States, providing employment to more than 700,000 people. The American Asian Hotel Owners Association estimates the cumulative market value of these hotels at about $36 billion (http://www.ahla.com; http://www.aahoa.com).

The success of people of Indian origin and the impact that their community has had are most notable in the IT industry.[1] The 200,000 Indians in the San Francisco Bay Area represent one of the most successful immigrant groups in the United States. The companies they own are worth $235 billion, and Indian millionaires are investing in new ventures.

Nearly 40 percent of Silicon Valley start-ups in the 1990s had at least one founder of Indian origin (Economic Times [b]). Evalueserve, a business intelligence and research firm, estimates that in 2004, 650–700 companies in Silicon Valley were owned, either partly or wholly, by people of Indian origin or had at least one person of Indian origin on their executive management team.

In 2004, there were more than 200,000 Indian millionaires in the United States, many of them engineers living in the San Francisco Bay Area. Some of these technocrat millionaires are investing money, time, and expertise in mentoring other people of Indian origin (Economic Times [b]). In 1992, they established The Indus Entrepreneurs (TiE), a network through which experienced Indians mentor others. Doug Leone, a partner at Sequoia Capital, a venture capital firm, said: "At Sequoia, we love Indian entrepreneurs, because they are extremely smart, they know the value of a dollar, and they hate the devaluation of dollar [sic] in terms of Indian rupees. That is an attitude that we like to be on the side of" (personal communication with the author).

Many factors have contributed to the success of Silicon Valley Indians. These include their technical expertise; their familiarity with the West and ability to work within the U.S. system; their proficiency in English; their combination of technical abilities and good management skills, which some have used to move up the corporate ladder; and their connections with companies and entrepreneurs in India, which they can exploit to reduce their companies' operational costs without sacrificing quality.

Contribution of the Indian Institutes of Technology

In 1947, when India became independent, many Indians realized that the country lacked sufficient numbers of engineers, doctors, and scientists. To address the problem, in 1953, Prime Minister Jawahar Lal Nehru established the Indian institutes of

---

[1] This section draws on Wu and Economic Times[a].

technology. Today there are seven such schools. Admission is so competitive and so valued that they have stimulated a $400 million industry in admissions test preparation in India.

Students entering the institutes do not necessarily come from privileged or even commercial backgrounds. Indeed, 80 percent come from the Indian middle class.

The undergraduate education provided by the institutes is superb, but U.S. universities still provide the best graduate education. For this reason, beginning in the 1960s, many graduates started moving to the United States to pursue graduate education. After graduation, many of these students joined IT companies in the United States. Today many of these Indians occupy the upper echelons of the industry in the United States.

Projected Growth of the Indian Presence in the U.S. Technology Sector

According to a 2003 report by the U.S. National Science Board, the Indian presence in the U.S. technology sector is likely to grow. U.S. census data for 2000 indicate that in the science and engineering occupations, foreign-born students receive about 17 percent of bachelors' degrees, 29 percent of masters' degrees, and 38 percent of doctorates (U.S. National Science Board). Among foreign-born students, Indians account for the largest share of science and engineering degrees granted by U.S. universities (14 percent), followed by the Chinese, who account for 10 percent of such degrees.

The percentage of Indian scientists and engineers who plan to remain in the United States has risen. In 1990–3, 86 percent planned to remain in the United States; by 1998–2001, the figure had risen to 94 percent. The percentage of Indians who plan to remain in the United States for postdoctoral research appointments or jobs with enterprises increased from 63 percent in 1990–3 to 73 percent in 1998–2001. Out of 13,000 Indian science and engineering doctorate recipients at U.S. universities between 1985 and 2000, about 58 percent accepted jobs with U.S. firms. Of these, 24 percent were engaged in postdoctoral work and 34 percent were employed in industry. In 2001, 77 percent of Indian science and engineering doctoral degree recipients accepted offers of employment or postdoctoral research in the United States (Economic Times [a]).

In 2004, more than half of the technology workforce (those with science and engineering degrees) in the United States was older than 40. This implies a significant gap between the supply of and demand for talent, a gap that is likely to be filled by the increasing number of Indians staying in the United States after completing their education. Between 1985 and 2000, Indian students constituted the largest group of all foreign-born communities in terms of the number of doctoral degrees awarded in computer and information sciences. This translates into an increasing number of Indian technocrats entering the U.S. workforce in the years to come (Economic Times [a]).

Importance of Indian Doctors in the United States

Indian doctors are involved primarily in primary patient care in both urban and rural areas. They constitute about 20 percent of all foreign-trained doctors in the United States.

Many Indian doctors migrated to the United States after 1947 to pursue residencies. This trend gained significant momentum in the 1970s, when international medical graduates were actively recruited to meet the lack of U.S.-trained doctors.

In 1984, some Indian medical professionals founded the American Association of Physicians of Indian Origin. The key driver behind its formation was the need to meet the challenges that physicians of Indian origin often face because of cultural barriers and bias against international medical graduates, which often cause problems in immigrating and obtaining medical licenses. The American Association of Physicians of Indian Origin grew rapidly. It serves as an umbrella organization for about 100 professional associations and is the largest ethnic medical organization in the United States. It is active in spearheading legislative agendas on health care and influencing the advancement of ethnic medical organizations.

With the increasing medical needs of the aging U.S. population, the American Medical Association projects a shortfall of medical professionals. An increasing number of foreign-born—particularly Indian—doctors and nurses is likely to mitigate this deficit, increasing the size of the Indian medical diaspora (Raymer).

The Role of the Diaspora in the Emergence of the Indian IT Industry

The Indian diaspora has been extremely successful in knowledge-intensive sectors in the United States, particularly in the IT sector. Almost simultaneously, a competitive and successful IT industry emerged in India. This section analyzes the factors that helped this sector emerge over the past 35 years and the role that the diaspora community played in its evolution.

Evolution of the Indian IT Industry in the 1970s and 1980s

The emergence of a strong, Indian IT industry occurred partly by design and partly by accident. In the 1970s there was no separate software industry. Multinationals such as IBM and ICL were the largest providers of computer hardware, which was bundled with operating systems and a few basic packages, usually written in FORTRAN or COBOL.

Larger enterprises that needed customized applications, including public organizations in India, employed in-house teams that did everything from install systems to write software. When specific software applications became popular, stand-alone boxes were made for them. The concept of stand-alone word processing software did not exist. Later, when local companies grew (after IBM's exit in the early 1980s), these companies had their own proprietary operating systems, which generally executed only their computer programs.

Developments in the 1970s

India was among the first developing nations to recognize the importance of software, but the key driver behind software exports was the need for foreign exchange. To export software, Indian companies had to design it for hardware systems that were the standard worldwide, which in the 1970s meant IBM mainframe computers. Indian import duties on this hardware were extremely high, almost 300 percent (Khanna). To make the price affordable to Indian customers, during the late 1960s and early 1970s IBM sold refurbished, antiquated machines. Fortunately, within a few years, the Indian government lowered import duties on all IT equipment, with a precondition that exporters recover twice the value of the foreign exchange spent on importing computers within five years (a clause that was modified in the 1980s). Overall, the regulatory scenario was not favorable for software exporters.

The first Indian software exporting company was Tata Consulting Services, which started operations in 1968. After filling a few local orders, Tata Consulting Services received its first big export assignment in 1973–4, when it was asked to provide an inventory control software solution for an electricity generation unit in the Islamic Republic of Iran.

Developments in the 1980s

Despite the unfavorable import policy, by the early 1980s, India was the only developing nation to have any significant software exports—$12 million—a substantial increase over the 1979 level of $4.4 million. Thirty companies were already beginning to export software.

The main competitive advantage for Indian companies was cost and the ability to communicate in English. Charges for a software developer in India were $16,000–$24,000 a year in 1980, considerably lower than the cost of sending the developer to the United States ($32,000–$42,000) or using a U.S. software developer ($60,000–$95,000).

Despite the cost advantages, the Indian software industry continued to face challenges in the 1970s and 1980s. Importing hardware, especially mainframe computers, was cumbersome and expensive. In addition, there was a shortfall in trained manpower. Although the education system was producing a substantial number of talented engineers, few institutions were offering computer training or IT courses.

Three unrelated incidents contributed heavily to shaping the Indian IT industry. First, in the late 1970s, the Indian government passed a controversial law (repealed in 1992) that forced all multinationals to reduce their equity share in their Indian subsidiaries to less than 50 percent. As IBM did not want to reduce its equity in its subsidiary, it decided to leave India, thereby making Indian companies less reliant on mainframe computers. Second, the advent of personal computers in 1980s significantly reduced the cost of importing hardware, spawning an industry that now has more than 2,700 companies. Third, realizing that the Indian higher education system was unable to provide computer training, three Indian entrepreneurs (living in India) began providing tutorials and training classes in IT. In the early days, one man often drove a scooter or motorcycle while another rode behind with a personal computer on his lap so that they could impart this training in rented spaces in the evenings. The training institute they started (National Institute of Information Technologies) is now a $167 million company, and it continues to be the leader in providing IT courses and training to Indians (NIIT).

Government policies became more favorable in the late 1980s, and IT training and education gradually becoming strong enough to create a fully fledged industry. Industry associations were formed, one of which eventually became the National Association of Software and Service Companies.

During the early years, exporting software initially meant physical transfer either of the programmer (sometimes called body shopping) or of software on floppies. In 1985, Texas Instruments set up an office in Bangalore with a direct satellite link to the United States. In 1989, a government-owned Indian telecom company (VSNL) commissioned a direct 64-kilobits per second satellite link to the United States, offering software exporters a completely new way of functioning.

Diaspora Support during the Initial Years

Indian engineers in the United States were quickly recognized as excellent technologists, but during the 1970s and 1980s they had to fight a strong perception—in some cases a self-perception—that they did not have front office or general management capabilities. As a partial reaction, many engineers made a conscious decision not to emphasize their ethnicity, and there was remarkably little ethnic collaboration among Indians in the United States. Their emphasis was on their careers within corporations managed by Caucasians, and they were rarely even aware of the progress being made by Indians in other organizations.

Not only did Indian engineers and IT professionals in the United States not collaborate with each other, they also invested little in the Indian IT industry. Indeed, the few attempts at investments made by people of Indian origin in the 1970s and early 1980s were quickly abandoned because of bureaucratic obstacles by the Indian government and the limited capabilities of Indian partners. The role played by people of Indian origin was limited to being tolerant mentors of early Indian software development companies.

In the early 1980s, several small Indian companies came to Silicon Valley in search of low-end contract work in software development. Several executives of Indian origin were willing to help, but most found the Indian companies' work to be unsatisfactory and their development tools and computers inadequate. This situation partly reflected the fact that as late as 1986, the Indian government was promoting Russian computers over American computers and Indian companies had just started working with personal computers. Indian companies could not meet, or sometimes even understand, U.S. standards for quality and timeliness. To mitigate this problem, diaspora executives sometimes created programs within their companies in which Indian programmers could work in the United States with U.S. technology (at Indian wages plus travel-related costs). They coached and guided the Indian companies in improving their quality and performance standards.

During the 1970s and 1980s, the role of the Indian diaspora in the evolution of the Indian IT industry was largely limited to that of a patient mentor and brand ambassador. This situation changed in the late 1980s, when several Indians became CEOs of new public companies and it became apparent that the community had the complete range of skills for leadership within the IT industry in the United States.

The Formative Years: The 1990s

In 1993, the U.S. Immigration and Naturalization Service made changes that made it difficult to get B-1 visas for immigrants who wanted to come to the United States temporarily for business. Obtaining a new H-1B visa (the primary United States work visa for foreign professionals who want to live and work in the United States in a specialty occupation) required certification from the United States Department of Labor that immigrant workers were receiving prevailing market wages. As a result of these changes, U.S. companies had less incentive to hire software engineers from India. Indian software professionals who were brought in under the umbrella of the Immigration Act had to pay Social Security and related taxes to the U.S. government, which placed a burden on them and their companies.

These factors led a few IT companies in India to gradually move to a mixed model whereby some software programmers would work at the client's premises and others would continue to work in the IT company's back office in India. As the Indian IT industry adapted to this new business model, IT exports boomed, rising from $128 million in 1990 to $485 million in 1994 (Dataquest). The shift to the new business model was gradual, but the savings, even after sending Indian programmers to the United States, were large. Many IT companies continued to follow the old model, sending programmers to Canada, the United Kingdom, and the United States.

Then came the year 2000 (Y2K) problem, the Internet-telecom boom, and the dot.com boom, which forced companies in Canada, the United Kingdom, and the United States to hire thousands of computer programmers. As a result of the shortage of programmers, the U.S. government increased its H-1B quota from 65,000 in 1998 to 130,000 in 1999 and to 195,000 soon after. The change represented a good opportunity for the Indian IT industry, which sent increasing numbers of IT professionals to the United States, creating an expanding Indian diaspora.

The Y2K problem presented a unique opportunity for Indian firms. U.S. firms needed software professionals with COBOL programming skills, but COBOL had become obsolete in the 1990s and was no longer part of the U.S. university curriculum. In India, however, where most of the computer science curriculum was obsolete, COBOL was still taught. This provided Indian IT service vendors with a significant advantage. Y2K contracts helped Indian firms enter new markets and build trust with clients.

By the end of 1999, the Indian IT industry was at an all-time high, and initial public offerings of software companies in India were oversubscribed. This led to the creation of a venture capital industry in India. Venture capital investments grew from $24 million in 1996 to $480 million in 1999, with a substantial amount going to Indian dot.com companies in 1998 and 1999 (Dataquest).

The 1990s witnessed the real emergence of the Indian IT diaspora in the United States. Many Indian engineers who had moved to the United States in 1960s had become entrepreneurs, venture capitalists, or high-level executives in midsize and large companies. They had started to coalesce, especially because many had graduated from the same top-notch institutions in India and most knew their counterparts in India, who were often alumni of the same institutions. Some of these relationships led to the formation of nonprofit associations, such as TiE and the Silicon Indian Professional Association.

TiE, originally intended as a Silicon Valley organization to facilitate mentoring of promising, young, expatriate IT professionals, soon developed into a worldwide network of Indian professionals. It has had substantial influence on the Indian IT industry and government policies toward it. As of 2004, TiE had 42 chapters and more than 10,000 members worldwide (Bagri).

Many expatriate Indians knew their counterparts in India, and most were closely observing the growing Indian IT industry, in the mid- and late 1990s. Some of them started their own IT companies in India, for example, Cognizant, Techspan, and Mphasis; others invested in nascent IT and dot.com companies in India. Given the shortage of IT professionals in Canada, the United Kingdom, and the United States between 1996 and 1999, many in the Indian diaspora convinced their companies to hire Indian IT professionals. This strengthened the Indian IT diaspora.

All these developments facilitated another crucial diaspora role. Some Indians had become senior executives at major corporations, including IBM, General Electric, and American Express. In nearly every instance in which these companies invested in or outsourced work to India, a well-placed expatriate executive crucially influenced the decision. In part, the individual's own success supported the emerging reputation of Indian engineers. Indians' direct experience of India also gave them credibility in vouching for the fact that the problems inherent in India's infrastructure and bureaucracy could be overcome. For example, Kanwal Rekhi, one of the founders of TiE, gave a well-publicized series of speeches and interviews in India in which he challenged the government and the people to adopt a set of modernizing reforms. This U.S. investment and outsourcing drove annual growth in the Indian software industry to 40 percent during the 1990s. By 2003, the Indian IT export industry, which includes IT exports as well as exports of business process services, had become a $12.2 billion industry (NASSCOM).

The diaspora played other roles as well. Some younger Indians in the United States returned to India to start IT research and development (R&D) laboratories, for example, the IBM India Research Laboratory established in 1998. Others returned to supervise U.S. investments and outsourcing contracts and to train and manage Indian professionals to U.S. efficiency and standards.

However, among all these contributions by the diaspora, the crucial role continued to be that of mentoring early-stage companies and confidence building with major U.S. corporations. The diaspora was critical in convincing U.S. firms that India was a good place to get work done and that Indian companies had the ability to perform the work.

Some expatriates downplay their role in India's success. For them, the sudden skilled labor requirements caused by the growth of the Internet and the Y2K problem would have drawn India's engineers and technicians into the world IT industry without the help of the Indian diaspora. These expatriates may be minimizing their role. Other countries with trained graduates and skilled diasporas—Pakistan, the Russian Federation, and South Africa—were not drafted into the boom. Indian expatriates seem to have made the difference.

Growth of the Indian IT Sector in Recent Years

During 1997–2003, the Indian IT market grew 25.5 percent a year. The contribution of IT to India's GDP rose from 1.2 percent in 1997 to 3.6 percent in 2003 (figure 4.4).

Exports of software and IT services constituted about 62 percent of the Indian IT market in 2003. They grew 38 percent a year between 1997 and 2003, and their share of exports rose from 4.9 percent to 21.3 percent (figure 4.5).

Evalueserve projects that exports of Indian IT software and services will grow at 26 percent a year over the next several years, reaching $38.7 billion of export revenue by 2008 (figure 4.6).

In 2003, offshore activities accounted for 59 percent of Indian software revenues. Evalueserve believes that on-site revenues will stabilize to 25 percent of software revenues by 2007, because end-clients are interested in reducing travel costs and because the United Kingdom and the United States are becoming stricter about visa rules and regulations for temporary workers.

The Burst of the Dot.com and Telecom Bubbles

In 2000, the United States witnessed an economic slowdown: the dot.com bubble and the telecom bubble had both burst, and most companies had spent enormous

Figure 4.4 *Indian IT Revenues and Share of IT in GDP, 1997–2003*

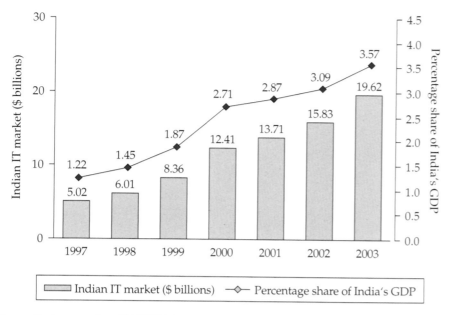

Source: Evalueserve data; NASSCOM 2004.
Note: The Indian IT market includes hardware, peripherals, networking, domestic and export markets for software, IT services, and IT–enabled services.

Figure 4.5 *Exports of IT Software and Services by India, 1997–2003*

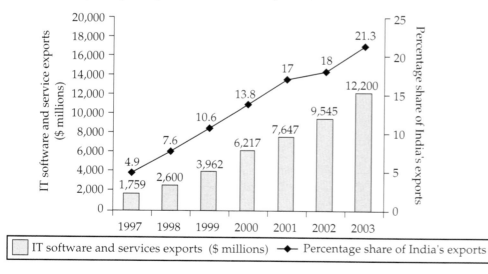

Source: Evalueserve and NASSCOM 2004.

amounts of money trying to fix the Y2K problem, with nothing to show for the money spent. U.S. companies began slashing their IT budgets and asking their IT departments for a return on investment.

The burst of the telecom bubble left a glut of unused telecom capacity around the world, and prices of long-distance telecommunications fell to a 10th of what

Figure 4.6 *Projected Growth of IT Exports by India, 2003–2008*

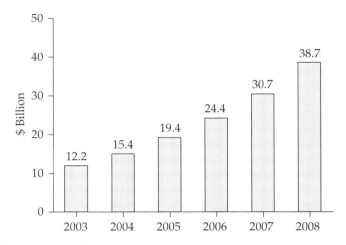

Source: Evalueserve data and analysis.

they had been a decade earlier. These developments spurred the development of the on-site–offshore model of IT services, in which a few people work on site, but most work offshore.

India's Growing Reputation in Offshore IT Services

An early-mover advantage and critical mass made India one of the most attractive global locations for companies looking to locate their IT work offshore. India offered strengths in application maintenance and support, application development, software package implementation, IT operations, and IT outsourcing and management. The 10- to 12-hour time difference between North America and India enabled overnight delivery of some of these services. This unique advantage helped U.S. firms operate two complete shifts in one working day, thereby enhancing their internal operations and customer service.

A large and talented labor pool has been the most prominent factor contributing to the Indian IT industry's success. India produces about 73,000 new IT graduates a year and had 656,000 IT professionals as of March 31, 2004 (Microsoft Malaysia). Of these, 376,000 are involved in exporting IT software and services, 318,500 of them providing services offshore and 57,500 providing services onshore, usually on site in Canada, the United Kingdom, or the United States. Of the 318,500 professionals providing services offshore, about 212,000 are being billed full-time (1,900–2,100 hours a year), and the remainder are undergoing training, moving from one job to another, or are being billed for part-time work. Average salaries for IT professionals with up to two years' experience are $5,400–$9,000 a year, a fraction of what comparable professionals earn in Canada, the United Kingdom, and the United States.

Evalueserve estimates that this pool of IT professionals will continue to grow by about 12 percent a year, creating 1.156 million professionals by March 2009. Of these, about 809,000 will be involved in exporting IT software and services.

Challenges for India's Offshore Sector

Going forward, India will need to take care of several shortcomings to remain an attractive offshore destination, namely:

- The power infrastructure is unreliable.
- The level of proficiency in English and of cultural compatibility with the United Kingdom and the United States are high in the 10 largest cities in India, but the next 4–6 cities are struggling in this regard. To mitigate this problem, many IT companies have started providing cultural training and accent neutralization programs. Addressing this situation will take five to seven years.
- The costs of labor have been increasing 14 percent a year in U.S. dollar terms. If they continue to rise at this rate, by 2010, costs will be $2\frac{1}{2}$ times what they were in 2003, raising salaries in India to $13,500–$22,500 a year. This expected rise in labor costs threatens to reduce India's competitiveness, opening up opportunities for other countries such as China, Romania, and the Russian Federation.
- A proper supply chain for talent is still not in place. Significant changes need to take place in the way people are trained in India, so that the students are better equipped to handle high-skill, knowledge-intensive jobs. A stronger focus on more niche areas and specializations in high-end domains are required.

Increased Involvement of the Diaspora

The Indian diaspora played an important role in the development of the IT industry in the 1990s in India, but its role was not pivotal. In contrast, by 2000 the Indian diaspora, especially in the United States, began to play a vital role in developing the IT and business process outsourcing industry in India as follows:

- To meet the needs of Indian IT companies, as well as those in other sectors, for project management and business expertise, the Indian diaspora established the International School of Business (ISB). Many Indian professors teaching in the United States, the United Kingdom, and Canada take one- or two-term sabbaticals to teach at the International School of Business.
- Many Indians living in Canada, the United Kingdom, and the United States returned to India to join large companies such as General Electric, Intel, and IBM or to start their own companies. Returning Indians have already started more than 200 IT and business process outsourcing companies.
- The Indus Entrepreneur and the Silicon Valley Bank have already taken two delegations of venture capital companies (which have collectively invested more than $40 billion in the United States) to India to explore potential investment opportunities. Many of these companies are actively considering investing in Indian companies, and some have already done so.
- With the rise of the Indian IT industry and the additional push by the Indian diaspora, many venture capital companies in the United States now require their start-up companies to have a back end in India in order to save on R&D costs. According to Evalueserve, as of March 2004, more than 150 start-ups had some form of their back end in India and front end in the United States, and this number is likely to have doubled by March 2006.

• Some venture capital companies in the United States—particularly those
run by people of Indian origin—are actively funding Indian companies that
are likely to produce intellectual property and innovative products in wireless technology, semiconductor design and technology, and new business
models for conducting R&D. Examples include Westbridge Capital, Kleiner
Perkins Caulfield & Byers, and Norwest Venture Group.

Global Offshoring of Knowledge-Intensive Services

What is driving the increase in global offshoring and how can Indian companies
already successful in the IT or low-end business process outsourcing sectors tap
this market? What role is the Indian diaspora likely to play in this gradual and
inevitable migration? What other opportunities can India—and other low-wage
countries—exploit in sectors other than IT?

To achieve global competitiveness and high profitability, companies worldwide
offshore some of their IT and non–IT services to lower-wage countries. The reduction in telecom costs and the increased digitization of services has facilitated this
trend in the services sector. Companies are offshoring their services in order to
reduce costs by using lower-wage labor; take advantage of time zone differences
to enhance flexibility (by adding another shift, for example), allowing them to
bring products and services to market faster and provide better service; access a
larger and more talented labor pool; access new markets; and localize products or
services.

Meeting the Labor Shortfall in the United Kingdom

On the basis of data from five independent forecasters (Cambridge Econometrics,
Experian Business Strategies, Global Insight, Item Club, Oxford Economic Forecast-
ing, and Evalueserve Analysis), Evalueserve projects that real GDP in the United
Kingdom will grow 2.49 percent a year between 2003 and 2010.[2] It projects that total
demand for labor will grow from 27.7 million in 2003 to 28.6 million in 2010. Given
an average rate of unemployment of 5.5 percent, the domestic supply of labor is projected to grow from 27.7 million in 2003 to 27.9 million in 2010. Hence the U.K. economy will face a labor shortfall of more than 700,000 workers in 2010 (figure 4.7).

This labor shortfall will result in a loss in potential output, which can lead to a
further loss in employment. Evalueserve estimates that the shortfall in domestic
labor supply will decrease GDP growth from the projected 2.49 percent to 2.08 percent, causing a cumulative loss in output of $200 billion.

Global sourcing of skilled professionals (both by letting people migrate to the
United Kingdom and by sending jobs offshore) can mitigate this shortfall. Evalueserve projects that the United Kingdom will allow 372,000 immigrants to enter the
workforce during 2003–10, send 272,000 jobs offshore, and hire temporary workers
and send additional manufacturing jobs offshore in order to meet the remaining
shortfall of 70,000 workers. Without offshoring and temporary workers, the U.K.
economy will face a cumulative loss in output of about $60 billion.

---

[2] This section draws on Evalueserve and NASSCOM [a].

Figure 4.7 *Projected Supply and Demand of Labor in the United Kingdom, 2010*

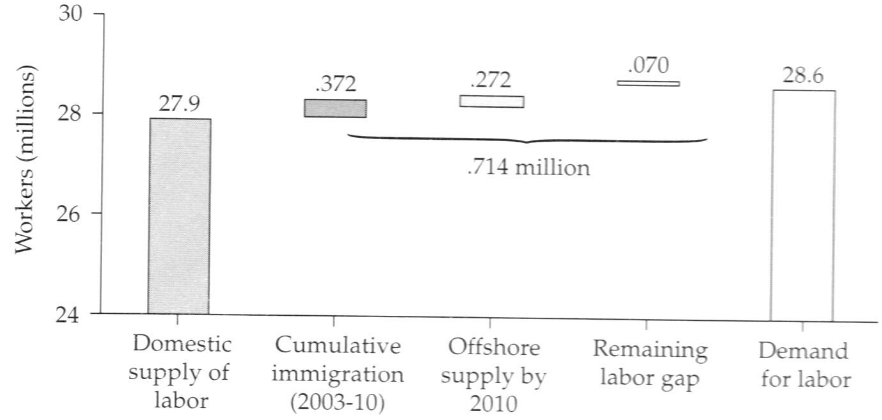

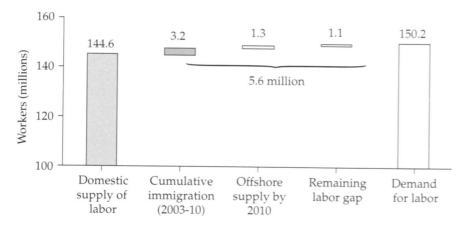

Source: Evalueserve and NASSCOM 2003[a].

Figure 4.8 *Supply of and Demand for Labor in the United States, 2010*

Source: Evalueserve and NASSCOM 2003[b].

Meeting the Labor Shortfall in the United States

According to the Congressional Budget Office, real GDP in the United States is expected to increase 3.2 percent a year between 2003 and 2010.[3] It projects that the demand for labor will increase from 137 million in 2003 to 150.2 million in 2010 (figure 4.8). According to Evalueserve, given a nominal unemployment rate of 5.2 percent in 2003–10 and no new immigration, the U.S. labor force would increase to 144.6 million by 2010.

A consequence of the labor shortfall will be an increase in wages and salaries, which will increase the prices of goods and services, potentially making United States companies uncompetitive in domestic and global markets. Overall output of the United States will be adversely affected, resulting in further loss of employment opportunities.

---

[3] This section draws on Evalueserve and NASSCOM [b].

According to Evalueserve, as a result of the projected shortfall in labor, GDP in the United States will grow at just 2.62 percent a year between 2003 and 2010. Compared with the Congressional Budget Office forecast of a real GDP growth rate of 3.20 percent, this represents a cumulative GDP loss of $2 trillion during 2003–10.

In the past, the United States has mitigated labor shortages by allowing immigration. The Chinese, the Indian, and other diasporas were created as by-products of this immigration. Evalueserve believes that this immigration trend will continue, helping reduce the labor shortage by adding 3.2 million new immigrants to the labor force by 2010. The addition of these new immigrants will reduce the cumulative GDP loss to $884 billion, but a gap of 2.4 million professionals (5.6 million minus 3.2 million) will remain.

Knowledge-Intensive Outsourcing

With the evolution and maturity of companies' outsourcing strategies, businesses are moving toward outsourcing high-end processes to offshore destinations. This knowledge process outsourcing involves outsourcing business processes that require substantial domain expertise or domain knowledge. Figure 4.9 illustrates two examples of knowledge process outsourcing, one in services, one in insurance.

Knowledge process outsourcing delivers higher value to an organization than traditional business process outsourcing and enhances the traditional cost-quality paradigm of business process outsourcing. It creates value for the client by providing business rather than process expertise. Hence knowledge process outsourcing requires moving from executing standardized processes to carrying out processes that demand advanced analytical or technical skills and some decision-making or decision-supporting process.

As businesses have become more competitive globally, the cycle for introducing products and services has become shorter and customers have become more demanding. Enterprises are being forced to adopt systems and business models that not only provide operational efficiencies, but also add strategic value.

According to Evalueserve, low-end outsourcing services are estimated to grow globally from $7.7 billion in 2003 to $39.8 billion in 2010, a compound annual growth

Figure 4.9 *Migration from Low-End to High-End Business Outsourcing*

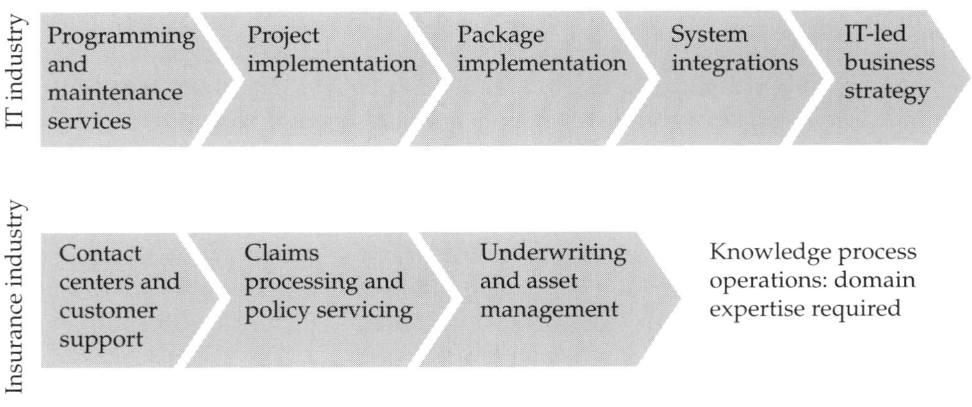

Source: Evalueserve data.

Figure 4.10 *Projected Growth in Global Business Process Outsourcing and Knowledge Process Outsourcing, 2003–10*

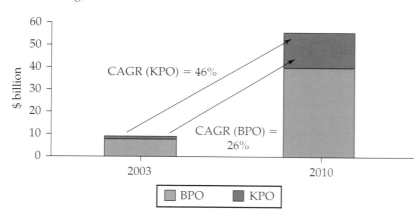

Source: Evalueserve data and analysis.
Note: BPO = business process outsourcing, CAGR = compound annual growth rate, KPO = knowledge process outsourcing.

rate of 26 percent. In contrast, total revenue for the global knowledge process outsourcing market, estimated at $1.2 billion in 2003, is projected to grow to $17 billion by 2010, implying a compound annual growth rate of 46 percent (figure 4.10). The business process outsourcing and knowledge process outsourcing sectors represent a huge potential market for Indian firms, most of which are strategically positioned to tap this opportunity in the coming years.

Opportunities in knowledge process outsourcing include intellectual property research, R&D in pharmaceuticals and biotechnology, and analytics and data mining services. For example, it costs about $10,000–$15,000 to draft and file a patent application with the United States Patent and Trademark Office. An intellectual property specialist at an offshore location can produce a preliminary draft of a patent application, which can then be reviewed, modified, and filed by a registered U.S. patent attorney, saving the client 50–60 percent of the cost. This model also allows lower-wage countries to provide other intellectual property services, including overlap, landscaping of technology domains, licensing, docketing, and commercialization and trademark searching and filing services, at much lower costs. Not surprisingly, some U.S. law firms have already set up back-end centers in India and others are working with Indian companies for this purpose.

The global contract research market was expected to grow to $20 billion by 2004. Destinations such as India offer significant cost advantages (as much as 40–60 percent) in contract research and clinical trials. AstraZeneca and Glaxo-Smith-Kline have set up drug discovery and R&D centers in lower-wage countries such as India.

Offshoring analytics and inventory management services can save companies as much as 60–70 percent after taking into account all the costs associated with offshoring, including overhead. Destinations such as India and the Russian Federation are ideal for these services, because of their large pools of low-cost engineers and people with doctorates. The average annual cost differential between a person with a doctorate in the sciences or engineering in India and the United States is $60,000–$80,000 a year. Similar cost differentials exist between the Russian Federation and the United States.

Challenges for Indian Vendors

Knowledge process outsourcing presents substantial opportunities to Indian players, but it also presents formidable challenges, namely:

- Processes executed require higher quality standards, because the stakes for clients are high. Because of these high stakes, clients may have apprehensions about the quality of the services delivered, especially from lower-wage countries, that may not be easy to allay.
- Some high-end services require significant investment in infrastructure. For example, a company doing simulation and finite element analysis will require very high-end work stations. Provision of services that require only simple data gathering, cleansing, and analysis will need only moderate amounts of capital.
- The lack of availability of domain expertise will pose a significant challenge to players in high-end knowledge services. The shortage of good midlevel managers in India will compound this problem.
- Knowledge process outsourcing projects will be characterized by a higher level of control, confidentiality, and risk management. Laxity in any of these parameters can jeopardize or eliminate the expected strategic value for clients. Traditionally, India has been known for its piracy of software and lack of respect for intellectual property and copyrights. Lack of a data protection act in India compounds concerns about data privacy.
- Scaling up knowledge process outsourcing operations will more difficult than scaling up traditional business process outsourcing services, because it is difficult to find highly skilled people with the domain expertise required and it takes longer to train professionals.

Indian professionals lack understanding of intellectual property and how to use it to make money. The model in which teachers or gurus used to provide knowledge to their students without any monetary rewards still exists in the Indian psyche, and most Indian IT and business process outsourcing companies have not even considered owning any of the intellectual property they are generating. If an Indian company that is working for an end-client generates intellectual property, the contract typically states that the end-client owns that intellectual property. However, if the Indian company knowingly or unknowingly infringes on someone else's intellectual property, it (and not the end-client) is responsible for all damages and fees. Unless Indian companies begin to innovate and own the intellectual property they generate, it is unlikely that they will succeed in some of the knowledge process outsourcing subsectors.

One of the greatest challenges for knowledge process outsourcing companies is hiring good talent and continuously training it. Outsourcing companies venturing into the knowledge process outsourcing business are advised to focus on initial training and development modules and then continue regular training with additional training modules, constructive feedback, appropriate coaching and mentoring, and identification of the right career paths for their professionals.

Firms need to work with end-clients to identify performance criteria. They need to set the right expectations and continuously assess and monitor projects jointly with the end-client.

Remaining Competitive

Salaries in India have been rising at 14 percent a year and are expected to continue to rise at the same rate in the coming years (BBC News). Given these increases, the most effective way to remain competitive and sustain growth will be by moving up the value chain and taking on high-value, knowledge-intensive work and ensuring that project management, as well as process management, is given the highest priority.

Among low-wage countries, China, with its huge diaspora network, strong economy, and low wages, is likely to pose a major threat. However, Belarus, Hungary, Poland, the Russian Federation, and Ukraine could also compete with India, especially in IT services and knowledge process outsourcing.

Evolving Role of the Diaspora in the Indian Knowledge Services Industry

In addition to providing some of the required capital (through investment), the Indian diaspora is expected to play several crucial roles in the gradual emergence of India's high-end knowledge services sector. Expatriate Indians are expected to

- Facilitate the gradual evolution of the IT and IT-enabled services sectors toward higher value-added, knowledge-intensive outsourcing by mentoring and coaching offshore vendors. This will involve imparting know-how about building knowledge-intensive service firms and transferring relevant best practices.
- Pitch for the Indian industry without appearing to favor India over other low-wage destinations. Their own brand equity as capable and successful professionals will lend credibility to the might and ability of Indian firms, increasing the equity of "Brand India."
- Leverage the Indian network to create win-win situations with other diaspora and other IT communities, such as the Chinese diaspora and the Chinese software and hardware manufacturing communities in China, Hong Kong (China), and Taiwan (China).

Opportunities for India in Medical Tourism

The model of cooperation between the diaspora and offshore services vendors in IT and business process outsourcing sectors can be replicated in other sectors. With the increasing maturity of Indian industry and skill-intensive sectors, successful diaspora communities in a variety of professions are likely to play a vital role in facilitating the tapping of emerging global opportunities.

Health care-related export services and medical tourism are likely to be significant businesses for India, thanks to unmet demand in countries such as the United Kingdom (box 4.1); the Indian medical diaspora in Canada, the United Kingdom, and the United States; and exceptional expertise within India, its cost advantage, and some world-class facilities. Worldwide, health care is a $3 trillion industry, and India is in a position to tap a small segment by highlighting its well-trained doctors and nurses and its facilities and services and by exploiting the brand equity of leading Indian health care professionals across the world.

India is emerging as a preferred destination for health care, because it has a large number of hospitals with world-class infrastructure and equipment and many medical practitioners who have been trained outside India. India has excellent

Box 4.1 The United Kingdom's Struggling Health Care System

The U.K. health care system has been struggling over the past few years because of a shortage of medical facilities and professionals. The shortage has made it difficult to provide timely treatment. In response, medical tourism, which allows patients to be treated by medical facilities in foreign countries, is an emerging trend in the United Kingdom.

The United Kingdom invests 8.3 percent of its national income in health care, a smaller percentage than the other Group of Seven countries. Measured by such parameters as cancer survival rates, the U.K. health care system performs poorly compared with systems in the United States and many European countries. It also performs poorly in terms of the number of people put on waiting lists for medical attention and the length of time they wait.

Every year, about 9 percent of the National Health Service workforce leaves, leaving a gap of about 100,000 employees. Some critical areas, such as emergency services, intensive care, and operating room nursing, face the most severe recruitment and retention problems. Hiring and retention difficulties are also common for specialists, such as physiotherapists, radiographers, dentists, and occupational therapists. The situation is exacerbated by the fact that a large proportion of the workforce is aging: according to the Royal College of Nursing, more than 70,000 nurses are expected to retire during the next few years (Hawkes).

At the same time, the population of the United Kingdom is aging. In 2001, about 21 percent of the population was 60 years or older, and another 1.8 million people are projected to join this group by 2011 (see the table below). This will exert increased pressure on the National Health Service and further strain available resources.

Projected Growth in the Elderly Population in the United Kingdom, 2001–11

Item	2001	2006	2011
Total population (thousands)	58,837	59,675	60,524
Population 60 and older (thousands)	12,238	12,874	14,040
Population 60 and older as a percentage of the total population	20.8	21.6	23.2

Source: Government Actuary Department data; Tinker 2002.

More than 1 million patients are on the National Health Service waiting list for treatment (National Health Service). On average, patients wait more than four months for treatment, and the waiting period can be as long as six months for a cardiac operation and nine months for cataract surgery. The waiting time for treatment of lung cancer is sometimes as long as six months, leaving little hope for remission.

The U.K. government is making efforts to meet the shortfall in health care services. It has announced a huge spending increase and a five-year investment program to bolster the National Health Service. The budget of the program, which was initiated in fiscal 2003/4, will reach $161 billion by fiscal 2005/6 and $195 billion by fiscal 2007/8. To meet the shortage, long-term recruiting targets have been set for various levels of medical professionals.

These efforts will not solve the problems: U.K. patients will have to move beyond their national borders to seek treatment. Indeed, medical tourism from the United Kingdom has already started, with more than 1,000 U.K. patients treated outside the United Kingdom in 2002.

In 2002, the National Health Service initiated a trial program in which patients could travel to France and Germany for surgery. If these trial programs prove successful, more patients could be sent to other destinations, such as India, Malaysia, and Poland.

U.K. patients seem quite willing to travel abroad. According to a survey conducted in June 2002, 42 percent of patients are willing to travel outside the United Kingdom for treatment and 51 percent believed that involving other organizations—including the private sector—would improve the current health care system.

Source: Evalueserve and NASSCOM [a].

medical facilities and skills in cardiology, angioplasty, and cardiac surgery; minimally invasive surgery; joint replacement; organ transplantation (liver, kidney, heart, and bone marrow); cataract surgery; cancer treatment, including radiotherapy; and neurosurgery, including stereotactic surgery.

Hospitals such as Apollo, Escorts, Hinduja, Max Healthcare, Manipal, and the Fortis Heart Institute are already becoming premier destinations for foreign patients. Indian hospitals are beginning to offer packages that include medical treatment, recuperation, relaxation, recreation, and tourism. Many foreign patients who come to India for treatment are spending two or three weeks at various tourist destinations after their treatment.

The setting up of Western-standard hospitals in India is now in full force. Evalueserve estimates that India generated $430 million from medical tourism in 2003. Indian hospitals are likely to generate about $2 billion in annual revenue by 2010, an annual growth rate of 21 percent (box 4.2).

Cost Advantages of Medical Tourism

Medical treatment in India is available at a fraction of what it costs in the United Kingdom (table 4.2).

Medical tourism has some significant challenges to overcome before it becomes an attractive alternative. An important challenge is that medical regulation and malpractice insurance in India and other lower-wage countries, such as Malaysia and Poland, are not well developed. Medical associations and courts in these countries are slow.

Recognizing these gaps, these countries are now beginning to implement regulations in order to bring these areas up to globally acceptable standards. In 1995, for example, the Supreme Court of India ruled that injured patients could sue doctors

---

Box 4.2 *Medical Tourism in India and Competition from Other Countries*

Patients from Bangladesh, Egypt, Mauritius, Sri Lanka, the Middle East, and elsewhere are beginning to come to India for cardiac bypass surgery. It costs $5,000 to have this surgery done in India, $25,000 in the United Kingdom, and $40,000 in the United States.

Europeans are beginning to come to have cataract operations done in India. Once their operation is done, they often spend two weeks in Goa recuperating. These patients avoid the long lines in Europe, and the insurance companies in Europe pay the entire costs (including those of recuperating).

Some Indian radiologists are beginning to read X-ray charts of U.S. patients and send their preliminary findings to radiologists in the United States, who verify their findings and do a thorough quality check. Eighty percent of the work is done in India and the remaining 20 percent in the United States (with proper quality checks by professionals with U.S. medical licenses).

Polish hospitals and organizations are also offering medical facilities to patients from developed nations, particularly the United Kingdom.

Guests at the Palace of the Golden Horses Hotel in Kuala Lumpur can undergo a full health checkup, including X-rays, blood pressure tests, and liver and thyroid screening, for about one-third the cost charged in the United Kingdom. The Gleneagles Intan Medical Center in Malaysia offers knee replacement for $5,000 and hip replacement for $6,000. At private hospitals in the United Kingdom, the procedures cost two to three times as much.

Source: Macer and Wilson.

Table 4.2 *Costs of Selected Medical Treatments in India and the United Kingdom ($)*

Type of surgery	Cost in the United Kingdom	Cost in India
Open heart	22,200	4,900
Hip replacement	12,025	7,300
Cardiac	11,100	4,900
Heart bypass	9,250	4,900
Cataract	3,700	740

Source: Evalueserve data and analysis.

and hospitals under India's Consumer Protection Act. Indian courts remain slow, however.

Another challenge is reimbursement. Because most payments in developed countries are made either by the government or by private insurance companies, hospitals and other medical organizations in low-wage countries will have to form ties with such bodies.

Potential of Medical Tourism for India

Medical tourism can play a crucial role in helping the health care system in some developed nations. It can overcome long waiting periods and help patients who cannot afford expensive medical facilities. In addition to providing surgery and Western-style medical treatment, India can also promote alternative medicine (yoga clinics; health spas; and aryuvedic, homeopathic, and *unani* treatment centers).

Traditionally, many patients from the Middle East sought medical treatment in the United States. Since September 11, 2001, the United States has implemented fingerprinting and other laws that many foreigners, especially Arabs, find discriminatory. In response, many Arabs are no longer going to the United States for medical treatment. Instead, they are traveling to India and Malaysia, which have good hospitals and doctors and sizable Muslim populations.

If India can overcome the challenges cited, medical tourism could represent a particularly attractive opportunity. More than 20 million people of Indian origin live outside India. Their combined personal earnings are $363 billion a year and they spend more than $7.2 billion on medical insurance and hospitalization a year. If India could attract 14 percent of the spending by people of Indian origin on medical insurance and health care outside India, it would earn an additional $1 billion a year.

Opportunities for the Diaspora to Contribute to the Indian Hospitality Industry

The Indian business diaspora can play an important role in the development of the travel, tourism, and hospitality industry in India by providing management experience, process expertise, and funding. Although the hotel industry in India is considered among the best in the world, most hotels are very expensive for Indians. There is a dire need for affordable hotels (those priced at $10–$15 per day) for middle-class Indians. Budget hotels are the types of hotels that people of Indian origin in the United States own. Their expertise in managing such hotels could be extremely valuable for India.

Conclusions and Lessons for Other Diasporas

The diaspora has played a crucial role in ensuring a first-mover advantage for Indian IT players, helping them exploit market opportunities before players from other low-wage countries such as China. The established model of cooperation between the diaspora community and Indian IT service vendors will need to be replicated in other sectors, such as knowledge process outsourcing and outsourcing of health care services. Further analysis of this experience and the effective adaptation of the existing cooperation model between the diaspora and Indian IT service vendors in several other emerging sectors will prove to be of significant importance in India's development strategy in the years to come.

For the following reasons, it will be difficult for other diaspora communities to duplicate the Indian experience:

- India has a long tradition of mathematics and science education, as well as a tradition of intergenerational mentoring that does not exist in most countries.
- Indian leaders injected large amounts of money in higher education in India, in most cases at the expense of primary education. Although India currently produces about 2.45 million graduates every year, including 200,000 engineers, 73,000 IT professionals, 117,000 doctors, and 40,000 with a masters in business administration, 59 million children between 6 and 14 receive no primary education. This dichotomy would be hard to find in other countries, and especially hard to find would be the high number of educated people that are graduating every year.
- Few governments are likely to maintain a hands-off policy toward services such as IT, business process outsourcing, knowledge process outsourcing, and medical tourism, especially once their potential has been demonstrated.
- Large-scale migration of labor from developing to developed countries has become more difficult since September 11, 2001.
- Few diaspora communities other than the Chinese will achieve the critical mass necessary to produce substantial numbers of influential people in any given sector.
- People of Indian origin in Canada, the United Kingdom, and the United States have friends and colleagues who studied with them in India and did not emigrate. This allows Indian expatriates with innovative ideas to contact friends and colleagues in India to help them execute them. In other developing countries, most good professionals migrate to developed countries, leaving too few behind to take innovative ideas forward.

Despite these differences, many other countries have the combination of low-wage graduates and successful expatriates living in the West. Some form of mentor-sponsor model may work for some countries in a limited set of industries and sectors if it is mobilized effectively.

Although replication of the Indian experience is beyond the reach of other diaspora communities, India's experience nevertheless has far-reaching implications for them. Smaller diaspora communities can help transform their home countries. Such transformations may not be significant from the global economic perspective, but they may have a substantial effect on the home country. In Armenia, for example, just 200 dedicated expatriates could constitute the critical mass needed to become role models for local businesses and nongovernmental organizations and to forge business linkages with the rest of the world. More important than the size or the strength of the diaspora is the creation of disciplined, dedicated, value-driven, visionary diaspora organizations, such as TiE. Such organizations can provide good networking platforms for diaspora executives, as well as local players, facilitating the mentoring and limited sponsoring of local players.

References

Agrawal, Subhash. "Putting India to Work." *Axess Magazine.* http://www.axess.se/english/archive/2004/nr2/currentissue/theme_indiawork.php.

Bagri, Apurva. "Chairman's Message." The Indus Entrepreneurs. http://www.tie.org/Home/AboutTie/ChairmansMessage/index_html/view_document.

BBC News. "Indian Pay Rises Highest in Asia." http://news.bbc.co.uk/1/hi/business/3264009.stm.

Center for Immigration Studies. "Doctors and Nurses: A Demographic Profile." http://www.cis.org/articles/1998/DocsandNurses.html.

Dataquest. "The Hot Verticals: The Great Indian Software Revolution." http://www.dqindia.com/content/20years/102122306.asp.

Economic Times [a]. "Indians in the U.S. to Rule American IT sector." http://economictimes.indiatimes.com/articleshow/670159.cms

———— [b]. "NRIs Create Jobs in Silicon Valley. http://economictimes.indiatimes.com/articleshow/msid-701176,curpg-4.cms.

Evalueserve and NASSCOM (National Association of Software and Service Companies) [a]. "The Impact of Global Sourcing on the U.K. Economy: 2003–2010." http://www.globalsourcingnow.com/gsn_reports.asp.

———— [b]. "The Impact of Global Sourcing on the U.S. Economy: 2003–2010." http://www.globalsourcingnow.com/gsn_reports.asp.

————. 2004. "Strategic Review 2004." http://www.nasscom.org.

Hawkes, N. "NHS Must Double Its Nurses from Abroad." *The Times.* Republished at http://www.bl.uk/collections/social/welfare/issue18/reform.html

Khanna, Vikram. "India's Software Patriarch Still a Pace-Setter." *Business Times.* Republished at http://it.asia1.com.sg/newsdaily/news004_20011105.html.

Macer, Hall, and Peter Wilson. "Beat the NHS Queue with a Medical Trip to Malaysia." Telegraph.co.uk. http://news.telegraph.co.uk/news/main.jhtml;jsessionid=OAGSK4SIX2OABQFIQMFCFFWAVCBQYIV0?xml=/news/2001/12/30/nmal30.xml.

Microsoft Malaysia. "Spice for Progress: Innovation." http://www.microsoft.com/malaysia/business/articles/linkpage4176.asp.

Ministry of External Affairs, India [a]. "Report of the High-Level Committee on the Indian Diaspora." New Delhi. Republished at http://indiandiaspora.nic.in/diasporapdf/chapter13.pdf.

———— [b]. "India–U.K. Relations." Europe West and Commonwealth Division. Republished at http://meaindia.nic.in/foreignrelation/united%20kingdom.htm.

NASSCOM (National Association of Software and Services Companies). "IT Software and Services Market." http://www.nasscom.org/artdisplay.asp?Art_id=1636.

National Health Service. "National Health Service Hospital Waiting Lists by Region, 1999: Social Trends 30." http://www.statistics.gov.uk/STATBASE/xsdataset.asp?vlnk=548&More=Y.

NIIT (National Institute of Information Technologies). "Our Organization." http://www.niit.com/niit/corporate/about niit/Org.asp.

Raymer, Steve. "Indian Doctors Help Fill U.S. Health Care Needs." *YaleGlobal.* http://yaleglobal.yale.edu/display.article?id=3340.

Tinker, A. 2002. "Aging in the United Kingdom: What Does This Mean for Dentistry?" *British Dental Journal* 194 (7): 369–72. http://www.nature.com/bdj/journal/v194/n7/full/4809996a.html.

U.K. Department for Education and Skills. "Employers' Skill Survey 2002." http://www.dfes.gov.uk.

University of Hyderabad. "The Indian Diaspora." Centre for the Study of Indian Diaspora. http://www.uohyd.ernet.in/sss/indiandiaspora/Indian.html.

U.S. National Science Board. "The Science and Engineering Workforce: Realizing America's Potential." http://www.nsf.gov/nsb/documents/2003/nsb0369/nsb0369.pdf.

Wu, Kevin. "The Silicon Valley Indians." BeBeyond.com. http://www.bebeyond.com/KeepCurrent/Indepth/Indians.html.

5

Mexico: Leveraging Migrants' Capital to Develop Hometown Communities

Federico Torres and Yevgeny Kuznetsov

Mexico is one of largest recipient of remittances in the world. Yet with about $19 billion expected to be sent in 2005, representing 2.7 percent of gross domestic product (GDP) in 2004 (World Bank 2005), it is not the largest recipient either in absolute terms (not surprisingly, China and India receive larger inflows), or as a percentage of GDP (it is far behind Haiti, Jordan, and Serbia and Montenegro, all of which receive the equivalent of about 20 percent of GDP from remittances). Nonetheless, this flow is significant and explains why remittances have been the subject of renewed interest in Mexico.

Recent attempts by several Mexican state governments to promote more productive use of remittances have led to interesting new forms of public-private collaboration for developing small-scale infrastructure and *maquiladoras* (firms allowed to import materials duty-free if output is exported) in migrants' hometowns through programs and projects partially financed with remittances.

This chapter assesses these new experiences and their potential in rural, low-income communities in Mexico. It is based on a survey of programs and projects in four Mexican states with high rates of out-migration and remittances: Guanajuato, Michoacán, Oaxaca, and Zacatecas. Per capita income in these states is among the lowest in Mexico, a large proportion of the population is rural, and the labor force is scattered across small localities and engaged in low-productivity agricultural pursuits. Michoacán, Oaxaca, and Zacatecas have channeled and used collective remittances to support small-scale infrastructure projects through a consolidated public-private program in Zacatecas and by means of projects autonomously undertaken by migrants or local organizations with some public support from the state government in Michoacán and Oaxaca. The state of Guanajuato was included because of its experience using remittances for small and medium projects.

This chapter is dedicated to the memory of its principal author, Federico Torres, who passed away in 2002. In 2000–1, Torres led a research project supported by the Private-Public Infrastructure Advisory Facility for a study of collective remittances in Mexico developed by Yevgeny Kuznetsov. The facility's generous support made this chapter possible. At the National Development Bank, Patricio Marcos was in charge of supervision and Adán González contributed to shaping the main conclusions and recommendations. Three teams undertook the fieldwork. The first, which conducted the fieldwork in Zacatecas and the United States, was led by Rodolfo García Zamora, with the participation of Miguel Moctezuma Longoria, Héctor Rodríguez Ramírez, and Raúl Delgado Wise. The second, in charge of the fieldwork in Michoacán and Oaxaca, was led by Almendra Carrillo and Roberto Ramírez Rojas. The third, the Guanajuato team, was led by Alejandro Márquez y Albo. The data were updated by Clemente Ruiz Duran.

The Importance of Migrants' Savings and Community Remittances

The projects studied were financed by migrants' savings or by community remittances. Both are new kinds of transfers that supplement traditional family remittances. These new transfers are closely tied to the growth and consolidation of organized groups of Mexican migrants in the United States, known as hometown associations (also referred to as migrants' clubs). The new and traditional remittances are related: regions and towns with higher family remittances also have higher volumes of migrants' capital and donations.

Community, or collective, remittances are voluntary donations that organized groups collect from their members to finance community investments or social events in their native towns. More and more Mexican migrants in the United States are looking for an opportunity to invest their savings in their hometowns on an entrepreneurial basis. The hometown associations are becoming a vehicle for the diffusion of information about investment opportunities in Mexico and, even more, a vehicle for pooling the financial resources of small-scale savers and investors in the United States, allowing them the opportunity to invest through an organized group.

There are no reliable estimates of community remittances or migrants' savings, but judging by the experiences of Guanajuato and Zacatecas, where partial estimates of those flows have been made, they are still a small proportion of family remittances. The importance of migrants' savings and collective remittances does not lie in their volume, but in their features. In contrast with family remittances, they show great flexibility for investment purposes and, having an organized network of migrants behind them, are often accompanied by personal and managerial skills. They have great potential for supporting local development. Migrants' capital can also be of great importance for rural regions and small towns in Mexico.

The inflow of remittances in Mexico is especially important for rural areas where out-migration is heavy. In these regions of Guanajuato, Michoacán, Oaxaca, and Zacatecas, per capita remittances reach $300 or more a year, comparable with or higher than those in the Dominican Republic and El Salvador, where remittances represent a high proportion of gross national product (GNP).

These increasing flows of dollars reflect the intensification of labor mobility in one of the most dynamic trade areas of the world. In the next 10 years, remittances in Mexico could exceed a cumulative total of $100 billion. Collective remittances and migrants' savings will be a rapidly increasing part of this figure.

Collective remittances and migrants' savings, along with the capabilities, entrepreneurial skills, and organization of migrants, are a manifestation of the human and social capital generated by labor-exporting regions with intensive international out-migration. The social networks themselves are a form of social capital that encourages and facilitates social cooperation.

Social capital is not explored in this book, nor are the social networks that Mexican migrants have developed after more than a century of movement to and from the United States. These topics were beyond the scope of the project, which was to study small-scale infrastructure and *maquiladoras* programs and projects financed by migrants in selected states. Along with financing, some of the examples studied indicated clearly that migrants contributed other "assets" as well: their managerial skills, their knowledge of a foreign market, the power of their organizations, and their leadership.

Migrants' clubs and hometown associations are part of the vast formal and informal economic and social networks being developed by Latino communities in the United States and in their countries of origin as these communities grow in size and importance. More than 35 million Mexicans live in the United States, with a total income of more than $400 billion, comparable to that of Mexico. The substantial economic assets now at the command of this community are beginning to circulate through the extensive social and economic networks that international migration has created between Mexico and the United States. These networks facilitate the flow of assets. To the extent that the economic situation in Mexico remains stable, these flows will continue to increase.

Public-Private Collaboration to Tap Flows from Migrants

Since the early 1990s, some state governments in Mexico have recognized migrants' potential and promoted new forms of public-private collaboration to increase the flows of community remittances and migrants' savings. These governments have recognized the potential to stimulate these flows through local policies and instruments (table 5.1).

Attention has centered on instruments and incentives to stimulate family remittances, mainly on how to reduce the transfer costs of such funds. Advancement has been slow, in part a reflection of the country's efforts to achieve macroeconomic stability and to liberalize the financial sector.

Two of the most interesting cases of public-private collaboration are those of the Mexican states of Guanajuato and Zacatecas, where two successful programs, My Community (Mi Comunidad) in Guanajuato and Three for One (Tres por Uno) in Zacatecas, are channeling migrant flows. Interviews were conducted with the

Table 5.1 *Policy Instruments Affecting Capital Flows by Mexican Migrants*

Type of flow	Motivation	Sent by	Sent to	Main instruments or incentives influencing amounts sent
Family remittance	Provision of basic needs for family members	Individual migrants	Relatives in hometown	Banking facilities, transfer facilities, transfer costs
Collective remittance	Social and philanthropic	Migrants' clubs	Local leaders or organizations, local and municipal governments	Local demands and local leadership, matching programs or funds
Savings for personal investments	Welfare	Individual migrants	Relatives, migrants themselves	Personal investment schemes (housing, other)
Savings for entrepreneurial investments	Business	Individual migrants	Investors, partners, migrants themselves	Investment environment in hometown, technical assistance, information

Source: Authors.

officials in charge of both programs and a field survey of nine of their projects was conducted. Ten other projects carried out independently or related to smaller programs in Michoacán, Oaxaca, and Zacatecas were also surveyed.

Guanajuato's program seeks to attract migrants' savings to *maquiladoras.* Twenty-one *maquiladoras* for garments and other textile products have been established, 15 of which are already in operation. The firms in operation have generated about 500 permanent jobs. Migrants invested about $2.2 million in these plants over four years.

The Zacatecas program channels community remittances to small-scale infrastructure projects. For each $1 contributed by migrants, the Mexican government contributes $1–$3 from the federal government, $1 from the state government, and $1 from the municipal government. This program has funded more than 400 projects in eight years, with migrants investing about $4.5 million, including $2.7 million between 2000 and 2002.

The Guanajuato and Zacatecas programs were the result of the interaction of state governments with the organized Mexican community in the United States (box 5.1). There are about 700 registered Mexican associations of migrants in the United States and many more that are not registered. Because these associations are normally linked to groups of migrants from the same town in Mexico, they are known as hometown associations.

The leaders and most influential members of hometown associations have been actively involved in promoting and operating the Guanajuato and Zacatecas programs and projects. Their participation has been key to the programs' success. Through the programs, migrants have been contributing not only money for projects in their native towns, but also organizational and managerial skills. This is one of the most promising features of this new form of collaboration, because it reveals a strong commitment and identification of migrants and hometown associations with the advancement of their hometowns.

Local communities recognize hometown associations and migrants as the most influential forces behind local progress and fulfillment of the most urgent needs and priorities of local communities. As the migrants are generally the youngest and ablest segment of the population, their influence and leadership permeate through the projects sponsored by the hometown associations in many ways.

State governments have succeeded in taking the first steps toward mobilizing the potential of migrants' capital, but they have not been able to take full advantage of it. Even in states where programs for matching or leveraging remittances for investment purposes have been put into practice, the number and quality of projects is not yet rising steadily and more innovative projects have not been attempted.

This uneven performance is explained by two limiting factors. The first has to do with state and municipal governments' inability to match the migrants' contributions and to improve the design of policies and programs. The second is related to the incipient nature of the institutional development of hometown associations and clubs in the United States, which prevents them from taking a more active role in programs and projects.

Even with their limitations, however, the projects reviewed have had a significant impact on local communities and have been recognized as new and effective forms of public-private collaboration. These efforts have shown that migrants' capital offers a clear entry point for local development. Such capital offers the possibility

Box 5.1 *Using Migrants' Capital to Finance Community Projects in Yuriria and Jerez*

Yuriria and Jerez have traditionally been labor exporters to the United States. Yuriria, in the state of Guanajuato, is a rural town of 74,000 inhabitants, with few employment opportunities, most of them related to agriculture and cattle activities. Only 23 percent of the economically active population has a job, and two-thirds of those who work earn less than $8 a day.

Jerez, in Zacatecas, has a smaller but more urban population. The municipal capital has 27,500 inhabitants and is a regionally important agricultural and commercial center. Just 29 percent of the economically active population is employed, and the average wage is less than $8 a day.

Given these circumstances, it is not surprising that the majority of young adults in both towns, especially men, migrate to the United States in search of a better life, where they soon earn in one hour more than they could earn in their hometowns in a day. In the 1990s, out-migration of native workers from both municipalities increased rapidly, leading to a decline in the population. In Yuriria, the population decreased at an annual rate of 0.5 percent; in Jerez it declined 0.6 percent a year.

As the local population diminished, the flows of family remittances started to increase rapidly. Today each town has annual revenues of at least $25 million from remittances. This amounts to per capita income from remittances of $339 for Yuriria and $457 for Jerez—substantial sums given per capita GDP of $4,100 in Guanajuato and $3,300 in Zacatecas.

In addition to family remittances, other revenues started to flow into these towns in the 1990s. These flows come from the clubs that migrants have established in several U.S. cities, mainly in California, to help their hometowns. Migrants' clubs have long sent donations to their hometowns to finance civic and religious festivities or community projects. In the 1990s, when the state governments set up programs to attract such donations and channel them to specific projects, these clubs began doing so more regularly and on a larger scale.

In 1993, Zacatecas took the first step with the Three for One Program. In 1996, the government of Guanajuato launched an alternative program oriented to attract migrants' savings to finance the establishment of textile *maquiladoras* in localities of high out-migration. The response of Jerez's and Yuriria's migrants to these initiatives was enthusiastic. Natives from Jerez have at least five active clubs in California. Since 1993, these clubs have contributed more than $30,000 in collective remittances, which have helped promote community projects worth more than $1 million in their hometowns. The grants have been growing every year. Between 2000 and 2002, they sent more than $160,000 for paving streets and constructing public buildings and schools.

In California, migrants from Yuriria joined the Casas Guanajuato in response to the government of Guanajuato's program, pooling their resources to set up three textile *maquiladoras* in their hometown. The *maquiladoras* were entirely financed with $220,000 of migrants' capital. The state government provided them with the technical design for the projects and helped them get organized. Two of these enterprises have 20 partners or more and have created more than 100 permanent jobs. In addition to their financial contribution, migrants have supported the projects with their managerial and entrepreneurial skills.

Migrants' capital in Yuriria and collective remittances in Jerez are two early manifestations of the enormous economic potential the Mexican community in the United States is developing. Both constitute resources of great importance for local economies. Mobilized on a larger scale with innovative schemes, such resources offer the possibility of contributing to the development of vast rural areas that are in a difficult phase of transition toward modernity.

of mobilizing seed funds or venture capital that, complemented with other tools of economic promotion, can make a real difference in regions of heavy international migration.

The federal government could assist the states in this pursuit through selective, light-touch interventions designed to encourage best practices, innovative projects, networking, and capacity building. The National Development Bank (Nacional Financiera or NAFIN) could be part of that effort given its experience in promoting *maquiladoras* and local development. NAFIN could mobilize seed capital, technical assistance, and training in relation to targeted programs and projects. The objective would be to develop a self-sustainable private system for the development of projects and local programs financed totally or partially with remittances and savings from the Mexican community abroad. Available international aid funds could be used to support some of the initiatives.

Remittances are an important source of foreign exchange for more than 20 states in Mexico. In about 100 towns in these states, the level of remittances is at least $300 per capita, one of the highest levels in the world. In the most backward rural areas of these states, migrants' funds may constitute the only source for investment.

Scope and Methodology of Research

The analysis of programs and projects assesses past and current trends in the use of remittances for community-level infrastructure and *maquiladoras* in low-income communities. It examines financing and institutional mechanisms to increase private participation in projects and leverage hard currency and identifies policy, regulatory, logistical, informational, and funding impediments to increased private sector involvement.

The fieldwork examined both traditional and innovative projects and included at least three projects in each state. The targeted sectors for small-scale infrastructure projects were water and sanitation, electricity, transport, and telecommunications, but only in Zacatecas was it possible to find examples of ongoing projects in all these sectors. For the other states, other kinds of public works had to be included.

Nineteen projects (11 for small-scale infrastructure and 8 for productive purposes) were investigated directly through fieldwork covering 15 towns in the 4 selected states. One hundred participants in those projects (76 for small-scale infrastructure and 24 for productive projects) were interviewed using a semi-open questionnaire. The main questions addressed to local participants in Mexico included the following:

- Are the needs of the community served by the projects?
- How are decisions made and by whom?
- What are the costs of the project and the contribution of the hometown associations? Who participates in the different activities of the project?
- Who is in charge of the maintenance of the project and what provisions have been made for that purpose?
- What are the main policy problems (regulatory, technical, logistical, informational, and financial) faced by the project?
- What solutions have been proposed to address those problems?

Fifteen migrants from Guanajuato and Zacatecas were interviewed in Chicago and Los Angeles, and three focus groups were held there with selected leaders and members of hometown associations. The questionnaires and focus group guides focused on stages of the project cycle: idea and original proposal, preinvestment activities, evaluation, approval, financing, implementation, and operation and maintenance. More specifically, the following questions were asked:

- How much and what types of collective remittances have been contributed and how are they raised?
- What opportunities are there for increasing the flows of remittances, making them steadier, and leveraging them with other sources of financing?
- How sustainable are the projects and how could their sustainability be improved?
- What opportunities are there to introduce innovative instruments or to improve the institutional or financial arrangements of the existing program?
- What needs are there for technical assistance and training?
- Do the programs meet the objectives of the clubs?
- Are the rules and procedures clear and transparent?
- Were the opinions and suggestions of leaders and members of the clubs taken into account in shaping the programs?
- Are the results of the programs and the particular projects satisfactory?
- Have the programs had a clear influence on the increase in collective remittances?

Family Remittances

Remittances in Mexico have grown rapidly over the past several decades (table 5.2). They now represent the second largest source of dollar revenues in Mexico, bringing in 80 percent as much as oil exports. In 2003, Mexican migrants remitted about $13.4 billion to Mexico, sending about 4.7 percent of total U.S. income to recipients outside the United States.

These increasing flows of dollars reflect the intensification of labor mobility in one of the most dynamic trade areas of the world. That mobility has been encouraged by the enormous disparities in wages and salaries between the United States and its neighbors and by many years of continuous growth of the U.S. economy. The signing of the North America Free Trade Agreement in 1994 further consolidated economic interchange.

Most remittances are sent through normal commercial channels, with about two-thirds sent by electronic transfer. Less than 10 percent are sent in cash or in kind. Money orders represent about 25 percent of the market and have been declining steadily since the early 1990s (Lozano-Ascencio 1997).

Family remittances are used mainly for basic consumption. Household surveys of receipts and expenditures show that the patterns of savings, investment, and consumption of households receiving remittances are similar to those of households that do not receive them. Family remittances raise the standard of living of the households and communities receiving them. In some traditional areas of migration to the United States, the entire economy is based on receipt of monies from abroad. The level of consumption is higher and the pattern of consumption

Table 5.2 *Current Account Receipts and Family Remittances in Mexico, 1980–2003*

Year	Total receipts		Family remittances		Family remittances as a percentage of total receipts ([2]/[1])
	Billions of dollars (1)	Annual rate of growth (percent)	Billions of dollars (2)	Annual rate of growth (percent)	
1980	24.9	n.a.	0.7	n.a.	2.8
1981	31.1	25.1	0.9	23.1	2.8
1982	31.0	−0.4	0.8	−1.8	2.7
1983	32.9	6.3	1.0	16.2	3.0
1984	37.8	14.8	1.1	14.8	3.0
1985	35.9	−5.2	1.2	2.7	3.2
1986	29.9	−16.5	1.3	11.5	4.3
1987	37.4	24.9	1.5	14.5	4.0
1988	42.1	12.7	1.9	28.4	4.5
1989	48.1	14.3	2.2	16.6	4.6
1990	56.1	16.6	2.5	12.7	4.4
1991	58.1	3.6	2.7	6.6	4.6
1992	61.7	6.2	3.1	15.5	5.0
1993	67.8	10.0	3.3	8.6	5.0
1994	78.4	15.7	3.5	4.2	4.4
1995	97.0	23.9	3.7	5.7	3.8
1996	115.5	19.0	4.2	15.0	3.7
1997	131.5	13.9	4.9	15.2	3.7
1998	140.1	6.5	5.6	15.7	4.0
1999	158.9	13.5	5.9	5.0	3.7
2000	193.3	20.1	6.6	11.2	3.4
2001	185.6	−4.0	8.9	35.3	4.8
2002	187.9	1.2	9.8	10.3	5.2
2003	195.0	3.8	13.4	36.5	6.9

Source: Bank of Mexico data.
Note: n.a. = not applicable.

more modern than in other rural areas. Throughout the year, migrants' families in these areas receive regular flows of remittances and goods from abroad. During the summer and holidays, thousands of migrants working abroad flow back into their hometowns, bringing household appliances and significant sums of dollars, which are spent on local goods and services and sometimes on commercial or financial transactions. Many local professionals, such as doctors, dentists, and notaries, earn more than half their annual revenues during these periods. In addition to the positive direct impact on the local economy, there is some evidence of favorable multiplier effects on the aggregate expenditures financed with remittances on several economic sectors of the national economy (Zárate-Hoyos 1999).

The savings and investment generated by family remittances may also be important. Households receiving remittances allocate 23 percent of their income to savings and investment. If income from remittances is subject to the same pattern of use, $1.5 billion in savings and investments can be attributed to family remittances. This is equivalent to about 25 percent of nationwide expenditures by the federal and state governments in antipoverty programs. There are some indications that investment opportunities in migrants' hometowns may have a positive influence on the amounts of remittances sent and earmarked for productive uses, but the issue has not been studied in depth. Little is known about the patterns of savings and investment of Mexican migrants in the United States.

Data on the profile of remitters, their motivations for sending money, and the relationship between the amounts remitted and migrants' income, family status, time of residence in the United States, and level of education are limited. A generally accepted view, however, is that the amounts sent tend to decrease after migrants settle down in the United States and become permanent residents. This tendency has been more than offset by increases of remittances from new migrants, however.

At the national level, remittances represent only 1.2 percent of GNP, but at the regional and local level, family remittances are extremely important, especially in rural areas (box 5.2).

Estimates of the regional distribution of remittances in Mexico show that 10 states plus the Federal District received 70 percent of remittances in 2003 (figure 5.1). Seven of the 11 states—Durango, Guanajuato, Guerrero, Michoacán, Puebla, San Luis Potosí, and Zacatecas—are among the states with the lowest per capita GNP in Mexico. There may be more than 50 high-remittance clusters in Guanajuato, Michoacán, and Zacatecas and perhaps as many as 100 in Mexico as a whole.

Most of the municipalities visited are areas of heavy international out-migration and high receipt of remittances. If what is happening there is representative of similar areas elsewhere, a spectacular increase in the flows of migrants' savings and donations can be expected in the near future. Current remittances are an indicator of significant potential: the potential of the less conventional transfers accompanying the massive transfer of family remittances. These transfers can be mobilized to fund innovative projects, develop human capital, and invest in local development.

Box 5.2 *The Importance of Remittances in Mexico's Central-Western Zone*

A large part of remittances is flowing to rural municipalities with high international out-migration. There are no reliable data on the remittance flows at the municipal level, but it is estimated that 47 percent of total flows ($3 billion) are concentrated in 463 municipalities, mostly rural, that represent only 16 percent of Mexico's population.

The pattern of origin and destinations of migration from Mexico to the United States are changing in many important ways, but the traditional labor-exporting rural zones will continue to enjoy large inflows of family remittances. States in Mexico's central-western zone have historically received about 60 percent of family remittances. Guanajuato, Jalisco, Michoacán, San Luis Potosí, and Zacatecas receive far more remittances than other states.

The areas with the highest family remittances also register the most important flows of collective remittances and migrants' savings. These flows have not been quantified, but they have grown rapidly in recent years, especially in Guanajuato and Zacatecas, where local governments have established programs to attract them.

If trends in those two states are illustrative of what is happening in the rest of the central-western zone, this area is becoming the axis of a vast, binational network of economic, social, and political interrelationships that will have a profound influence on Mexico's development. The growth of family remittances is only a partial manifestation of the great potential of such a network.

Figure 5.1 *Distribution of Remittances by State, 2003*
(US$ millions)

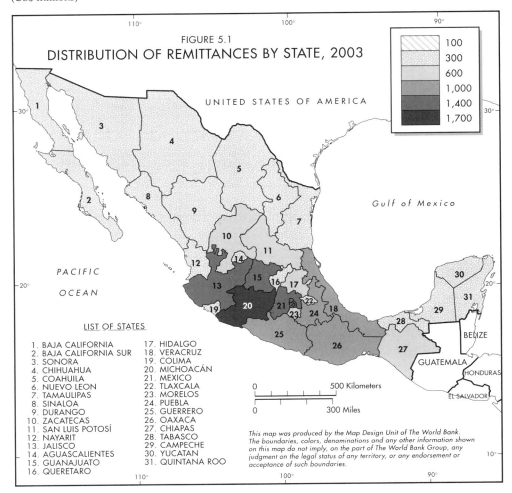

Source: Author's calculations.

Labor migration and remittances in the Latin American region have outstripped all forecasts and point toward a steady inflow of foreign earnings into labor-exporting economies. Demographic trends characteristic of an aging population in the developed countries will intensify international migration for a long time.

Community Remittances and Migrants' Savings

In view of the increasing flows of family remittances and their growing economic impact, state governments in Mexico have become increasingly interested in promoting better use of these receipts. In the past, efforts were aimed at stimulating the investment activities of local households receiving remittances, an approach that proved largely ineffective. Family remittances seem rather impervious to policy measures or incentives designed to influence their use. Attention has therefore focused on the migrants themselves, their savings, and their social networks and organizations.

Migrants have established new practices for supporting small-scale infrastructure development initiatives in their hometowns. Community remittances are voluntary donations that hometown associations of migrants in the United States collect from their members to finance social investment projects in their native towns. These remittances are associated with the development and maturation of a large number of associations of migrants in the United States during the 1990s, although some are much older. Associations of Latino migrants in the United States grew rapidly during the 1990s because of three main factors: the strong increase in migration flows caused by the economic bonanza in the United States; the tightening of U.S. immigration laws, which encouraged migrants to become better organized to defend their civil and labor rights; and the efforts of several Latin American governments to initiate a constructive dialogue with their migrants and give them better support through their consular procedures.

Organizations of migrants from Mexico, the Caribbean, and Central America are identified with the region or community of origin of their members. Each major regional or local source of emigrants in these countries is represented in the largest cities of the United States by one or more associations. Thousands of migrants' associations from the Dominican Republic, El Salvador, Guatemala, Honduras, and Mexico exist in the United States, especially in Atlanta, Chicago, Dallas, Houston, Los Angeles, Miami, New York, San Francisco, Seattle, and Washington, DC.

Migrants' associations are involved in a variety of cultural, social, and other activities. They offer legal advice, English courses, and assistance in transferring remittances. They also support trade with their home countries or communities.

Migrants' associations have long financed social and religious festivities in their hometowns. Lately they have also begun to direct their efforts toward improving their native communities by financing the paving of streets, the provision of water and electricity, the construction of roads and small dams, the improvement of secondary schools, and other development projects. In El Salvador, Guatemala, and Mexico, the impact of the activities of these kinds of associations is already visible and widely acknowledged.

The amount of these collective donations has not been documented in a systematic way, and it is difficult to estimate their size. During 1997, a midsize Salvadoran group from Los Angeles collected $10,000 that it donated to several charitable and cultural institutions in El Salvador. A smaller Salvadoran association in Washington, DC collected $37,000 in six years (CEPAL 2000a). Associations of migrants from Zacatecas, Mexico, regularly send annual donations of $5,000–$25,000, depending on the size of the club, its degree of development, and the project being sponsored.

Clubs of Mexicans have begun to exchange information on possible investment projects in their hometowns, to pool resources from their members, and to channel them to such projects. In 1998, Zacatecas had the largest number of registered hometown associations, Guanajuato was in third place, Oaxaca was in sixth place, and Michoacán was in eighth place. In Zacatecas, the large network of migrants' clubs has given birth to second-tier organizations: federations of migrants' associations.

Increasing numbers of Mexican migrants in the United States are looking for an opportunity to invest their savings in their hometowns for their personal use or on an entrepreneurial basis. Until a few years ago, the most frequent cases were those of migrants who had amassed savings in the United States and wanted to retire in their hometowns. In the states studied, many examples were found of personal investments in the form of a house or a ranch and formal investments in businesses such as restaurants.

More recently, migrants with less substantial savings have been looking for ways to invest in their hometowns. In these cases, the exchange of information and the transactions themselves are often accomplished through the network established by leaders and members of the hometown associations.

Hometown associations have become one of the most important links between migrants and their hometowns and an indispensable source of information for Mexican migrants. It would be difficult for a government initiative to reach the Mexican community in the United States without the intervention of these clubs. The hometown associations are becoming a vehicle for the diffusion of information about investment opportunities in Mexico and for pooling the financial resources of small-scale savers and investors in the United States.

There are no systematic estimates of the amounts of collective remittances or migrant savings flowing into Mexico. However, as they are related in many ways to family remittances, they are expected to grow along with them.

In Zacatecas, there are documented and updated partial estimates of the community remittances that have been channeled through the Three for One Program. They have been growing steadily, reaching about $1.3 million in 1999 (http://www.zacatecas.gob.mx/), or about 0.5 percent of total remittances in the state. But there are additional donations that are not channeled through government programs.

Some leaders of hometown associations have estimated the amounts of community remittances collected and sent to Mexico by their associations at $15,000–$20,000 a year for a medium club. The records of the Zacatecas program indicate that some of these clubs contribute more than $50,000 a year.

Whatever the size of these contributions, they are small relative to family remittances. The potential of community remittances lies not in their current size, but in that an organized force backs them, they are generally earmarked for investment, and they show a clear tendency to grow.

If current trends of Latin American migration to the United States continue, hometown associations will continue to grow at a rapid pace. It is also expected that the clubs will become better organized.

The Latino community in the United States is enormous and has turned into a new economic and political force, with continental ramifications. The economic and social networks of Latin American migrants, both formal and informal, are becoming more extended and complex and are developing the characteristics of an organized and strong diaspora. According to the U.S. Census Bureau (2000), there are some 10 million Latino households in the United States, with a total of about 35.3 million members. Average family income is about $40,500 a year, which amounts to a total of more than $400 billion a year for the community as a whole.

Latino workers in the United States remit $16 billion to $17 billion a year to their home countries. These flows are important to the economies of labor-exporting regions and countries, but they amount to only about 4 percent of the community's total income in the United States, suggesting that even greater flows could be possible. Within the Latino community, 20.6 million, or about 58 percent, are of Mexican origin. The number of Mexicans increased by 7.1 million during the 1990s, accounting for 55 percent of the 12.9 million increase in the Latino population (U.S. Census Bureau 2001).

Box 5.3 *Stages of Assistance from the Diaspora*

Diasporas have played important roles in the economic and social change of their countries. Burki (2000) identifies three phases in this process. The first phase involves sending remittances to families in the homeland. The second phase, which begins after migrants have established themselves in their host countries and accumulated economic assets, involves long-term investment in the home country if conditions permit. The third phase involves charitable giving, done largely through nongovernmental organizations.

Despite the increasing importance of migrants' clubs, few studies have focused on them and the possibilities they offer to improve development in their hometowns (box 5.3). Attention has focused on the recipients of remittances rather than on the remitters and their associations. Undoubtedly, this situation has contributed to a bias in the policies and instruments designed to stimulate more productive use of those receipts.

There has also been little analysis of other, no less important, developments in the United States that are also related to Latino immigration. For instance, there is a large, rapidly expanding business network owned by small and medium investors of Latino origin. In New York, hundreds of businesses are owned by Dominican, Mexican, and Salvadoran entrepreneurs, especially in Latino areas. Many of these entrepreneurs are well organized and have started to look for opportunities to invest in their countries of origin. The Latino business network is in part related to the boom in the market for Latino products, especially food products, in several U.S. cities. Chains of carriers, importers, and retailers have been established, with important repercussions for the people and regions producing such goods.

Interaction with migrants' associations is expensive and difficult. The associations are dispersed, there is no systematic information about them, and they do not always have regular meetings or working hours. Members do almost all the work of the clubs on a voluntary basis. In Mexico information about these associations is limited to a directory of clubs of Mexicans in the United States issued by the Mexican Ministry of Foreign Affairs, which lists only the names, addresses, and telephone numbers of the clubs.

State Government Institutions and Programs

Hometown associations in the United States are organized by state or locality. Leaders and members of hometown associations are interested in becoming political and economic actors in their hometowns. Aware of this situation, state governments have taken steps to consolidate their relations with their communities abroad. All states with significant out-migration have offices to help Mexicans living abroad. These offices have developed regular relations with migrants' clubs and have updated information about the cities in which they are located and their current leaders and general activities (box 5.4).

Basic information about projects and sites to be included in the field research was gathered initially from government officials in each state. Fifteen government officials were interviewed and asked to provide detailed information about the state's programs for migrant affairs in general and the use of remittances in particular. The

---

Box 5.4 *Helping Migrants from Guanajuato*

The main institution set up by the government of Guanajuato to help migrants is the General Directorate. Inaugurated in May 1994 as the Department of Migrants, in 1999 its status was elevated to that of General Directorate.

The General Directorate has a staff of 40 people, 5 of whom are on the state government's payroll and 35 of whom are independent professionals. Among these are researchers, advisers, and those who operate and promote the General Directorate's programs in the United States. The General Directorate has an annual budget of about $850,000.

---

main contacts were with the new specialized offices, the Offices of Attention to Citizens Abroad (Oficinas de Atención a Oriundos en el Exterior or OFAOE). All four states have such offices, and their objectives are similar, but their programs, institutional development, and links with migrants and hometown associations are at different stages of development.

Policies to increase the channeling of remittances and their productive use are just one of the concerns of the OFAOEs. These offices help migrants defend their human and working rights by providing legal support and advice and provide consular services in emergencies. They also promote cultural activities among Mexican communities in the United States.

The OFAOEs are normally attached to the political branches of state governments and coordinate with the Ministry of Foreign Relations and its consulates in the United States. Efforts related to remittances are only weakly linked to the other social and economic programs of the state and to general economic promotion policies.

In terms of their work on remittances, the most advanced OFAOEs are those of Guanajuato and Zacatecas. Both have well-established means of communication and collaboration with migrants and hometown associations and have strengthened links with economic and social programs. In Michoacán, the OFAOE is still trying to consolidate its relationship with migrants and establish procedures.

Of the four states studied, only Guanajuato and Zacatecas have systematic programs to attract remittances for investment purposes. Both programs rely on the mediation of hometown associations to promote projects and collect contributions. Hometown associations have different characteristics in each state, but in both states clubs recognize and endorse the programs and show a strong commitment to them, which is the main key to their success.

Guanajuato's program, My Community, seeks to attract migrants' investment in a *maquiladora* that has a social impact in the home community. Members of a hometown association, along with local investors, are stockholders in the enterprise and have a business motivation, but they are also concerned about their hometown's development. This combination is one of the most interesting features of the program. *Maquiladoras* in Guanajuato's program were originally planned as joint public-private ventures, with the migrants or local investors contributing half of the capital ($60,000–$100,000) and the state government contributing the other half. In the end, the state government participated only as a facilitator, developing the business plan, covering two months of wages and training courses for the new workers, and making low-cost loans available. Other government officials offered legal, administrative, and technical advice when necessary.

The program started in 1996 with the promotion of the establishment of 10 *maquiladoras* in seven municipalities. It was well received and accepted by migrants from Guanajuato and their clubs. By June 2000, 12 *maquiladoras* had been put into operation and 9 more were under way. The capital contributed by migrants is estimated at $2.2 million for the 21 firms. The 12 firms in operation employed about 500 people (table 5.3). The associations participating in the program were mainly from Illinois and California.

Zacatecas' main program, Three for One, is one of the oldest and most successful initiatives in the field of remittances. The initial idea of this program was that for every $1 contributed by the hometown associations for community projects, the federal government would contribute $1 and state governments would contribute another $1. In 1999, municipalities also agreed to contribute $1 for every $1 collected by the hometown associations. Contributions go to a fund for community investments in the clubs' hometowns. Investment decisions are made by a committee made up of local government and hometown association representatives.

Between 1993 and 2000, the program financed $16.2 million of projects ($5.4 million under the Two for One Program and $10.8 million under the Three for One Program). Hometown associations contributed $4.5 million (table 5.4). The amounts committed to the program by the hometown associations have been increasing rapidly, and in the last few years some contributions could not be accommodated because of government budget restrictions.

Typical projects include construction of roads; street paving; provision of water, sewage, and electricity; and construction and improvement of other community facilities, including churches, cemeteries, parks and squares, community centers, and sports grounds (table 5.5). Recently, investments have also been made in the purchase of computers for high schools and the construction of small dams and water treatment facilities.

Most projects are small, with an average cost of $56,000. The cost of some of the projects, especially the most expensive, may be underestimated, however, because construction is typically divided into phases, each accounted for as an individual project in order to accommodate a larger number of communities and clubs within budget restrictions. A few of the projects are budgeted at standard costs. For instance, the drilling of a deep well for water supply, a common demand of the smaller communities in the Three for One Program, was budgeted at about $62,000

Table 5.3 Maquiladoras *Promoted under the My Community Program in Guanajuato as of June 2000*

Item	Maquiladoras *in operation*	Maquiladoras *being implemented*
Number of *maquiladoras*	12	9
Number of municipalities affected	9	9
Total investment (dollars)	1,230,000	980,000
Average investment per plant (dollars)	102,500	108,888
Maximum investment per plant (dollars)	200,000	250,000
Number of employees	505	420

Source: Program officials.

Table 5.4 *Community Infrastructure Projects Developed under the Two for One and Three for One Programs in Zacatecas, 1993–2000*

Municipality	Number of projects	Cost ($ thousands)	Migrants' contributions ($ thousands)
Valparaíso	66	1,878.3	574.7
Villanueva	25	1,637.7	411.1
Fresnillo	26	1,189.9	313.9
Jerez	47	1,020.3	286.5
Juchipila	18	994.6	263.0
Sombrerete	7	948.5	251.5
Tlaltenango	11	947.4	252.1
Jalpa	26	925.8	259.0
Río Grande	13	717.5	191.2
Fco. R. Murguía	9	718.6	222.8
Nochistlán	15	625.3	160.5
Monte Escobedo	28	466.4	149.9
Saín Alto	2	444.6	111.2
Pinos	7	412.5	113.1
Tepechitlán	16	365.3	112.0
Tepetongo	23	364.5	115.5
Others	76	2,599.7	728.1
Total	415	16,256.9	4,515.9

Source: Program officials.
Note: Data for 2000 are based on amounts budgeted.

in 1999. The same year the cost per kilometer of road paving was $30,000–$64,000 (the specifications of the work done was not available).

The average size of the localities served by the projects was 3,600 inhabitants, but this figure is biased upward by the inclusion of six towns of more than 10,000 inhabitants each that account for less than 10 percent of the projects. Almost two-thirds of the projects were located in small communities of less than 2,000 inhabitants.

The main advantage of the Three for One Program is that it provides a clear mechanism for channeling collective remittances to projects in migrants' hometowns. Its main disadvantage is that it does not encourage deeper involvement of migrants in the projects, because hometown associations' contributions are solicited mainly as matching funds by municipal authorities and local communities.

In Michoacán and Oaxaca, where formal programs do not exist, local governments support traditional, small-scale infrastructure projects financed wholly or in part by hometown associations. The limited information available shows that fewer projects are being supported in these areas and that they are more scattered geographically than in Guanajuato and Zacatecas. In Oaxaca, there appears to be an increasing number of autonomous projects with little or no support from the state and municipal governments.

The programs face various problems, namely:

- Public resources to support projects sponsored by migrants are more restricted.
- Gaining state approval for proposals for small-scale infrastructure support by hometown associations and local groups is more difficult.

Table 5.5 *Sectoral Distribution of Community Infrastructure Projects Developed under the Three for One Program in Zacatecas, 1999–2000*

Type of project	Cost ($ thousands)	Percentage of total costs	Number of projects	Percentage of total projects	Average cost of a project ($ thousands)	Average size of population of localities served (number of people)
Construction and paving of roads	3,324.2	30.7	19	9.8	175.0	1,702
Construction of community facilities	3,026.3	27.9	65	33.5	46.6	4,745
Paving of streets	1,636.1	15.1	42	21.7	39.0	4,932
Water and sewage	1,578.5	14.6	29	14.9	54.4	898
Construction and furnishing of education and health facilities (including scholarships)	671.0	6.2	29	14.9	23.1	4,400
Construction and maintenance of small dams	512.2	4.7	6	3.1	85.4	282
Electricity	88.4	0.8	4	2.1	22.1	1,218
Total	10,836.9	100.0	194	100.0	55.9	3,660

Source: Authors.

- Entrepreneurial projects are generally not eligible for support. At best, they are referred to other promotion schemes, which are not very relevant for migrants.
- Small-scale infrastructure projects depend heavily on the leadership of particular individuals for taking the initiative and collecting funds. Without local leaders, it is difficult for migrants' clubs to take the initiative.
- Technical and implementation problems are more frequent.
- Projects' social and economic impact remains limited, even if constraints can be overcome, because they rarely attain sufficient scale or are replicated.
- Constraints are exacerbated by the difficulties imposed by distance and by the fact that migrants do not have easy access to information about their hometowns, investment opportunities or needs there, and local institutions or about the regulatory environment for projects. Distance and the lack of information increase the transactions costs of these projects.

Guanajuato, Michoacán, and Zacatecas, along with other states, such as Jalisco and San Luis Potosí, have announced or implemented other investment funds designed to support productive projects undertaken by migrants or their families. To date, none has achieved significant results.

Experiences, Attitudes, and Opinions of Local Participants

People interviewed included direct beneficiaries, public officials, investors, local leaders, project employees, building contractors, and community members. Agreement was almost unanimous that the projects sponsored by migrants and hometown associations were important for the communities. It was widely recognized that the small-scale infrastructure projects addressed communities' most urgent needs.

It is not always clear who generates the original idea of a new project, although, according to local people, the idea has to be approved by hometown association leaders. The community is always consulted for final approval of infrastructure projects. Almost all local participants acknowledged that the quality of these projects was good, that the financial accounts were clear and well managed, and that all the people who benefited from projects had contributed to them.

Most of the people interviewed had a clear idea of the cost of the infrastructure projects and the amount the hometown associations contributed. They were not clear about the costs of *maquiladoras* projects.

As infrastructure projects are submitted to the community for consultation and are shaped to meet local needs and priorities, strong commitment and participation could be expected from local groups and beneficiaries, but in practice, these groups, as well as hometown associations, are not heavily involved in project implementation, operation, or maintenance. As a result, the main problem faced by the projects is lack of sustainability. Interviewees had only minor complaints about technical deficiencies.

Local beneficiaries of the infrastructure projects do not have many ideas on how to improve projects or cope with implementation and maintenance problems. Local leaders and public officials recommended more active involvement of hometown associations. Building contractors have limited contact with local groups or hometown associations. They follow the standard procedures issued by local authorities for public works and interact directly with them.

When asked what would be the next priority that a project should address, a large number of local participants expressed their preference for education and more community facilities. Only a minority believed that productive or entrepreneurial projects were more important. Leaders and members of hometown associations tended to hold the opposite point of view.

Participants in My Community faced more difficulties than participants in the Three for One Program, but they managed to overcome them. The original joint venture scheme proposed by the government of Guanajuato for the establishment of *maquiladoras* could not be carried out as expected. The state government had announced its intention of providing 50 percent of the capital required for each plant, but instead ended up offering a low-cost loan to the investors. Those loans were used in only two cases. In the rest, migrants preferred to provide the other half of the capital required. They considered the credits too expensive.

The first three *maquiladoras* also faced other problems: the machinery and equipment originally selected for the plants was inadequate, the commercialization plan was not fulfilled on time, and there were difficulties recruiting able managers for the plants. When the state government failed to provide solutions, issues were tackled and solved by the migrants themselves, acting as concerned investors. In at least two cases, the managers of the *maquiladoras* were recruited from among the members of the hometown associations. During the process, there was a transfer of managerial and organizational skills from investors to local groups. The main investors and leaders became involved in the implementation and supervision of the projects, keeping constantly in touch with local managers and public officials.

In contrast, the Three for One Program and the small-scale infrastructure projects funded partially with remittances conform to the norms and operational procedures of the social programs of the Ministry of Social Development. These programs normally require that the beneficiaries of a project make some contribution in cash or in kind to cover part of its costs. The contribution varies from place to place and across states, but it is generally about 10–25 percent of the total cost of the project. In the Three for One Program, the contribution of the community, if any, is a small part of the 25 percent contributed by migrants.

The norms and operational procedures of the programs assign responsibility for the implementation, supervision, and maintenance of the projects almost entirely in the hands of the municipal governments for two main reasons. First, the intermediation of a government agency facilitates the use and disbursement of federal funds. Second, municipal governments have access to a network of services (suppliers, contractors, supervisors) that facilitates the building process, making it speedier and less expensive than would otherwise be the case.

These advantages are offset by the bureaucratic rigidities of the Three for One scheme itself and the lack of motivation for active participation by communities. In the Three for One Program, migrants' clubs are active members of the technical committee, which reviews and grants final approval to projects. At the project level, however, participation by migrants and members of local communities is weak. Sometimes the beneficiaries get involved in supervision through a project committee they create for that purpose. Occasionally, they also get involved in maintaining projects.

The margin for improvement, innovation, or increased involvement by the private sector is very narrow under the Three for One Program. Suppliers, building contractors, and other people interested in the projects are regularly invited to the meetings of the technical committee, where they can obtain all the information necessary to plan their activities and work up their bids. Contractors are generally small companies working in the town or in a neighboring city. There has been an effort to mobilize state associations of professionals, such as civil engineers, to advise on supervision procedures and technical standards.

No advances have been made in terms of the organization of local and migrant communities and the financial arrangements for the scheme, and little has been achieved in terms of introducing new types of projects. The state and municipal governments lack the technical capabilities to promote such changes. The migrants' clubs are aware of many of the shortcomings of the Three for One Program, but they find it a practical mechanism for channeling their donations, increasing their impact, and gaining wider recognition. The scheme is already well known and accepted by the Mexican community in the United States.

Local beneficiaries are not organized to participate meaningfully in the project cycle, and the hometown associations generally do not have an active local counterpart. Less than a third of the local participants interviewed were members of a community organization, usually a working committee for a particular project. More structured organizations were not observed.

In conclusion, the Three for One Program itself and the rules governing it do not encourage wider or deeper involvement of migrants, local communities, or other actors participating in the scheme. Other regulatory issues do not seem to be a problem for the small rural projects of the Three for One Program. The construction of community facilities and the paving of streets account for 55 percent of the total number of projects in the Three for One Program. These types of projects are normally under the direct regulatory control of municipal governments.

As for the rest of the projects in the Three for One Program, regulatory issues do not pose special problems, though they may be of some significance for larger projects in larger communities or in cities. In some states, for example, rates for water distribution and consumption must be approved by the state congress or a state agency. While in the small communities this is not a concern, because there are usually generic rates to which municipal authorities can resort, in large and expensive projects this provision often leads to bureaucratic problems and financial difficulties for local operators. To a large extent, the experiences of Guanajuato and Zacatecas reflect the contrasts between an entrepreneurial approach and a social philanthropy approach (box 5.5). In Guanajuato, migrants invest their money and ensure that it is well invested. Their investments have a social impact in their hometowns by creating jobs. In Zacatecas, migrants are motivated by humanitarian concerns and the desire for prestige. They are conscious of their social role, but they rarely become deeply involved in the projects they sponsor.

Experiences, Attitudes, and Opinions of Migrants

The development of their hometowns is one of the main concerns of members and leaders of hometown associations. As they do not have a clear idea of the needs of their native communities, they respond to local initiatives, mainly to those of municipal authorities. Those initiatives are discussed and approved by the migrants' clubs, which collect funds for particular projects. There are no strategies for fund-raising based on a broader vision. There is no doubt among members of

---

Box 5.5 *Differences between the My Community and Three for One Programs*

Both the My Community and the Three for One programs have achieved acceptance by local residents and migrants. In both cases, migrants' clubs have been active promoters of the programs and the programs have evolved more slowly than the clubs expected.

The two programs differ in several respects. In the My Community program

- Migrant participation in the general functioning of the program, as well as in the operation and follow-up of projects, is high.
- Migrants invest their money in projects and the approach is entrepreneurial.
- Migrants actively participate in solving problems faced during project development.
- Migrants have contributed more capital than originally planned, mobilizing more savings.
- Migrants have modified the selection of machinery.
- Migrants have actively collaborated in the selection of technical staff and in marketing.
- Problems faced by the projects are attributable to their original design.

In contrast, in the Three for One Program

- Migrant participation in the general functioning of the program is high, but of the extent of involvement in the operation and follow-up of projects is low.
- Migrants respond to humanitarian and prestige motivations, that is, the approach is based on social philanthropy.
- Local governments are responsible for project implementation.
- Migrants' clubs and local beneficiaries do not participate in follow-up once the project has been approved.
- Provisions for maintenance are not made.
- Projects have sustainability problems.

---

hometown associations that the existence of a systematic program for attracting and leveraging the clubs' contributions is a necessary vehicle for increasing the flows of community remittances and channeling them to particular uses.

Contributions raised for small-scale infrastructure projects are collective remittances raised as small cash donations from a large number of individuals or collected through a fund-raising event organized to support the cause of the native community, for example, a party, a raffle, or a competition. Donations are made for humanitarian reasons or out of the desire for prestige.

In the case of *maquiladoras* or other "productive" projects, contributions (or "investments") are made on a more businesslike basis. They are not collective remittances in the strict sense, although they are frequently channeled through hometown associations.

The state governments of Guanajuato and Zacatecas took into account the opinions of the main hometown association leaders when shaping the programs and have maintained consultations with them about changes and improvements.

According to hometown association members, both the Guanajuato and Zacatecas programs have been progressing slowly and have rejected many project proposals because of budget limitations. The Zacatecas government has not been able to match collective contributions, and many proposals are subject to prioritization criteria or are waiting in line indefinitely. Some migrants' clubs have been insisting that productive projects be included in the Three for One Program.

Several improvements could be made within the framework of the current programs according to members of the hometown associations. In the case of My Community, project design and business plans could be developed not only for *maquiladoras,* but also for other kinds of enterprises. Promotion activities could be complemented with some general orientation for potential investors and with training courses for managers or administrators of the *maquiladoras.*

In the case of the Three for One Program, the list of eligible public works should be more precisely defined and projects should be considered for support sequentially. Special efforts should be made to attain sustainability by ensuring the proper functioning of the project committees at different stages of the project cycle. During the operating stage, these committees should be in charge of making the necessary provisions for maintaining the project and collecting contributions from community members. More attention should be given to the use of funds to supervise projects.

Migrants' clubs are satisfied with other aspects of program and project management by the state and municipal governments. No criticisms were expressed about the behavior of the public officers in charge of the program or the lack of transparency or accountability.

Technical or regulatory problems are seldom discussed by the hometown associations. From time to time, when these problems threaten the progress of a project, the hometown association presses the state government for solutions.

Members of hometown associations believe that collective remittances and migrants' savings would rise and become steadier if state governments enhanced the scope of programs or developed new formulas for collaboration with the migrants' clubs. They are willing to experiment with new methods, increase their donations, and take more risks in entrepreneurial activities.

Hometown associations expect state governments to come up with more and better projects (box 5.6). In this respect, dialogue with authorities and policy makers is not flowing easily, because the hometown associations are far away and the transactions costs associated with discussing new programs and projects with them is high. Leaders of hometown associations are conscious of the limitations they face and of the need to develop the institutional capacity that allows them to play a more active role in future initiatives.

Alternative Financing Mechanisms

Microfinance institutions have expressed interest in remittances, but their actions in this field have been limited. Recently, credit unions have developed an international remittance network for their members (Grace 2000). This experience is still at a pilot stage, however, and examples of microfinance institutions or other financial intermediaries successfully mobilizing migrants' savings and investments are rare (Portugal and Spain are perhaps the only exceptions).

Hometown associations are willing to explore the possibilities of strategic alliances with microfinance institutions. There have been some interesting experiences in the labor-exporting countries of Asia (Villalba 2000), but they are at a early stage of development and their scale is small. The successful experiences of microfinance institutions in Latin America have been only marginally related to migrants and hometown associations.

> **Box 5.6** *Migrants' Club Members Views on Collective Remittances*
>
> Three focus group meetings were held, one in Chicago and two in Los Angeles. In each city, seven in-depth interviews with key migrants from Guanajuato and Zacatecas were also held. Leaders of both communities participated in the focus groups.
>
> The focus groups and interviews were carried out by a team from the University of Zacatecas. In Chicago, migrants from Guanajuato and Zacatecas met in a single focus group. In Los Angeles, separate focus groups were held for each community.
>
> Strong differences are apparent between the approaches of the migrants from the two states, differences that reflect their relationships with the state governments. Each group defended its government's approach, though there were strong criticisms of the operation of the programs. At the focus group in Chicago, representatives of both communities discussed the advantages and disadvantages of the two approaches, concluding that the two programs could complement each other.
>
> The focus groups revealed that a great reserve of migrants' savings could be mobilized for projects in Mexico. The capacity of migrants' clubs for fund-raising or for summoning their members to participate in business endeavors is impressive. The problem is that there are not enough projects or mechanisms to channel such resources. In the Three for One Program, for example, municipal governments and the state government of Zacatecas cannot match the contributions the clubs are able to offer. In Guanajuato, My Community has developed very slowly relative to migrants' expectations.
>
> Neither the clubs nor the federations of clubs have the capacity to formulate and negotiate their own projects, and neither has seriously considered developing such capacity. They expect local governments to develop attractive alternatives for new programs and projects—expectations that have not been met.
>
> Hometown associations have discussed the possibilities of leveraging remittances with other sources of financing in order to increase private participation in programs and projects. They are not interested in borrowing in Mexico, however, because they consider the cost of credit in Mexico very high, especially compared with rates in the United States. Moreover, they believe that financial resources are not a constraint for the types of projects hometown associations are sponsoring, and they are ready to increase their fund-raising and contributions if necessary. In their view, training and technical assistance for project development and management are needed more than financial resources.
>
> The great majority of migrants are not familiar with the different funds state governments have established to support investments by migrants or their families. The mechanism did not seem to interest them much. The financial issue will be one of the crucial points to integrate migrants into a wider system of economic promotion.

The Mexican experience is also limited. Only a few microfinance institutions have explored the remittance market, and still fewer have explored the possibility of mobilizing migrants' savings and investments. Some financial companies that transfer remittances to Mexico have also tried to take some action in this respect, with discouraging results.

Two constraints are at work. First, migrants separate their decisions to send money to their families from their savings and investment decisions. Second, they do not rely on Mexican financial intermediaries, because of bad experiences with these institutions. In addition, the great majority of transfer companies have a bad image among Mexican migrants and hometown associations because of the high commissions they charge.

Some groups of Mexican migrants have expressed interest in joining reputable international microfinance institutions as active members or investors or in developing their own financial or development instruments based in Mexico. It would be worth helping the most advanced hometown associations undertake some pilot projects along any of these lines.

In the international arena, the credit union model is one of most attractive to migrants, because it provides access to regular banking services, such as savings accounts, loans for consumption and investment, and credit cards. In addition, credit unions are developing an international network that will eventually enable them to provide an efficient and inexpensive way of transferring money.

In Mexico, alternative financing mechanisms range from a savings association to more complex institutions, such as investment funds. NAFIN has launched a program to create several investment funds (NAFIN 2000). Under this institutional and financial arrangement, members of a community can undertake a self-managed program of local microentrepreneurial development. A fund is established with the contributions of the members of the community, who join a microentrepreneurial project group. The fund has components for operation, competitiveness, and development, each of which can be enlarged with contributions from external donors and leveraged by NAFIN with credit lines that increase over time. The investment funds model can be adapted to a local development initiative with the participation of migrants and hometown associations.

The record of investment funds for migrants or their families is still not good in any of the states that have launched them, and international experience with such instruments is not encouraging (CEPAL 2000b). In El Salvador, an ambitious program of funds for financing migrants' investments was launched in 1992 through the Salvadoran banks. The program produced no observable results.

One of the reasons for poor performance is undoubtedly the lack of interest of migrants in receiving credit, not only because they think it is expensive, but also because they distrust doing business with financing institutions (box 5.6). In addition, the funds lack the tools needed to identify good projects. As a result, projects eligible for financial support are scarce.

Policy Recommendations

Funds sent by Mexican migrants to their hometowns include family remittances, by far the most important flow, but also the most difficult to affect by policy; collective or community, remittances (donations contributed by clubs of Mexicans in the United States and normally earmarked for community investment purposes); and migrants' savings channeled to personal or business investments (remittance-like funds that are different from, but linked to, traditional family remittances). The motivations for remitting, the recipient or beneficiary, the sums involved, and the use of the funds differ for each of these types of capital. They also offer different opportunities for investment and for innovative use. Community remittances and migrants' savings represent only a small proportion of family remittances, but they can have a large impact on local development, especially because they can be used to finance innovative projects. Policies and programs for promoting the more productive uses of remittances must take these differences into consideration.

It is not a coincidence that Guanajuato and Zacatecas both have promising programs for attracting remittances for investment and a strong and organized network of hometown associations. The governments of these states have devoted much time and effort to encouraging and promoting the development of migrants' clubs and to building a network for collaboration with them. Other states in Mexico lag behind in this respect. But even among migrants from Guanajuato and Zacatecas, only a small proportion belong to hometown associations in the United States. In addition, the transaction costs of dealing with these associations are high, not only because they are distant and dispersed, but also because most Mexican migrants do not trust government initiatives. These factors restrict the interaction of hometown associations with other agents and institutions of the Mexican private sector.

It will take time to develop a more extensive network that facilitates business contacts and the interchange of information with the migrants' clubs. A critical factor for developing this network and for the future prospects of economic cooperation with migrants will be the institutional strengthening of hometown associations. The federal government should support the efforts of state governments in this field more actively. Support could be tied to program or project innovation. There is also room for cooperation from nongovernmental organizations and international agencies, such as the International Labour Organization and the International Organization for Migration.

Before adopting new schemes, policy makers should consolidate and improve the Three for One and My Community programs. My Community and the Three for One Program can coexist because they do not compete for the same funds. Combining them would enhance the ability of local communities to achieve results. Despite their shortcomings, these programs can be considered promising practice for states that have not been able to set up mechanisms for attracting collective remittances and migrants' investments.

Critical problems for both small-scale infrastructure and productive projects and programs include the lack of technical capacity of hometown associations and state governments, the high transaction costs of working with hometown associations, the budget restrictions of local governments, and the lack of sustainability of projects. It will be difficult to overcome these problems within the framework of current programs. New schemes are needed through which state and municipal governments pool the tools and resources available for social investment and *maquiladoras* promotion. Establishing a new basis of collaboration with the migrant community is likely to increase the financial and managerial participation of hometown associations and local groups. The design and implementation of such new schemes will require external assistance and capacity building. This is where the main focus of future work should be.

The prospect of improving programs and policies by increasing private participation through financial intermediaries does not seem very promising in the near future. A more promising avenue is the participation of migrants and hometown associations as active partners in savings associations or credit unions. Technical assistance is needed for institutional strengthening and for program and project development in order to reinforce best practices and introduce innovative new schemes and solutions. As they now stand, small-scale infrastructure projects do not encourage innovation or deeper private sector involvement and they are subject to rigid rules and procedures. They have been a good starting point, but they have not evolved to take full advantage of the potential for improvement. Few *maquiladoras* have been established.

To undertake more ambitious projects, migrants and hometown associations must increase their membership, improve their fund-raising practices, and develop basic capacity for project management and promotion. State governments must improve the design of their policies, programs, and projects and enhance their promotion schemes for attracting more remittances for investment purposes so they can make better use of the resources and opportunities available. Establishing an appropriate link with the existing promotion schemes is important.

Improving small-scale infrastructure projects will be especially difficult. Financial instruments that may be important for larger projects, such as bulk contracting, guarantee funds, and leasing, do not seem possible within the rigid financial scheme of the Three for One Program. Migrants' clubs have been reluctant to accept the proposals of the National Bank of Public Works (Banco Nacional de Obras y Servicios Públicos) or other financial intermediaries to borrow to enhance the scope of or to complement projects. No evidence was found that microfinance institutions are financing small-scale infrastructure projects with the exception of home improvement. Some improvements could be achieved by piloting new types of services, such as water treatment, computers and software for schools, and specialized training workshops. Different arrangements for fund matching and leveraging could be tried for these new kinds of projects, and new organizational formulas could be found to induce more active participation by local and migrant communities in their implementation, operation, and maintenance.

In general, migrants' clubs are willing to undertake innovative schemes, but setting the example will require external technical assistance from the federal government or multilateral organizations. Only after some experience has been gained will it be possible consider creating a local development institution for the promotion of small-scale infrastructure projects in which migrants could play a significant role.

To follow up on these recommendations, the federal government should provide support to state governments' promising practices and to program and project innovation (box 5.7). It should preserve the concept of a decentralized scheme, because it is at the state level that meaningful initiatives can be undertaken. Migrants identify with their native communities and are tied to them through complex social networks.

The autonomy and creativity of the hometown associations and migrants' clubs should be encouraged. Migrants and hometown associations are willing to explore a large variety of initiatives—ranging from new, innovative projects to savings funds and strategic associations with microfinance institutions—but they urgently need technical assistance, training, and institutional strengthening to cope with current projects.

Any attempt to attract community remittances and migrant savings must be backed by a systematic program to produce meaningful results. The program has to be endorsed by hometown associations in the United States. In Michoacán and Oaxaca, where formal programs do not exist, it is difficult to pool resources and bring parties into agreement. Each project has to be negotiated on a different basis in a long process in which transaction costs increase. The many initiatives that promote new projects should be considered in a wider context. Good programs are thus critical.

Box 5.7 *Recommendations for the Federal Government*

1. *Develop technical assistance tools to help the federal and state governments consolidate and disseminate best practices.*
   1.1. Prepare a strategic plan and a general proposal for instruments, including a small fund for technical assistance to state governments.
2. *Support experimental model projects for* maquiladoras *in different states with seed capital, technical assistance, and training.*
   2.1 Design and operate a special program of seed capital, technical assistance, and training.
3. *Advise state governments on how to improve small-scale infrastructure projects by increasing sustainability and private involvement.*
   3.1 Elaborate the basic design and rules for the sustainability funds.
4. *Advise hometown associations and other migrants' groups on the options for mobilizing savings and investments through existing or new institutions of their own creation. Provide technical assistance for project development and implementation.*
   4.1 Prepare basic information for analyzing options.
   4.2 Elaborate specific strategic and detailed business plans for new institutions.
5. *Promote pilot projects for microregional development in targeted communities together with state governments.*
   5.1. Prepare basic proposals and general terms of reference for pilot projects.
   5.2 Prepare information about other instruments available for *maquiladoras* and small-scale infrastructure at the national and local level.
   5.3 Elaborate specific strategic and business plans for selected projects.
6. *Launch a long-term strategy for the development and strengthening of hometown associations and other migrants' organizations.*
   6.1 Prepare materials and training courses for hometown association investors.

States with no systematic programs could adopt the Three for One or My Community schemes. A combination of them could enhance results, but budgetary restrictions mean that it will be easier to get only one started. If restrictions are very tight, the scope of the program can be limited to targeted areas or migrants' clubs.

States initiating collaboration with clubs must establish mutual understanding about basic objectives, rules, and procedures for supporting projects. That means creating a program that will have to be limited and selective.

The Three for One and My Community schemes can be modified if the changes are discussed and negotiated with the hometown associations. Some improvements can be attempted from the outset. It would be advisable, for example, to take into account suggestions by hometown associations.

More profound changes could take a longer time and demand a greater effort, but they are worth trying on a gradual basis. In the case of *maquiladoras*, selected projects with a strong impact in targeted communities can be supported with seed capital, technical assistance, and training. The funds for this purpose can be supplied by state governments or by a program of the federal government.

In the case of small-scale infrastructure programs, new rules can be discussed with hometown associations and local groups that focus their role on the operation, maintenance, and restoration of public works. Projects could be released to local organized groups (beneficiaries, suppliers, and representatives of hometown associations) for the supervision, operation, management, and eventual replacement or rehabilitation of works. Remittances could be used directly for these purposes, along with maintenance charges or contributions from local residents. This would foster sustainability and deeper involvement of the community in the solution of their local problems. In some cases, it could also lead to the creation of small private firms or public utilities. Funds for sustainability would be created in each community.

In states such as Guanajuato and Zacatecas, with consolidated programs and numerous and well-structured migrants' clubs, more ambitious projects can be explored. With technical assistance from NAFIN and in coordination with the state government, hometown associations can explore the possibility of joining existing or developing new microfinance institutions. This is an initiative that demands time and specialized technical assistance and supervision.

For Guanajuato and Zacatecas there are also other possibilities. One of the most promising is targeting migrants' hometowns and microregions for projects in which tools and resources are pooled in a local development initiative.

In clusters in which the per capita level of remittances is high, a combination of *maquiladoras* and small-scale infrastructure projects financed by migrants could be launched to kick-start local growth. My Community and the Three for One Program could be used as the basic platform for project promotion and support, but other available instruments could be used as well.

As the great majority of the clusters are predominantly rural, projects for agriculture and cattle-raising could gain additional support from rural development programs. Tools for promoting *maquiladoras* could be used to reinforce the central projects or support complementary projects. Microcredit could be used for household investments. This comprehensive approach could increase the impact of remittances.

The central idea would be to stimulate growth in neighboring communities long enough to achieve a critical mass of investment and local entrepreneurs. The microregional dynamic should lead to self-sustainability. That is why the careful selection of municipalities and local activities is essential to the success of the initiative.

The microregional approach has great potential. Most of Mexico's 100 or so clusters are located in the poorest regions of the country. All suffer from demographic stagnation, lack of employment opportunities, and low productivity.

This approach requires a more complex institutional arrangement, in which hometown associations and local groups assume a leading role in promoting and implementing programs and projects and the state government develops a more flexible and professional scheme for local promotion that is capable of providing information and resources for specific regions. Clearly, such a scheme must be linked to the national and state systems for spurring economic development. This linkage could be achieved through NAFIN, which could promote the implementation of a few model projects to prepare the ground for a more comprehensive program.

NAFIN can also play a crucial role in mobilizing migrants' capital for the benefit of the whole country. As a development bank, NAFIN should tap the potential of the flourishing Mexican diaspora in the United States. That community can be the source of savings, investment, donations, and technical skills for the development of *maquiladoras* and of new commercial and productive chains in Mexico. But this source must be linked to local investors and to Mexican financial intermediaries. This is no easy task, because the migrants have their own networks and distrust government initiatives. NAFIN must gain the confidence of the key actors before it can accomplish greater tasks. For small-scale infrastructure projects financed with community remittances, the National Bank of Public Works can play a similar, albeit more limited, role.

NAFIN could mobilize a wide variety of instruments to facilitate business associations and networking between migrants' clubs and selected Mexican institutions or business groups at the local level. It could provide seed capital, project development, institutional strengthening, entrepreneurial and managerial training, and information exchange. In the short run, the most demanded tools will be seed capital, entrepreneurial training, and technical assistance for project development.

NAFIN should establish a self-sustainable institution that channels migrants' remittances and savings into socially and economically productive projects. The enterprise would perform the following functions:

- Establish a system for identifying microregional potential and translating that potential into viable and profitable projects that generate employment and revenues for local communities.
- Establish a system for attracting and channeling resources from migrants' clubs, migrant investors, and local investors to programs and projects.
- Link migrants' clubs, different levels of government, and the local private sector.
- Build a financial mechanism that allows different types of financing to be used, depending on the needs and potential of each project.
- Provide technical training and assistance that improves the sustainability of projects.

Conclusion: Juxtaposing the Development Impact of Low- and High-Skilled Migration

This chapter focused on collective action by low-skilled migrants (hometown associations) and the projects these hometown associations cofinanced by means of collective remittances. Hometown associations have displayed significant creativity in leveraging funds to finance a diverse set of community infrastructure projects; however, the developmental impact in terms of diversifying local economies and triggering new institutions is quite limited. This is not to disparage the progress made by hometown associations, but to put in a proper context. It is useful to distinguish the poverty reduction impact and the development-related impact of remittances. Poverty reduction is significant. It is seen in nicer streets, street lights, community centers, schools, medical centers, and bullrings, but all based on income from development far away.

As Ellerman notes in chapter 2 (see, in particular, box 2.1), the crux of the matter is to trigger economic diversification, that is, local economic development in hometown communities that would not be dependent on remittances, whether collective or family remittances, although they can serve as an initial trigger for such a process. This is the thrust of a development agenda with a high-skilled diaspora. As chapter 6 on the Armenian diaspora demonstrates, transition from a remittances agenda to a broader development agenda is not easy and far from trivial, but this is a direction for the future of hometown associations. In practical terms, it would mean a shift of focus from financing projects to designing new projects characterized by new institutional practices. That means identifying high-skilled migrants from Mexico who could bring new skills and practices to their hometown communities. Projects could (and probably should) be quite mundane and inexpensive: coming home for a summer to teach a new course in a local university, introducing new methods for teaching socially disadvantage children, participating in local economic development planning, and so on, but this first-mover perspective should be present in all projects.

References

Burki, Shahid Javed. 2000. "Diasporas, Remittances, and Homeland Development." Paper presented at the International Labour Organization project planning meeting "Making the Best of Globalization: Migrant Workers Remittances and Microfinance," Geneva, November 20–21.

CEPAL (Economic Commission for Latin America and the Caribbean). 2000a. "Informe de la reunión de expertos sobre remesas en México: Propuesta para su optimización." LC/MEX/L.452. CEPAL, Mexico City.

———. 2000b. "Uso Productivo de las Remesas en Centroamérica. Estudio Regional." LC/MEX/L.420. CEPAL, Mexico City.

Grace, Dave. 2000. "The Development Potential of Remittances and the Credit Union Difference." Paper presented at the International Labour Organization project planning meeting "Making the Best of Globalization: Migrant Workers Remittances and Microfinance," Geneva, November 20–21.

Lozano-Ascencio, Fernando. 1997. "Immigration, Settlement in the United States, and Remittances: Evidence from the Mexican Case." Paper presented at the 20th International Congress of the Latin American Studies Association, Guadalajara, Mexico, April 17–19.

NAFIN (National Development Bank). 2000. "Programa global para el desarrollo de la microempresa." NAFIN, Mexico City.

U.S. Census Bureau. 2000. "Historical Income Tables. Households, Table H-11C, Size of Household. Households of Hispanic Origin by Median and Mean Income." December 13 revision. Washington, DC. http://www.census.gov/hhes/income/histinc/h11c/html.

———. 2001. "Census 2000 Paints Statistical Portrait of the Nation's Latino Population." May 10. Public Information Office, Washington, DC. http://www.census.gov/Press-Release/www/2001/cb01-81.html.

Villalba, María Angela C. 2000. "Migrant Remittances and Investments May Serve as Local Engines of Growth." Paper presented at the International Labour Organization project planning meeting "Making the Best of Globalization: Migrant Workers Remittances and Microfinance," Geneva, November 20–21.

World Bank. 2005. *Global Economic Prospects 2006. Economic Implications of Migration and Remittances.* Washington, DC: World Bank.

Zárate-Hoyos, Germán. 1999. "A New View of Financial Flows from Labor Migration: A Social Accounting Matrix Perspective." *E. I. A. L.* 10 (2).

6

Armenia: What Drives First Movers and How Can Their Efforts Be Scaled Up?

Victoria Anahí Minoian and Lev M. Freinkman

This chapter examines ways to expand the contribution of the Armenian diaspora to Armenia's long-term development agenda. It identifies factors that could explain the involvement and dynamics of a small group of entrepreneurs from the diaspora who have been active in and with Armenia. Based on these findings, it develops recommendations, consistent with the diaspora's institutional capabilities, for increasing the number of such business activists and transforming diaspora efforts from humanitarian relief campaigns to business initiatives and development projects.

Armenia's independence—achieved on September 21, 1991—opened up a new chapter in Armenia-diaspora relations. For generations the large Armenian diaspora, dispersed across five continents, had preserved the nation's aspirations for independence. Together with a strong sense of pan-Armenian solidarity, this nationalistic tradition helped mobilize an unprecedented level of diaspora support for the new state. For more than a decade, the Armenian diaspora generated international political support for Armenia, developing, funding, and implementing humanitarian aid programs and mobilizing private transfers.

The humanitarian contribution of the diaspora has been massive. Much more modest has been the diaspora's participation in Armenia's economic life (Freinkman 2001; Manasaryan 2004; Samuelian and others 2003). The level of diaspora investments and business participation is low, and the diaspora plays only a limited role in the debate on Armenian development policies, despite broad consensus that it is an invaluable and fundamental resource for Armenia's economic, social, and political development.

The lack of participation is noteworthy given the large relative size and wealth of the diaspora, which numbers about 5.5 million people (Samuelian and others 2003), far more than the number of Armenia's residents (3 million). About two-thirds live in the Russian Federation and the United States. Estimates prepared for this chapter conservatively suggest that the aggregate annual family incomes of the 1 million Armenians living in California may be 15 times higher than Armenia's gross domestic product. About 1 million people are believed to have left Armenia since 1988. This latest emigration is highly skilled, with about 30 percent estimated to have university degrees and about half having completed at least high school (World Bank 2002).

The authors are grateful to Yevgeny Kuznetsov and Thomas Samuelian for comments and suggestions on an earlier draft. Preparation of this chapter was partially supported by a Department for International Development grant to the World Bank Institute.

Review of the Literature on the Armenian Diaspora

The literature on the sociological, psychological, historical, ethnographical, gender, and identity aspects of the Armenian diaspora is large. Recently, studies of the economic and business aspects of Armenia-diaspora relations have also been conducted.

Amirkhanian (1997) examines the diaspora's contributions to the socioeconomic development of Armenia before and after independence. He emphasizes the complex relationship between the Armenian government and the diaspora, which has limited diaspora investments. The rules for Armenia-diaspora interactions are defined largely by the government in Yerevan, which has provided limited and selective support to diaspora investors. Amirkhanian underlines the demand side of the diaspora investment process, concluding that the "significance of the diaspora will come down to whether the local Armenians can afford to share their limited resources and opportunities with the outsiders" (p. 21).

Gillespie and others (1999) examine the determinants of interest in investing in the country of origin among four diaspora communities in the United States (emigrants and their descendants from Armenia, Cuba, the Islamic Republic of Iran, and the West Bank and Gaza). Across all four communities, they find that altruistic motivations and perceptions of an ethnic advantage in home country markets have a positive effect on interest in investment and that perceptions of business impediments have an insignificant effect.[1]

Among the four groups, Armenians showed the least interest in foreign direct investment in the home country. However, the Armenian respondents in the survey differed considerably from those from the other diaspora groups in that they belonged to the "old diaspora" (people whose ancestors left Armenia several generations ago) and lacked family ties in modern Armenia (they came from what is currently Turkey and other countries in the Middle East). Thus it is natural that the individual propensity to invest in the homeland should be weaker among Armenians relative to more conventional and younger diasporas. Among Armenian respondents, the self-employed had the strongest interest in investing in Armenia.

Freinkman (2001) uses the example of the Armenian diaspora to explore the potential role of the diaspora for a home country in transition to a market economy. While noting the significance of diaspora contributions to the mobilization of both humanitarian aid and foreign development assistance to Armenia, he highlights the imbalance between these successful efforts and the lack of diaspora contributions to the development agenda in the form of foreign direct investment, business partnerships, advisory services to local businesses, and participation in the local debate on improving the investment climate. He argues that such an imbalance has been detrimental to both the quality and sustainability of Armenian growth and that diaspora assistance has been suboptimal in terms of job creation, poverty reduction, and a decline in emigration.

The *Human Development Report on Armenia* (UNDP 2001) analyzes the first 10 years of Armenia-diaspora relations since independence. The report notes that a large and affluent diaspora represents a potential competitive advantage for Armenia and calls for more intensive participation of diaspora communities in developing and implementing Armenia's foreign economic policy.

---

[1] This study looked at interest in investment. There is a considerable gap between intentions and actual investment decisions.

Samuelian and others (2003) analyze the determinants of broad social trends in the modern Armenian diaspora, including factors that shape its members' attitudes toward Armenia. They emphasize the serious weaknesses of diaspora institutions, which are narrow, too personality driven, and often seen by community members as controlled by specific individuals and groups. Moreover, diaspora institutions continue to focus on the historical agenda, developed by and for immigrants, rather than expanding and diversifying the agenda to reach a larger number of Armenians in the diaspora. This explains why the diaspora's contacts with Armenia rely on ad hoc personal ties rather than diaspora institutions. Whether the new generation of diaspora leaders, who are largely disconnected from traditional organizations and who are beginning to build links across the traditional diaspora divides, are ready to make a long-term commitment to building Armenia remains to be seen.

Gevorkyan and Grigorian (2003) examine the extent of the diaspora's current involvement in Armenia's development. They propose introducing nontraditional financial instruments (such as diaspora bonds and investment funds) and creating a Pan-Armenian Development Bank to facilitate diaspora investment in Armenia.

Gillespie and Adrianova (2004) present a case study of three large Armenian diaspora initiatives to support business development in Armenia, launched on the principles of social entrepreneurship. They point to the serious institutional constraints such initiatives face whereby diaspora sponsors are either unable or unwilling to become personally involved in managing project implementation, but instead delegate management to various local partners, such as government agencies or commercial banks. The programs they analyzed were demanding in their management requirements and prone to implementation risks, but the sponsors were not prepared to deal with these risks in a systematic way. Instead, they reacted to the implementation problems by reorienting the initiatives toward the financing of more traditional charitable or infrastructure projects. Gillespie and Adrianova contend that the lack of direct diaspora management contributions has been a major flaw of programs. It robbed participating small and medium enterprises in Armenia from the key advantage that "angel investors" usually bring to the businesses they help develop: strategic advice on customers, suppliers, and key personnel. Armenian enterprises need this kind of help much more than the funding provided to them by diaspora programs.

Manasaryan (2004) identifies the core factors hampering Armenia-diaspora cooperation in the area of economic development, noting that the actions of both sides are affected by the lack of a strategic approach to the development agenda. After 1998, the government of Armenia made numerous attempts to expand the diaspora's business potential and to facilitate its political unification. However, no strategic cooperation plan aimed at mobilizing the diaspora has been prepared. Two large diaspora conferences in Yerevan were mostly symbolic and resulted in few tangible outcomes. At the same time, traditional diaspora organizations failed to adjust their established cultural and nationalistic agenda to place greater emphasis on supporting the development of the independent state. In the almost 15 years since independence, they have failed to offer any significant reform or modernization project for Armenia. Manasaryan doubts the potential of the traditional Armenian diaspora to become more effective in this respect, because their historical and cultural connections with Armenia are weak. He suggests that more emphasis be given to the mobilization of the newest diaspora, for whom Armenia remains an everyday concern and who show a much higher tolerance for the potential risks associated with doing business in Armenia.

Roberts (2004) analyzes the impact of remittances and private external transfers to Armenia on the country's macroeconomic performance. He concludes that the annual aggregate amount of private transfers may be three times official estimates of remittances. Roberts highlights the importance of private transfers for poverty reduction, as well as for savings and the financing of household investments in home improvements, land acquisition, and children's education. He finds no systematic evidence that transfers fuel business development, for example, through the creation of small and medium enterprises.

Views from the diaspora

Fifteen business people from the Armenian diaspora were interviewed. They included people living in Argentina and the United States (mainly the East Coast), as well as those living in or having lived in Armenia while running their businesses or working on the development of future business projects.[2] Most respondents' business experience was in the services sector (finance, transportation and communication, information technology, health care, hospitality, and legal services). The sample included only members of the old diaspora. It does not reflect the views of the new diaspora activists, including those from the Russian Federation.

A semistructured questionnaire was designed for the in-depth interviews, which were conducted either face-to-face or by telephone. The purpose of the interviews was to identify and understand the factors that triggered the engagement of these entrepreneurs in business development in Armenia.

The interviews focused on three areas. The first concerned visiting Armenia before making an investment. The second explored how informed respondents were about business opportunities in Armenia. The third explored the role of professional associations and collective projects.

Visits to Armenia and other Drivers of Initial Engagement

The Nagorny Karabakh conflict, the 1988 earthquake, and independence increased interest in exploring Armenia and renewed a sense of pan-Armenian solidarity in the diaspora. This sense of solidarity increased visits by the diaspora. As one respondent noted: "I started going to Armenia after the earthquake, that's how I got really involved in Armenia, sort of an opportunity to begin to have some understanding and relationships with the people in Armenia. I now go to Armenia every three months."

Respondents who had first visited Armenia under Soviet rule were curious to see the changes since independence:

> I first went there in 1981. I wanted to get involved ever since all the changes in the early 1990s. This independence, it's something we waited for a long time. It is very exciting to be part of a whole transformation process.

---

[2] A lack of funds prevented the sample from being expanded to other geographical areas.

I traveled to Armenia for the first time in 1982. I got very connected there. It is not real until you actually visit. When you actually see all the signs and all the people speaking Armenian, it becomes reality. Ever since then I knew I wanted to do something to get involved in Armenia, even when it was Soviet Armenia. I never dreamed in those days that the opportunity would come.

For some entrepreneurs, their initial direct experience of Armenia came when they accepted an international assignment in Armenia or came as part of a government or community delegation. According to one such entrepreneur: "I went for the first time with the official visit accompanying President Menem, when they signed an Argentine-Armenian health agreement. We visited the Pediatric Hospital in Yerevan, where we have started some projects."

Historical considerations, as well as a strong sense of Armenian identity, have been the main triggers of their business engagement in Armenia. As one interviewee stated: "Since I was a little kid my father bought me history books, but it did not produce that tangible feeling until I actually went there. I felt sort of a sense of nation building. We have been waiting for this for centuries, and here is the opportunity to do something. As idealistically as it sounds, it really comes down to that. I know the people by now, I have a connection to them."

For some of the respondents, investing in Armenia represents making a commitment to the legacy of their parents and extended families:

I decided to do business in Armenia because I believe this is a way to help Armenia. My father died before seeing a free Armenia, he never imagined that Armenia would be independent that fast. How many thousands and millions of Armenians would have given their lives to see that? I have the luck to witness it, but I am an intermediate generation, neither a full Argentine nor a full Armenian, but enough Armenian. This intermediate situation makes me do something for the memory of my parents. If my father were alive, what would he have done? For sure he would have created a venture in Armenia or done some work over there.

Intensive engagement in charitable activities in Armenia was not common among respondents. The following comment is typical: "I do not favor donations. I have contributed and still contribute a lot to the church. These donations are aimed at the religious structure, not because of strong religious feelings but because I believe the church has supported, over the centuries, the permanence of Armenianness and the unity of the diaspora in the absence of a state as an institution."

Sources of Information about Business Opportunities in Armenia

None of the respondents described the information channels in the diaspora as providing useful information on business opportunities or the positive experiences of other investors. Very few were able to cite examples of diaspora members investing in Armenia. None found existing diaspora organizations or formal information resources helpful in exploring business opportunities.

Word of mouth in the diaspora has been only sporadically used to obtain information about business opportunities and experiences in Armenia. The lack of efficacy of both formal and informal informational channels reveals an underutilization of existing diaspora resources for dissemination and outreach.

Respondents expressed concern over what they view as incoherent and unprofessional government policies to promote local industries and attract foreign investment. The institutional reputation of the government of Armenia is also of concern. Respondents also indicated that the government underutilizes their business and technological expertise:

> The real issue is the perception that there is no real effort made [by the government] to create an environment that is favorable to business. Armenia should become "Armenia Inc." I think Armenia should become the Singapore of the region. The government might need to strengthen the public sector as opposed to its current excessive involvement in private sector activities.

> The government of Armenia is not a homogeneous synthesis of thought. There are some officials with a certain mentality, and there are others with another one. This clash of cultures is at the core of the government, and it becomes evident when somebody in the government says: "The service this businessman is going to privatize is the last thing we are interested in. Let him come in but set up a dairy farm." I don't want to set up a dairy farm! I want to set up a business in my specialty, which I do very well. This points to the very core of the question: freedom.

Respondents strongly believe that diaspora members could play a critical role in Armenia's economic development, including by establishing new ways of operations in the still difficult business environment and by bringing in new business practices and role models. They expressed dissatisfaction about the level of professional and business contributions made from the diaspora:

> What most bothers me is to see the potential Armenia has, the potential Armenians from the diaspora have to help the country, and to witness that it does not get materialized.

> One of the things that disturbs me is that there are not more diaspora Armenians doing something directly, not contributing to church or anything like that but doing something for the country.

> What I have noticed is that those diaspora members who have succeeded in their professional life are not contributing properly to the Armenian nation. I do not mean making a donation and then leaving. I think people have to involve themselves, they have to invest. With an investment, I don't know if I win or lose, but it is an investment. I create jobs and I contribute to a mentality change, which is so needed. Through donations you don't change minds.

> Armenia's biggest threat is our own failure, despite our tremendous wealth in the diaspora, to come to the rescue of the country from the economic standpoint. We should change our attitude. As a diaspora we should say: this is a new country and yes, there are a lot of weak points, but this is it, the best we have, and if we are going to turn our backs on this little country, it is not going to survive until 2050.

> Oh! The great deals diaspora can do. They talk about it at a lot of symposiums and seminars. A lot of handkerchiefs wiping away tears, but there is usually no action. That's the tragedy.

Respondents believe that successful diaspora entrepreneurs should be more active in sharing their Armenian business experience with other members of the diaspora in order to improve Armenia's business image. Despite years of high economic growth and considerable government efforts to improve the country's investment climate, there is still insufficient trust in the government's economic policy. The media in the diaspora do not report positive economic news from Armenia, exacerbating the information gap between reality and much grimmer perceptions. It is up to the first movers themselves and other diaspora business leaders to close the gap. They need to call on their peers to launch businesses in Armenia, promote collective investment projects, and expand efforts to strengthen public awareness in the diaspora of the role of foreign investments for Armenia's future and the need to improve the business environment in the country.

At the same time, the government has to find a way to upgrade its communication tools and outreach practices. The diaspora lacks access to timely, reliable information on Armenian business development and economic policies.[3] This lack of information represents an additional stumbling block to mobilizing the diaspora. The Internet offers a unique possibility to connect Armenian communities worldwide. A Pan-Armenian, Internet-based information network could be cost-effective, and it could be developed quickly enough to address existing needs (box 6.1).

Box 6.1 *Internet Chat on Small and Medium Enterprise Development in Armenia*

The text below is taken from the transcript of a 2002 Internet chat session sponsored by Armenia's Ministry of Foreign Affairs. The participants included members of the diaspora who live and do business in Armenia and members of the diaspora who live outside Armenia.

Vazken:	Hi everyone, is living in Armenia fun?
Menua_Nane:	You bet!
Ponchig:	Living in Armenia is the BEST!!!
Dolmama:	All the time I am here I always wondered when and why we are not all here so please if you have any intention to give more meaning to your life don't let us stop you.
Menua_Nane:	It is great to work and live in Armenia. I would not think of moving back for a second.
Vazken:	Are all of you running profitable businesses in Armenia?
Ponchig:	I think most of us are in successful operations.
Voske_Hats:	Most businesses Diasporans run are successful in general.
Ara:	Would you guys encourage me to think about moving?
Menua_Nane:	We need some accountants here in Yerevan. Are you thinking of openeing a business here in Armenia?

---

[3] The recent experience of the U.S. Embassy in Yerevan in broadening diaspora outreach could be relevant. Pressure from the diaspora to increase accountability over how the Armenian government spends donor funding generated a new market for information about donor assistance programs in Armenia and more generally about Armenia's development. In response, the embassy developed an outreach strategy (Sherinian 2005).

Role of Diaspora Professional Associations

Professional associations are a forum for information dissemination, technical assistance, two-way business networking, and exchange of professional experiences. Professionals use these organizations to share common professional concerns and interests:

> Professional associations are basically facilitators. They also protect investors from getting into problems.
>
> Professional associations already exist for the IT [information technology] industry. They are very good, because you learn about other companies, what kind of products they are doing. If you go to Armenia for the first time and you need contacts, you join the association.
>
> I belong to two professional associations. I think both are very good associations, where professionals come together. For no other reason it brought Armenian-American lawyers and high-tech professionals together. They have a place to discuss issues that are relevant to each other's business here in the United States and in Armenia. It creates a forum for discussion.

Some respondents confused professional associations with associations that deal with social, cultural, and educational issues that help preserve the core of the Armenian identity. Such confusion is not surprising, because Armenian professional associations are rare in the Armenian diaspora.

Representatives of the few professionals associations indicated that their core activities are quite pragmatic and directly linked with their field of expertise. They serve the needs of their immediate local community, but they are also involved in Armenia's economic development. In this respect, professional associations are quite different from traditional diaspora organizations:

> Professional associations could have a strong role, almost like a mentor, either as advisors or maybe having seminars there or exposing students and teachers to their industry needs. To do these things through a professional association adds credibility, it provides a forum, a way or a physical place to do it, and it immediately discloses information to members, so more people can benefit from the information. Associations can then participate in international forums and trade shows, where you get exposed to different organizations, potential clients.
>
> I think that as Armenians you bring a cultural element to the work in Armenia, which helps you link to the people on the ground easier. You are able to create the linkages that perhaps are not available or feasible for those who are not connected to the people this way. If our association had more resources, we could be key partners to development agencies, adding experience, connections.
>
> We did a very extensive needs assessment based on our visits to the hospitals in Yerevan. We called people who were involved in health care issues and then based on their recommendations we looked at certain areas. Our work is pro bono.

Collective Diaspora Projects

According to respondents, even diaspora first movers know little about collective development projects and initiatives in Armenia. This reflects the fact that only a limited number of such proposals have been sponsored by the diaspora, and it points to the weak informational capabilities of the diaspora. The last diaspora conference, held in May 2002 in Yerevan, produced a list of seven collective project proposals, only one of which—a regional health center—differs from the traditional projects focused on cultural and historical issues.

Respondents showed some hesitation about participating in collective diaspora projects. Their reluctance to participate is suggested as well by the failure in 2002–3 to raise adequate funding for the Armenia investment fund sponsored by the International Financial Corporation:

> Armenians have a serious problem. They like to control what happens with their money, which is fairly reasonable. However, when it comes to investing, most do not know how to invest in Armenia, and the approach by which each individual makes his or her own investment usually backfires, because some investments will make money and some others by definition are going to be losers. That's why the idea of a portfolio approach, where people come together and invest together, so that they diversify the risk, makes a great deal of sense, but they do not understand that. It's a combination of not quite understanding the concept of a fund, as well as prejudices toward giving money to someone, particularly someone who is not recognized, has not a brand name, even though the International Financial Corporation is supporting the fund.

The reluctance to invest in collective projects for Armenian reconstruction may reflect preferences of diaspora Armenians to achieve quick but tangible goals through charitable donations and avoid the discomfort associated with both potentially longer-term risks of future business failure and the lack of direct control over invested funds. For individuals with such an incentive framework, making a contribution is easier and more comfortable than investing in a collective business development venture.

Even large charitable donations do not contribute to Armenia's economic long-term agenda in a sustainable fashion. As one respondent indicated: "Money from the Lincy Foundation [a charity set up by billionaire Kirk Kirkorian] is very significant, but it is a one-time shot, it is not going to act as a multiplier as effectively as if that money were spent in the private sector."

Recommendations from First Movers

Respondents were asked to give advice to other Armenians who may be willing to start businesses or provide development assistance in Armenia. Their recommendations are summarized below:

- *Do business in Armenia in the same mode as you do in the rest of the world, but be patient and do not expect immediate results.*

You have to follow the same instinct that you do in starting a company in any country. Where you should give the benefit of the doubt, give the little extra benefit of the doubt or use that to fuel your passion of doing business in Armenia. Don't let that passion cloud your business judgment. Treat doing business in Armenia like you would any other business: have a contract, do things right, don't just do things on a handshake. Don't just trust the person because he is Armenian. Don't think they are going to do you any favors or that you should do them any favors. Just have a little extra patience and explain things.

The expectations that diaspora Armenians have about Armenia are sometimes absolutely incredible. We should manage expectations. Armenians from the diaspora who go there expect favors from the government, like tax holidays. In fact, as responsible citizens, we should be paying taxes.

I think that if you are going to have Armenianness drive you, you have to be a little bit patient, maybe take an extra step to teach, an extra step to explain that maybe you wouldn't take in other circumstances, allow one mistake or two mistakes, more maybe. But I would say, don't use that Armenianness to a point that you're being stupid or foolish in a business. You do business the way you do business anywhere.

You have good opportunities, you have good talented people and . . . you say, "For Armenia, I can make it." There is altruistic reasoning, trying to help develop the country. But business is business, you have to go in there in profit mode.

- *Have realistic expectations.*

Non-Armenian investors are more successful than Armenian investors in Armenia because they do not come with prejudgments and expectations. They know that this is an emerging country, they know how to cope with it.

Armenians have a serious problem trusting each other. They have always been loyal servants to others, but when it comes to other Armenians they won't support each other.

- *Use diaspora professional associations to teach the basics of business.*

The people in our association came together and we discussed things like how to behave in a trade show, because for many companies it was going to be the first time they exhibited at an international trade show. Just simple things, like you smile, you look the person in the eye, you shake hands. Stupid things like this, but they add up! An association might be a good way to spread that information.

- *Share your success story with others to motivate them and let them know that they could be successful in Armenia.*

Lessons from Armenia-Diaspora Cooperation Since Independence

Since independence, 14 large diaspora organizations have mobilized about $900 million in assistance to Armenia. Much of this funding came from non-Armenians (Manasaryan 2004). The government-sponsored Pan-Armenian fund Hayastan, one of the main channels of diaspora aid, spent $75 million on 138 different infrastructure projects in Armenia and Nagorny Karabakh in the first 10 years of its operations. Private transfers to Armenia that are outside official charity channels are estimated at $900 million a year, about 30 percent of Armenia's official gross domestic product (Roberts 2004). Only one-third of these funds are transfers from the diaspora; the rest are traditional remittances by Armenians who are working abroad on a temporary basis.

The diaspora clearly has the potential to help Armenia, and it members express a strong desire to do so. The global survey of Armenians in the diaspora undertaken for the Armenia 2020 project in early 2003 indicates that about 70 percent would be willing to help market Armenian products in their countries of residence (Manasaryan 2004).[4] The same number of respondents claim that the most effective way to help Armenia is to make business investments there. About 90 percent of Armenians in Armenia would like to see the diaspora play a more active role in the country's economic development.

The reality of diaspora mobilization remains below this potential. The level of mutual trust between the government and the diaspora is low, and too few influential champions have tried to change the status quo (Samuelian and others 2003). Manasaryan (2004) describes the situation as a classical Catch 22: to get the diaspora more intensively engaged in its development, Armenia needs to modernize, but modernization is impossible without more substantial diaspora support. Armenia has to become much more liberal, diverse, and tolerant to be attractive to the modern diaspora, but internal forces that could lobby for such diversification remain weak in Armenia.

The principal lesson from the diaspora experience in Armenia since independence is that a massive program of humanitarian assistance that is not complemented by active business support and an investment program is not sustainable (Freinkman 2001). It eventually fuels emigration and the concentration of economic power. It does not help (but just delays) resolution of the most important challenges of transition and economic reconstruction. If the diaspora is wealthy and powerful enough to mobilize considerable resources in support of the home country, it should make sure that a substantial portion of the resources it provides are channeled for business development and the private sector.

Humanitarian assistance and unconditional political support provided by the diaspora to the Armenian government helped delay critical domestic reforms, especially in the business environment, in the second part of 1990s. Against expectations, the diaspora organizations did not advocate for economic reform, which eroded local demand for further reforms. Thanks to massive diaspora support, the ruling elite in Armenia received additional resources for survival that provided a breathing space for delaying necessary reforms, despite extreme poverty and emigration of the skilled population.

Provision of massive humanitarian assistance suggests that the diaspora community is concerned about Armenia. That concern requires that it play a more active role in the country's economic development. Future diaspora assistance should have a different structure and target different recipients.

This does not mean that Armenians living abroad should change their lifestyles and devote all their time to serving as investors, business managers, consultants, or

---

[4] As discussed later, the project aimed to spell out various development scenarios for Armenia.

advisers to Armenia. While some from the diaspora will indeed be needed to play these roles, this is not the main challenge for the diaspora as a group. The diaspora has to serve as a bridge to the rest of the world, a translator and intermediary. A good diaspora network is a search network, which generates and disseminates information (knowledge and skills), identifies opportunities and projects, and helps people take advantage of those opportunities.

The following recommendations could become elements of an alternative strategy for the Armenian diaspora:

- Find a way to participate in the debate on Armenia's development strategy. Develop the capacity of diaspora organizations (probably in cooperation with local think tanks) to become partners (and sometimes critics) of the government in policy discussions on key development challenges.
- Work to help liberalize the Armenian economy at the micro level (creating equal economic opportunities, removing entry barriers to new businesses, reducing the costs of doing business, and so forth).
- Emphasize new types of diaspora-backed projects in Armenia—not just humanitarian relief but the transfer of business skills (helping Armenian enterprises enter world markets, supporting business and managerial training of new business owners and managers in new companies).
- Support independent business associations that are not linked to the political structure of the ruling elite. With time these organizations will become the main drivers of further domestic reforms.
- Strengthen diaspora professional organizations. A new type of diaspora activist is wanted: people who do not just sponsor fund-raisers and lobbying campaigns, but get involved in day-to-day development efforts, including private sector advocacy, regulatory reform, and participation in technical assistance programs.

Because the business realities in Armenia may remain difficult for individual investors, diaspora leaders may want to consider collective investment instruments, such as equity funds or a diaspora development bank. These could be umbrella projects that could facilitate new private entry into the Armenia economy from the diaspora and elsewhere.

Another lesson to be drawn from the diaspora experience in Armenia relates to the utilization of international assistance. The Armenian diaspora mobilized record amounts of U.S. assistance for Armenia, but until very recently, it did not participate in designing assistance projects or monitoring how funds were spent. There has been a striking contrast between the diaspora's activism in pushing relevant appropriation bills through the U.S. Congress and the lack of interest in seeing how the appropriations actually benefit Armenia. Diaspora organizations and diaspora activists need to play a more active role in implementing U.S. government–funded projects, including the conventional funding opportunities provided by the National Science Foundation and other agencies that support international cooperation in technological and business development between U.S. and foreign firms. Professional organizations in the diaspora could become contractors of the U.S. Agency for International Development (USAID) and other development partners. Individuals could go to Armenia to become advisers in local nongovernmental organizations, government agencies, and consulting firms.

Once the diaspora is ready to play a more active role in setting a development agenda for Armenia, it would help to restructure existing programs of bilateral technical assistance toward more productive instruments and projects. Examples include direct support to new private sector organizations, short-term internships for new business owners in foreign firms, and matching grant schemes for diaspora entrepreneurs who could try to pilot projects in Armenia.

Professional Associations and Nonprofit Efforts

Armenian diaspora communities are organized around four major institutions: the church, political organizations, schools, and the media. These institutions represent centers of gravity, creating and supporting diaspora networks, regulating communities' participation in various activities, and facilitating the dissemination of information. Individuals and families develop their community lives by participating in extracurricular activities at school; attending political meetings and church; and listening to radio programs and reading the Armenian press, both in Armenian and in the local language. Their socialization into the Armenian cultural, intellectual, religious, and political environment helps preserve their ethnic identity.

The traditional focus of Armenians' engagement in their communities has been noneconomic and nonprofessional. The traditional diaspora organizations are therefore ill-suited for engagement in economic development. Changing this situation would benefit both the diaspora communities and Armenia.

Diaspora Professional Associations

The formation of Armenian diaspora professional associations is a relatively new phenomenon, which appears to be consistent with the international trend. Globally, immigrant networks have become an important source of shared information, contacts, and trust that allow local producers (even rather small ones) in developing countries to participate in the global economy. In the modern economy, the scarce resource is often not money but knowledge: the ability to locate foreign partners quickly and to manage complex business relationships across cultural and linguistic boundaries. Knowledge is particularly crucial in the high-tech sector, where product cycles are short. Diaspora networks could help reduce the transaction costs of cooperating over long distances (Saxenian 1999).

The primary objective of diaspora association activities in Armenia is to facilitate the development of their professions in Armenia by harnessing the collective expertise of their members (box 6.2). These activities include providing technical assistance to investors and local businesses that operate in these sectors, advising on educational curricula (including retraining) and educational reforms in general, and supporting exchange and internship programs.

With support from USAID and the World Bank, Armentech launched a high-tech Web portal, Silicon Armenia (http://www.siliconarmenia.com/index.jsp?sid=1&id=10000&pid=50). This Internet-based platform supports cooperation among Armenian information technology (IT) businesses around the world. Developed in cooperation with the association of IT firms in Armenia (the Union of IT Enterprises), the portal provides profiles of about 100 Armenian IT companies; information on jobs, training, and tender opportunities; and updates on sectoral

---

Box 6.2 *Objectives of Selected Armenian Diaspora Professional Associations*

Several ethnic professional associations in the diaspora are committed to assisting in Armenia's development agenda.

Armentech, the association of high-tech professionals of Armenian descent, was established in 2002 in the United States, and by 2005 it had about 150 members. Its master strategy—which focuses on Armenia rather than the diaspora—was developed as a collaborative effort between the World Bank, USAID, foundations, academic institutions, and private sector entities. Armentech seeks to

- Encourage the successful development of high-tech and information technology sectors in Armenia in order to create jobs and improve the economy.
- Support efforts to provide the infrastructure, facilities, equipment, and competitive telecommunications services necessary to incubate and expand software, e-commerce, Internet, and other high-tech companies.
- Assist in the development of professional training programs in software engineering, project management, application development, and information technology services marketing.
- Promote the education of high school and university students in Armenia, to prepare them for careers in the high-tech and software industries.

The Armenian Jewelers' Association seeks to

- Establish a worldwide Armenian jewelry network and develop the jewelry industry in Armenia.
- Increase communication and cooperation among Armenian jewelers.
- Enhance the professional image, promote the interests of, and assist in the development and expansion throughout the world of Armenian jewelry businesses.

The Armenian-American Health Association of Greater Washington seeks to facilitate the following activities in Armenia, Nagorny Karabah, and Washington, DC:

- Provide and facilitate the development of health care services.
- Educate and train health care providers and the general public.
- Provide biomedical and technical support.
- Assist in health-related research and development.

Source: http://www.armentech.org; http://www.aja.org; http://www.aahagw.org.

---

and macroeconomic trends. It is seen as an important first step in the longer-term strategy of promoting Armenia as a modern economy that can compete for high-tech foreign direct investment. Armentech has also been marketing the portal as a model for other diaspora professional organizations to replicate in their sectors.

The activities of diaspora professional organizations have a public good element. As such, they deserve public support in both home and host countries. Without such support, diaspora professional initiatives are likely to remain sporadic, with limited development results (Expert Group Review of Scientific Diasporas 2003).

Turning professional associations into mainstream Armenian diaspora organizations could be an important medium-term objective. Transforming these institutions would require the redistribution of resources within the diaspora. Such a shift appears to be justified given recent changes in both the diaspora itself, where due to the generational shift there are new demands for community institutions, and Armenia, where needs have shifted from humanitarian relief to development assistance.

Collective Nonprofit Ventures

Collective nonprofit ventures are also making a difference in Armenia. Recent diaspora collective initiatives include projects by the Land and Culture Organization (http://www.lcousa.org/asp/default.asp) and the Armenian Volunteer Corps (http://armenianvolunteer.org/main.htm). Both are nonprofit ventures with agendas that go far beyond the traditional charitable operations of more established diaspora nongovernmental organizations. They emphasize specific projects, cooperation among Armenian organizations (in and outside of Armenia), skill transfer, and the promotion of diaspora travel to Armenia. So far the activities of both organizations have remained limited.

The Land and Culture Organization's mission is to preserve Armenian historic sites all over the world and to connect Armenians in the diaspora to their ancestral lands by offering them volunteer work opportunities. The organization was registered in Armenia in 1994. It has organized summer programs in which volunteers from around the world come to Armenia to participate in architectural preservation, land cultivation, and community development. These programs help participants strengthen their sense of being Armenian and provide them with the opportunity to act in line with their feelings.

The Armenian Volunteer Corps provides assistance to local Armenian organizations by bringing skilled volunteers from the diaspora to work with them for one year. The Armenian Volunteer Corps aims to help Armenians in the diaspora and in Armenia reap the benefits of working together for the common goal of building a strong country and nation. Since 2001, it has helped scores of volunteers find fulfilling placements in schools, nonprofit organizations, churches, and businesses.

Collective Investment Projects

A peculiar feature of diaspora investments in Armenia has been the relatively small size of individual investment projects. The World Bank's (2002) analysis of Armenia's development challenges points to a demand for collective, umbrella-type diaspora projects that pool funds and expertise from a number of diaspora sponsors. The strategic advantages of such collective initiatives are several, namely:

- Consolidating many small, individually noninvestable, contributions could trigger a broader transformation of the inflow of humanitarian assistance into real sector investments. It would also diversify risks for investors.
- Monitoring the performance of investments sponsored by collective projects would provide investors with first-hand knowledge of business realities and help assess economic liberalization in Armenia. Project visibility would provide sponsors with additional opportunities to lobby for improvements in the investment climate.
- Obtaining political backing from the broader diaspora community is more likely for collective projects. Such grassroots support could help manage project implementation risks, such as those associated with corruption and other deficiencies in the investment climate.

Two types of priority actions could help accelerate the creation of mutual trust in diaspora-Armenia relations: broadening the dialogue about Armenia's future and implementing pilot projects that could have signaling effects. Broadening the dialogue among individuals and organizations facilitates mutual trust. Credible commitments made by diverse participants are a cornerstone in the traditional process of building a local partnership, but mutual trust is a precondition for such commitments. Trust develops gradually as stakeholders engage in dialogue and commit to each other incrementally and experimentally. Initially, the process is driven by individuals (not organizations), who are champions of the process of innovative, joint problem solving. Honest brokers—individuals with an established reputation in the community—are usually critical to launching and facilitating a fruitful dialogue.

Stakeholders need a shared strategy for and confidence in the longer-term prospects of the local economy before they will make investments in a risky business environment, but to gain credibility, some progress in implementing tangible projects must be made. The institution that combines vision with action is a private-public partnership that formulates a strategy in the context of specific, low-cost but visible projects. Once these pilot projects demonstrate signs of success, the partnership could scale them up and break up into specific organizations. Candidates for such pilots could be identified in higher education, innovation, and information and communication technology.

Distance education and the Millennium Science Initiative (boxes 6.3 and 6.4) are potential models for diaspora-government cooperation on pilot projects. The early Zionist movement successfully combined a long-term, shared vision based on broad dialogue and mass participation with implementation of specific projects, which helped preserve momentum and keep the enthusiasm of participants high (box 6.5).

Another promising area for potential diaspora pilots is associated with the formation of hometown associations, that is, groups of migrants from the same town or region of the home country (chapter 5). Hometown associations grew rapidly in

---

Box 6.3 *Involving the Armenian Diaspora in a Pilot Distance Learning Project*

Participation in upgrading the education systems of home countries is widely viewed as a priority direction for diaspora mobilization (Expert Group Review of Scientific Diasporas 2003). Distance learning could be a low-cost way for Armenia to accelerate the transfer of global knowledge and upgrade the quality of teaching at its universities.

For a landlocked, remote country like Armenia, modern technology could provide

- Access to high-caliber professors and lecturers who would demonstrate how core modern curricula should be delivered to students, modeling teaching for local professors. Many diaspora members might be ready to lecture on a pro bono basis. Recent examples from Thailand and Turkey confirm the feasibility of such an educational model.
- Online access to modern research facilities and academic libraries.
- Low-cost dissemination and sharing of popular courses by various local universities and training centers.

Participation in distance training could provide Armenian professionals in the diaspora with an opportunity for a "virtual return" to Armenia, which could be just a first step toward closer and more intense engagement. As with many other collective diaspora initiatives, a distance learning project, especially in engineering, is likely to lead to a second generation of (indirect) benefits. As experience from other countries suggests, professionals participating in advanced education projects abroad often launch new business ventures with their local partners and former students.

Box 6.4 *Chile's Experience with the Millennium Science Initiative*

The Millennium Science Initiative was launched in Chile and several other Latin American countries to establish national centers of research excellence. The initiative channels resources to high-priority research areas, selected competitively on the basis of scientific merit. Resources are channeled to fields in which the country has shown some comparative advantage and that can contribute to its long-term economic development.

The original project in Chile had a budget of $15 million ($5 million from the World Bank and $10 from the Chilean government). This funding was channeled to three local research institutes and 10 smaller research groups to support their projects for three to five years.

Source: Agapitova and Watkins 2004.

Box 6.5 *Lessons Learned from the Early Zionist Experience*

Almost from the moment of its establishment, the Zionist Organization operated simultaneously in two different capacities. It acted as the Jewish national government in exile, representing and defending the political rights of Jews worldwide. It also obtained the status of chartered corporation, modeled after the West India Company, with the objective of facilitating the Jewish colonization of Palestine. The original Labor Zionist strategy was designed for long-term implementation (it was expected that at least a century would be needed to attain its targets), during which time it aimed to populate and develop Palestine with Hebrew-speaking agricultural communities.

Financing this colonization effort was always seen as critical. The financial institutions of the new movement were established immediately after the First Zionist Congress in 1897. Those institutions included the Jewish Colonial Bank, which supported the development of Palestine, and the Jewish National Fund, which channeled charitable donations for land purchases in Palestine. In addition, the Zionist Congress supported the introduction of a voluntary poll tax on Jews living outside Palestine to finance the Zionist Organization's operational expenses.

Source: Avishai 2002; Hozany 2001.

---

the 1990s among Mexican and other Latin American emigrants in the United States. Some hometown associations pool philanthropic contributions by members to fund small infrastructure projects in their hometowns or villages. The governments of El Salvador and Mexico cofinance some hometown association investments. Hometown associations may have potential for mobilizing the new Armenian diaspora, especially migrants living in the Russian Federation, who have much tighter links with specific locations in Armenia than old diasporas and do not have well-established organizations with preset agendas (Roberts 2004).

In several countries, successful public dialogue and trust building emerged over the past 20 years within the framework of a "vision-building exercise." In the case of Armenia, the diaspora played a key role in preparing the Armenia 2020 vision (http://www.armenia2020.org/) (box 6.6). So far the government has shown inadequate commitment to this initiative.

Building trust and better understanding is not just critical for Armenia-diaspora relations, it is also a priority for development within the diaspora. Fragmentation of the modern Armenian diaspora is the result of various historical events (the

---

Box 6.6 *Increasing the Impact of Armenia 2020*

The Armenia 2020 process has been highly successful in engaging members of the diaspora in designing and communicating various development scenarios for Armenia. Armenia 2020 differs from best international practice, however, in that it focuses exclusively on vision building. The second pillar of a successful public-private partnership—designing and implementing specific projects—has not been adopted yet. Small, bottom-up projects are critical for lending credibility to the process, expanding its support base, and ensuring its sustainability. Without such a practical component, the process can easily be discredited and painted as nothing more than a feel-good social event for wealthy Armenians in the diaspora that makes little difference to the lives of people in Armenia.

One potential direction for the future evolution of Armenia 2020 could be the establishment of an Armenian Development Foundation. Such a foundation could operate as a think tank that would generate ideas about Armenia's development agenda, support design and feasibility studies for pilot development projects, and administer specific development initiatives, such as matching grant schemes.

Foundation Chile could be considered a highly successful prototype for such a foundation (Kuznetsov 2003). A high-level diaspora leadership conference could provide the venue for discussing the principles and objectives of the foundation. A main lesson of Foundation Chile is the critical importance of placing capable individuals on the senior managerial team of the organization, individuals who are motivated and capable of getting things done, despite obstacles. Identifying and nurturing such individuals, who are in short supply everywhere, would be the greatest contribution the diaspora could make to Armenia's development.

---

genocide, the domination of the Russian and Ottoman empires, Sovietization). As a result of these factors, trust within the diaspora is insufficient to ensure efficient networking. Difficulty mobilizing the Armenian diaspora could in part be attributed to its weak ability to communicate and cooperate as a large informal group. Participation in collective projects, which initially would be small, could be a strategic way of addressing this deficiency.

Conclusions

Like other small, low-income countries with relatively educated populations, Armenia will face growing demographic pressure for migration over the next 50 years. The aging population in the developed world; the income gap between Armenia and the developed countries; the declining cost of migration; and the extremely negative demographic outlook in the Russian Federation, which may motivate it to adopt an aggressive immigration policy, will increase emigration from Armenia (Ndulu 2002; Vishnevsky 2004). Migration pressures could be the most serious development challenge Armenia will face in the medium to long term. At the same time, migration would provide an opportunity for the diaspora to expand its engagement in Armenia and transfer its support for the homeland in line with new national needs.

The fundamental cause of skilled migration is the low local demand for high skills and the low return on investment in education (Ndulu 2002). Diversified private sector growth and professionalization of the public sector are needed to address these problems. Diaspora engagement could be critical to help Armenia raise adequate amounts of foreign direct investment and create a sufficient number of professional jobs, but the diaspora will have to become much more committed to Armenia's development before it will make a difference.

Our analysis suggests several priority directions for cooperation between the government and diaspora organizations to facilitate broader diaspora engagement in Armenia's development agenda. First, because visits to Armenia often change attitudes, motivating members of the diaspora to become more involved in Armenia, targeted programs should be developed that facilitate travel by successful diaspora professionals and community activists, who could combine tourism with the development of professional contacts and the provision of consulting services. There is a need to expand opportunities for the diaspora to participate in summer programs, internship exchanges, and business volunteer programs, including through established international programs for retired business people and managers.

Second, efforts should be made to strengthen diaspora professional networks and organizations and encourage them to get involved in ongoing debates about Armenia's development strategy. This may require considerable redistribution of resources within the diaspora from more traditional institutions and causes. Providing diaspora activists with the opportunity to contribute professionally (in addition, to providing charitable and political support) could become a natural entry point for building mutual trust between the government and diaspora organizations, which in turn may lead to more productive cooperation on mutual development projects. A practical way to expand the diaspora's professional involvement in Armenia could be through targeted use of its members as partners and contractors for international development partners providing technical assistance to the Armenian government, such as USAID and the European Union's technical assistance program for the former Soviet republics.

A related priority is support for the establishment of organizations in the newest diaspora. On average, people who left Armenia in the past 15 years have the strongest links to the country. Most live in the Russian Federation and other former Soviet republics, but some live in Canada and the United States , where they are not well represented by traditional diaspora organizations.

Third, the government and the diaspora should try to address the information gap in the diaspora with respect to Armenia's development challenges and efforts to improve the business environment. The government should try to improve its investment image and build awareness of business opportunities in Armenia. A new communication strategy should be developed to promote success stories of business people from the diaspora as well as their professional contributions to Armenia's development. Partnerships between Armenian and diaspora media outlets should be established, with the aim of expanding access to information on development progress and providing the opportunity to participate in policy debates. The government should also reduce information barriers for diaspora and other foreign investors. This includes, in particular, increasing the availability of legal and business information on Armenia in English and Russian over the Internet.

Fourth, with the help of international partners, the government and the diaspora should try to identify and implement visible collective projects, which could broaden the engagement of the diaspora in development, support the formation of new types of diaspora organizations, and strengthen the diaspora's accountability for Armenia's development progress.

References

Agapitova, Natalia, and Alfred Watkins. 2004. "Creating a 21st Century National Innovation System for a 21st Century Latvian Economy." Policy Research Working Paper 3457, World Bank, Washington, DC.

Amirkhanian, Alen. 1997. "The Armenian Diaspora and Their Contribution to Socio-Economic Development in Armenia in the Soviet and Post-Soviet Periods." Background paper prepared for the World Bank's Country Assistance Strategy for Armenia, Europe and Central Asia Region, Washington, DC.

Avishai, Bernard. 2002. *The Tragedy of Zionism: How Its Revolutionary Past Haunts Israeli Democracy.* New York: Helios Press.

Expert Group Review of Scientific Diasporas. 2003. "How Can Developing Countries Benefit from Their Expatriate Scientists and Engineers?" Paris. http://www.dev.ird.fr/pdf/diasporas_ang.pdf.

Freinkman, Lev. 2001. "Role of the Diaspora in Transition Economies: Lessons from Armenia." Paper presented at the 11th annual meeting of the Association for the Study of the Cuban Economy, Coral Gables, Florida, August 2–4. http://lanic.utexas.edu/project/asce/pdfs/volume11/freinkman.pdf.

Gevorkyan, A., and David Grigorian. 2003. "Armenia and Its Diaspora: Is There a Scope for a Stronger Economic Link?" Paper presented at the Armenian International Policy Research Group conference, Washington, DC, January 25. http://www.armpolicyresearch.org/Publications/WorkingPapers/index.htm.

Gillespie, Kate, and Anna Adrianova. 2004. "Diaspora Support for Business Development in Armenia: Examining Paradigms of Social Entrepreneurship." Paper presented at the Second Armenian International Policy Research Group Conference, Washington, DC, January 17–18.

Gillespie, Kate, Liesl Riddle, Edward Sayre, and David Sturges. 1999. "Diaspora Interest in Homeland Investment." *Journal of International Business Studies* 30 (3): 623–34.

Hozany, Yoram. 2001. *The Jewish State: The Struggle for Israel's Soul.* New York: New Republic Books.

Kuznetsov, Yevgeny. 2003. "Moving to Knowledge-Based Competitiveness in Russia: Implementation Options." World Bank, Washington, DC.

Manasaryan, Tatul. 2004. "Diaspora: The Comparative Advantage for Armenia." Paper presented at the Second Armenian International Policy Research Group Conference, January 17–18, Washington, DC.

Ndulu, B. J. 2002. "Human Capital Flight: Stratification, Globalization, and the Challenges to Tertiary Education in Africa." World Bank, Washington, DC.

Roberts, Bryan W. 2004. "Remittances in Armenia: Size, Impacts, and Measures to Enhance Their Contribution to Development." Report prepared for the U.S. Agency for International Development, Yerevan.

Samuelian, Thomas J., Aram Hajian, Hakob Martisossian, and Tamar Hajian. 2003. "Diaspora-Homeland Issue Paper." Paper prepared for the Armenia 2020 project. http://www.armenia2020.org/index.php/en/activities/researches/13.

Saxenian, AnnaLee. 1999. "Silicon Valley's New Immigrant Entrepreneurs." Public Policy Institute of California, San Francisco.

Sherinian, Aaron H. 2005. "Marketing Assistance Programs to the Diaspora: The U.S. Embassy, Yerevan Experience." Paper presented at the Third Armenian International Policy Research Group Conference, January 15–16, Washington, DC.

UNDP (United Nations Development Programme) 2001. *National Human Development Report: Armenia.* New York: UNDP. http://www.undp.am/publications.

Vishnevsky, Anatoly. 2004. "Alternatives of the Migration Strategy." In Russian. http://www.polit.ru/research/2004/12/23/vishnevsky.html.

World Bank. 2002. *Armenia. Growth Challenges and Government Policies.* Country Study. Washington, DC: World Bank.

Part III
Expatriate Talent and Home Country Development: Emerging Diaspora Networks

7

Argentina: Burgeoning Networks of Talent Abroad, Weak Institutions at Home

Yevgeny Kuznetsov, Adolfo Nemirovsky, and Gabriel Yoguel

Half a century ago, Argentina's economy was at least as large as those of Australia, Brazil, Canada, and Denmark, economies that are now far larger and more vibrant than Argentina's. How can Argentina transform its economy into a knowledge economy in order to reverse its decline and compete in the global market?

Around the world, a growing number of professional diasporas have been playing key roles in the economic development of their home countries. This chapter examines how the scientific and technological diaspora could be used to develop a knowledge-based economy in Argentina. It identifies the conditions and requirements for the diaspora to play a transformative role and assesses its interest in doing so.

The Growing Value of Knowledge: Challenges and Opportunities for Argentina

Knowledge plays an increasingly critical role in scientific, technological, and business endeavors. It powers the emerging knowledge economy. In response to the increasing value of knowledge, the industrial countries have made significant changes in their productive structures and in the dynamics of innovation in order to facilitate the generation, circulation, and capture of knowledge.

This process requires good coordination and strong collaboration among academia, industry, and government. Governments and development agencies are showing strong interest in bridging gaps between business organizations and research and development (R&D) organizations in order to accelerate the transformation of scientific and technological developments into products and wealth. Bridging these gaps is particularly important in fields that offer economic payback in the medium term and that reflect local or regional competitive advantages in

The authors would like to thank Marco Bressan, Emilio Bunge, Delia Crovi, Gabriel Cwilich, Joaquín Espinosa, Daniel Farias, Myriam Giambiagi, Pedro Gromöller, Benjamín Hadis, José Kenny, Ignacio Martini, Diego Melamed, Enrique Mesri, Rodolfo Milito, Mario Nemirovsky, Nora Sabelli, José Sericano, and Gloria Silva for useful feedback.

high-growth areas, such as biotechnology, information and communications technology, and nanotechnology.[1]

The Transition Toward an Economy Based on Knowledge

The term knowledge economy is usually used to emphasize the importance of knowledge in almost every economic endeavor. This definition has evolved. Initially, the term was used to indicate manufacturing activities that make intensive use of technology. Today it usually designates knowledge-based services.

In the developed countries, the knowledge economy includes about half of all nongovernmental economic activities. High-tech and medium-tech industry accounts for only 20 percent of knowledge-based activities; the remaining 80 percent is made up of knowledge-intensive services. Fueling the development of the knowledge economy requires public investment in education and training, global information exchange, and commercialization of intellectual property.

Industrial countries have made substantial efforts to improve the qualifications of their workforces through continuing education programs offered by universities and corporations (box 7.1). In contrast, most developing countries have failed to train their workforces to be competitive in the global economy.

Technological advances have changed the structure and dynamics of economic units and their activities. In the past, corporations, universities, laboratories, and government organizations were weakly linked and largely independent of one another. In contrast, the current environment requires coordination among agents involved in the various stages of knowledge (and wealth) creation, from workforce education and training to production and commercialization. In the past, it took many years for innovations developed at universities or national laboratories to become products. In contrast, today innovations move from laboratory to market in less than two years. Once products were well defined, universities did not worry about commercializing intellectual property, and the need for the government to link parties in order to accelerate the construction of systems of innovation and the education and training of the workforce was much less than it is today. The new dynamics require "coupled" structures, such as innovation clusters and incubators, that reduce the uncertainties of the investors, corporations, and universities involved and provide a dynamic framework for generating, circulating, and appropriating knowledge generation.

---

[1]This dynamic has given rise to a new concept of competition that sees the generation of competitive advantage as stemming not only from macroeconomic factors, but also from microeconomic and mesoeconomic factors. Competitive advantage is dynamic. It can be created, changed, and destroyed, and its development depends on the degree of knowledge complexity that a society generates through its education and production systems; on the degree of development and complexity of its productive, professional, and other networks and on its institutional systems and civil society. A key factor in developing a competitive advantage is the development of multiple levels of communication and coordination among disparate actors, organizations, and disciplines that enable knowledge generation, valorization, circulation, and so forth within a society. In this framework, the degree of development of the education system and its interface with the production system are key for the development of competitive dynamic advantages.

Box 7.1 *Worldwide Trends Associated with the Growth of the Knowledge Economy*

Investment and trade in intangibles have skyrocketed in recent years. Public investment in education, R&D, and software represents almost half of total investment in the Organisation for Economic Co-operation and Development. As the importance of intangibles has grown, trade in intellectual property has increased: royalty and license fees reported in international trade increased from about $10 billion in the early 1980s to more than $60 billion by the late 1990s. High-income countries receive almost 98 percent of all royalty and licensing payments, while low- and medium-income countries pay out an amount that is disproportionate to what they receive.

Education and training are more important than ever. Between 1970 and 1997, the proportion of adults in industrial countries who completed high school rose from 44 to 72 percent, while the proportion of adults with some tertiary education doubled from 22 to 44 percent. The number of students enrolled in tertiary institutions rose from 28 million in 1970 to 88 million in 1997. But the gap between the number of tertiary education students in developing and industrial countries widened, from 21 million in 1970 to 45 million in 1997, even though the population is larger and growing more rapidly in developing countries.

Foreign investment, one of the key agents of globalization, is increasing, spurred mainly by the desire to exploit knowledge assets—technology; management; and access to markets, finance, labor, and natural resources—on a global scale. Foreign investment inflows increased by a factor of 15 between 1982 and 1999, and their share in world gross fixed capital formation rose from 2.6 percent to 14.3 percent. Exports of foreign affiliates rose from 31 to 46 percent of world exports and sales of foreign affiliates increased from 23 to 45 percent of world gross domestic product (GDP). The value added of these sales reached $3 trillion in 1999, roughly 10 percent of world GDP. In 1997, the estimated value added of home and overseas production by transnational corporations was $8 trillion, more than 27 percent of world GDP.

Firms are investing more in R&D. In most countries of the Organisation for Economic Co-operation and Development, R&D spending has risen faster than GDP. Businesses in Japan increased their spending on R&D to 2.32 percent of GDP from 2.12 percent in 2000 and 1.89 percent in 1995, and business in the European Union increased their spending on R&D to 1.17 percent of GDP from 1.15 in 2000 and 1.06 in 1995. By contrast, spending by U.S. firms fell to 1.87 percent of GDP in 2002 from more than 2 percent in 2000.

Multinational companies, now conducting R&D in countries other than their home countries, are establishing more strategic alliances—even mergers and acquisitions—to collaborate on technology and acquire technological assets. International collaborations in patenting and technical publications are also on the rise. The share of scientific publications written with foreign coauthors more than doubled to an average of 26 percent in 1995–7. An important implication is that all countries need to focus on how to obtain knowledge produced outside their borders.

Source: World Bank 2005.

The generation, exchange, and transformation of knowledge is highly influenced by national and regional competencies and available human resources (Novick and Gallart 1997; Yoguel 2000); the degree of association with virtuous networks (Gereffi 2001); and the degree of integration or coordination of key local actors, namely, academia, industry, and government (Hirshman 1996; Poma 2000; Rullani 2000). These elements constitute key objectives of scientific and technological development programs by industrial countries.

Need to Incorporate More Complex Technologies and Organizational Structures

For the past 10–15 years, the industrial countries and many developing ones (Armenia, Brazil, China, India, the Republic of Korea, Malaysia) have been taking advantage of new opportunities in the knowledge-based global economy. In contrast, Argentina's productive specialization, which is based on natural resources, has not being altered to exploit the growing value of knowledge. Argentina's attempts to develop comparative advantages based on the generation and transformation of knowledge have been unsuccessful (Albornoz, Milesi, and Yoguel 2002; Bisang and others 1999a, 1999b). As a result, it has been unable to generate a sustainable process of growth, wealth creation, and wealth redistribution.

In 1965, Argentina's per capita gross national product (GNP) was about three times that of the Korea; by 2000 it had declined to less than half of Korea's (figure 7.1). Korea's phenomenal growth reflects its incorporation of knowledge into productive activities, without which its GNP would have remained below that of Argentina.[2]

A key challenge for Argentina is to build the necessary competencies to generate productive chains that incorporate more complex technologies and organizational structures. This is not an automatic and linear process that follows as a natural evolution from the current production system. It requires structural changes, coordination, planning, and good execution.

Argentina has significantly more scientists and engineers per million inhabitants (703) than Brazil (167), Chile (366), or Mexico (213). The average number of years of schooling in Argentina (8.75) and the percentage of the population enrolled in tertiary institutions (35 percent) are the highest in Latin America (Holm-Nielsen and Thorn 2003). However, Argentina has difficulties benefiting from these advantages and generating wealth through technological and productive developments, for several reasons:

- Relative to GNP, the level of investment in R&D (by the productive system and the government) is low: about a 10th of that of Korea and a 3rd of that of Brazil.
- Linkages between academia and the productive sector are weak.
- Argentina's workforce is trained to produce simple commodities and natural resource–intensive products rather than knowledge-intensive goods and services, which it imports.

---

[2]To decompose total productivity into factors, consider a neoclassical aggregated production function that takes into consideration the qualifications of the workforce. (A Cobb-Douglas production function that includes human capital is used here to simply the discussion.) This function assumes perfect competition in markets and constant returns to scale:

$$Y = AK^{\alpha}(HL)^{1-\alpha}$$

where

A = total productivity of the factors or the knowledge contribution,
Y = aggregated product level,
K = stock of capital,
H = stock of human capital ,
L = size of workforce,
α = contribution of capital to national income.

Figure 7.1 *Per Capita GNP in Argentina and Korea, 1965–2000*

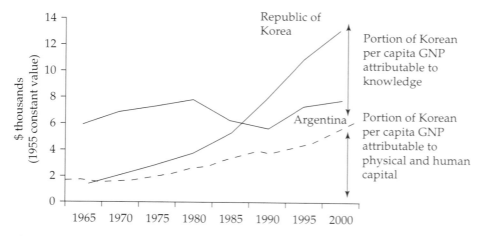

Source: Authors' calculations.

The lack of opportunities for scientists and engineers in Argentina has led to brain drain, which has increased dramatically in the past few decades. Professionals have emigrated mainly to the United States and Europe, but also to Australia, Brazil, Israel, and Mexico (Albornoz, Polcuch, and Alfaraz 2002; Albornoz, Luchilo, and others 2002).

Turning Brain Drain into Brain Circulation: The Argentine Diaspora as a Key Resource

The long-term or permanent migration of people with tertiary education was long referred to as the brain drain. Recently, the concept of brain circulation has gained currency. It implies two-way benefits for the country of origin and the host country. This phenomenon played a critical role in the rise of the Indian software industry (chapter 4).

The challenge for Argentina is to make significant changes in the way knowledge is generated, transformed, and exchanged and to leverage local and diaspora knowledge to create and sustain competitive advantages. This entails deep changes in both productive and institutional systems. Inserting Argentina into the global knowledge economy requires the development of demand-pull changes in the education system to generate a supply-push with spillovers into society; the development of mechanisms for disseminating knowledge among disparate actors in productive supply chains; and the creation of diverse forms of mediation to facilitate links between science, technology, and production.

Surveying the Diaspora

From May to July 2003, 185 Argentine professionals residing in the United States, Europe, and elsewhere were surveyed by means of written questionnaires and some telephone interviews. Most have technical or scientific backgrounds and work in academic institutions, research laboratories, corporations, or start-ups.

Thirty-eight percent of the respondents had been living abroad for more than 20 years. Most left Argentina in 1966 or 1976, with the arrival of military governments and political persecution.[3] Sixty-one percent of these people are over 40, with half of those over 50. Many of these people occupy positions of responsibility in corporations and R&D institutions.

Most of the sample emigrated before 1983, when democracy was restored. About 15 percent emigrated in the mid-1980s, probably because of dissatisfaction with the policies of the democratic government. More than half the sample have been abroad for more than 15 years. The rest of the group emigrated more recently. Fourteen percent left since 1998, during the deep recession that culminated with the end of the De la Rua government after a popular uprising. About 13 percent emigrated in the early 1990s as Menem's convertibility plan got established; 20 percent emigrated between 1994 and 1997.

About three-quarters of the sample (72 percent) are male. Forty-five percent reside in the United States; 37 percent in Europe; 10 percent in Latin America; and 6 percent in Israel, New Zealand, and Australia (in decreasing order of importance). The European population resides mainly in Spain, France, the United Kingdom, and Italy, in decreasing order of importance. Most of the diaspora in Latin America lives in Brazil, followed by Mexico.

About 73 percent of the sample works in academic institutions or corporate or government laboratories. Fourteen percent hold corporate positions; 8 percent are independent (company owners, consultants); and 5 percent work for international or national organizations involved in science and technology policy or other institutions.

Eighty percent of the sample hold doctorates. Ninety-seven percent received their undergraduate degrees in Argentina. A large group (65 percent) holds an undergraduate degree from Argentina and a doctorate from abroad.

The largest number of Argentines in the sample work in medicine, pharmacy, and biochemistry (16 percent), followed by biotechnology and molecular biology (14 percent) (table 7.1).

About half of those interviewed believe that their influence over their organization is moderate to high. About a quarter of the sample group reports having no or little influence. The degree of influence increases with age and depends on the nature of the organization where the professional works.

Almost half of those surveyed belong to at least one formal or informal network. About 70 percent of the networks are formal and more than half have at least 20 people. Half of the networks are international, a quarter are in the United States, and a quarter are in Europe.

---

[3]There have been several waves of immigration of Argentine professionals since the mid-1960s, each associated with a crisis in Argentina. Many scientists and technologists left the country after the 1966 military coup, many of them settling in the United States. These emigrants are now in their 60s. A second wave left in the mid-1970s during the Videla dictatorship. These emigrants are now in their mid-40s or older. A third wave left Argentina in the late 1980s and early 1990s. It included both young scientists and technologists emigrating for the first time and older colleagues who had gone back to Argentina after the return to democracy in 1983 but were disappointed by the slow economic and institutional progress. A fourth wave of young scientists and technologists left the country in the late 1990s.

Table 7.1 *Professional Specializations of the Sample of Diaspora Argentines*

Specialization	Percentage of sample
Medicine, pharmacy, and biochemistry	16
Biotechnology and molecular biology	14
Business, management, finance, law, marketing, and administration	12
Social sciences and education	10
Natural resources, environment, and food science	10
Basic science (physics, chemistry, and biology) and mathematics	10
Enterprise software, applications, and other software (artificial intelligence, security)	8
Superconductors, polymers, new materials, nanotechnology	7
Software tools (simulation, computer-assisted design, technical and scientific software)	6
Engineering and applied science	3
Electronics, photonics, electronic devices	2
Other (including arts and tourism)	2

Source: Authors' survey.

Links Between Argentina and its Diaspora

Argentines in the diaspora stay in touch with Argentina professionally in a variety of ways.

Visiting Argentina

Almost half (46 percent) of the sample visits Argentina once a year, and 15 percent go more than once a year. Only 4 percent rarely visit Argentina. Sixty percent of those surveyed visit Argentina for academic exchanges, 46 percent attend courses or conferences in Argentina, and 23 percent have other professional contacts there. Contacts with or facilitated by national or international organizations are rare, indicating the neglect of the diaspora by the government. The frequency of visits is independent of the length of time sample members have lived abroad, suggesting that ties to Argentina do not weaken over time.

Obtaining Information on Activities in Argentina

According to survey respondents, the most relevant information sources about opportunities to develop scientific, technological, and commercial activities in Argentina are colleagues in Argentina (70 percent), friends and relatives (38 percent), and newspapers and the Internet (34 percent). Institutional sources are not an important source of information, indicating the lack of a successful policy by the government to promote joint activities with the diaspora and the fact that the diaspora is not part of the agenda of public and private organizations in Argentina. Ten percent of respondents belong to Argentine professional organizations, 11 percent to international professional organizations, 11 percent to organizations associated with governments other than the government of Argentina, and 6 percent to organizations associated with the Argentine government.

Key factors that could catalyze the participation of the diaspora in projects with Argentina include support from colleagues and institutions in Argentina (47 percent of sample respondents) and recommendations from colleagues and institutions in Argentina (37 percent of respondents) (table A7.1). Eighty percent of those surveyed believe that there are institutions (universities, laboratories, corporations) with which they could collaborate. About 18 percent are not sure if such institutions exist and 2 percent believe they do not.

Professional Advantages of Coming from Argentina

Eighty percent of those surveyed believe that being Argentine is an advantage in developing technical exchanges or commercial relationships. Forty-five percent believe this advantage is marginal and 35 percent believe it is significant. Women are less likely than men to believe that having been born in Argentina is an advantage.

Among those who believe that being from Argentina is an advantage for technological and commercial exchanges, the main reasons cited are knowledge of local idiosyncrasies (82 percent), maintenance of informal networks with colleagues and friends (87 percent), and better awareness of opportunities (63 percent). Institutional factors do not play an important role: only 18 percent of respondents believe that connections with local networks of professionals are important and only 2 percent believe that the favorable tax treatment afforded investments by Argentines living abroad makes a difference

Experiences Collaborating with Argentina

Almost half (45 percent) of Argentine professionals in the sample—83 percent in the private sector—had negative experiences collaborating with Argentina (table 7.2). One quarter had positive experiences and 30 percent were ambivalent about their experiences.

About 56 percent of those in the sample that have moderate to high influence in their organizations have had negative experiences, and only 19 percent of this group have had a good experience. In contrast, among respondents with little or no influence, 37 percent have had positive experiences and 33 percent have had negative ones. This difference probably reflects the fact that people with influence usually

Table 7.2 *Quality of Experiences of Diaspora Argentines in Collaborating Professionally with Argentina*
(percentage of respondents)

Type of employment	Negative	Positive	Ambivalent
Independent, owner, partner	33	0	67 *
Employee in a private company	83 *	17	0
Employee in an academic organization, or laboratory	36	36	28
Other	100 *	0	0
Total	45	25	30

Source: Authors' survey.
Note: * = significant at the 5 percent level.

deal with public or private institutions (including local or national governments), while people without influence usually deal with other researchers or engineers.

Complaints about experiences are diverse (box 7.2). Respondents who work in academic institutions cite the limited involvement of the National Council for Scientific and Technical Research and of diaspora institutions, excessive bureaucracy, and lack of a strategic vision and clear program. Other problems include the following:

- lack of national policy on education, science, and technology;
- weak articulation between science, technology, innovation, and business development and commercialization;
- failure of the government to implement or sustain programs, including several that appeared promising and involved no cost to Argentina;
- abuse of influence in the scientific system and bureaucratic demands on researchers;
- lack of competence, informality, passivity, and weak engagement of local researchers.

Professionals who had had positive professional experiences in Argentina cite personal rather than institutional competence. They cite the capacity, creativity, honesty, professionalism, and excitement of local scientists as the key factor for the success of programs. According to one respondent: "These qualities of our scientists are, without any doubt, the only reason that good science still exists in Argentina, in spite of a quite harsh environment (low salaries, lack of incentives, and so on)." Some respondents cite the institutional support, infrastructure, and equipment of organizations such as the National Atomic Energy Commission, the Bariloche Atomic Center, the National Research Council of Argentina, the Naval Hydrographical Institute, the National Institute of Oceanography, the Patagonian Center at Puerto Madryn, the Marine Biology Center, and some national universities.

Box 7.2 *What's Wrong with Science and Technology in Argentina?*

Respondents from the diaspora cite many problems that hamper science and technology in Argentina:

"The lack of institutional support is aggravated by the lack of a national scientific policy, which is not consistent and lacks continuity. This limits the possibility to sustain credible programs. In addition, corruption leads to an inadequate use of the limited funds, and there are difficulties meeting international standards for evaluating proposals, reporting results, and so forth. Thus mid- or long-term planning is not possible."

"The only initiatives that work are because of a strong personal push by leading participants to overcome Kafkaesque difficulties in spite of the institutions."

"The combination of the country's internal problems, such as lack of political, economic, and social stability, and the corruption of many institutions, the lack of justice, and petty politics make the system incompatible with the ethics and standard rules of international transactions."

"In certain cases, there is a lack of interest in the achievements of Argentine professionals that reside abroad. Many Argentine scientists consider their job a 9 to 5 job."

"There is limited understanding of international rules. There is a naïve believe that the Argentine workforce is highly qualified, when in reality it is outside global knowledge networks."

Source: Authors' survey.

In regard to institutional problems, respondents cite the lack of fulfillment of financial promises by the Argentine side, which has limited progress. According to one respondent: "If we have succeeded in our bilateral projects, it is because of the strong will of the participants. The programs are not clearly defined, they are poorly funded, and they require time-consuming efforts to get the blessing of bureaucrats, in processes that are usually not transparent or well organized. In several bilateral projects, the Argentine institutional side did not respect agreements."

According to respondents, these institutional problems cannot be fixed by individual efforts. "It is difficult for isolated groups to work well when they are immersed in a system and society that does not work properly," noted one respondent. Respondents cite the existence of feudal characteristics, in which "owners of territory" do not want an "invasion." The result is clientelism instead of meritocracy. Professionals from abroad may be viewed as dangerous, particularly by Argentines over 40.

Willingness to Contribute to Argentina's Development

Many respondents manifested a strong willingness to help develop science, technology, and education in Argentina. They expressed their desire for Argentina to develop a strong and sustainable cooperation program with the diaspora (box 7.3). Sixty-two percent of respondents believe they could provide moderate help to other Argentines in their areas of expertise and 35 percent believe they could offer substantial help.

The majority of respondents believe that scientific, technological, or professional exchanges between the diaspora and Argentina are possible. In contrast, few are likely to start a business in Argentina or invest there (table 7.3).

Argentina's Strengths and Weaknesses

According to respondents, the key factors that could facilitate scientific and technological exchanges and economic development in Argentina are the creativity of Argentine professionals (70 percent), the high qualifications of the workforce (51 percent), the

---

Box 7.3 *What Do Argentine Professionals from the Diaspora Think about Collaborating Professionally with Argentina?*

"I live in the United States, have built a research group there, and will not be returning to Argentina. But I have a strong interest in making a contribution from here."
"I would like to help and return to the country what it has given me."
"It is important to develop a network of Argentine professionals that links those of us abroad with our colleagues in Argentina to catalyze interactions and collaborations. It is clear that those in the diaspora that have reached leading positions could make important contributions to the country, but we need some infrastructure and programs to initiate collaborations and make them sustainable."
"My contribution could be along several dimensions: generating links with high-tech agents in the United States, creating programs or contributing to programs to educate professionals in Argentina on business opportunities in the United States, establishing links between U.S. and Argentine research centers."

Source: Authors' survey.

Table 7.3 *Probability of Initiating Scientific, Technological, or Commercial Activity in Argentina*
(percentage of respondents)

Activity	None	Unlikely	Possible	Probable	Likely
Start a new business	43	30	17	8	2
Invest	53	29	11	4	3
Engage in scientific exchange	5	9	35	21	30
Engage in technological exchange	13	20	41	13	13
Engage in other types of exchanges	8	19	43	16	14

Source: Authors' survey.

country's excellent natural resources (44 percent), and the ability to work in loosely structured and continuously changing environments (42 percent). The creativity of local professionals and the highly qualified workforce were cited by both older and younger members of the diaspora group surveyed. This suggests that the deterioration of the formal educational system over the past three decades has been offset, at least partially, by informal education, teamwork, mistrust of authority, and ability to quickly overcome unpleasant surprises or last minute changes.[4] For these factors to contribute to the building of competencies that would allow Argentina to capture niche markets in the global economy, they must be properly integrated into a realistic plan of action.

On the negative side, Argentina's wealth of natural resources has kept it from developing innovative productive sectors tied into local and global systems of innovation and with multiplier effects on society. Factors limiting economic development and scientific and technological collaboration include the corrupt legal system (57 percent of respondents), the lack of capacity of the national government (53 percent), the instability of the financial system (51 percent), the lack of capacity of local governments (46 percent), the lack of investment in relevant areas (37 percent), the lack of insertion of Argentina in the global economy (table A7.2).

Recommendations from the Diaspora

Many respondents submitted recommendations with their questionnaires; others contacted the authors with recommendations or suggestions. In many cases, the questionnaire created expectations that the investigation would lead to a meaningful project for involving the diaspora. Several respondents inquired about the next steps in developing an effective network in the diaspora that could collaborate with Argentina.

Many respondents stressed the strategic importance of developing a specialization profile that will help Argentina develop knowledge-intensive industries. Several respondents cited the need to coordinate and integrate efforts in science, technology, and economic development. They mentioned the need to involve companies that invest in R&D and in the development of new ideas, concepts, and products in generating a specialization profile that gives more weight to sectors

---

[4]Referred to in Argentina as *viveza criolla or picardia criolla.*

that provide high value added products. In contrast to older industries, such as metals or oil, many new areas, including biotechnology, nanotechnology, software, and food science, do not require large investments.

The issues that received the most attention were scientific and technological policies and possible strategies to start sustainable growth. Some respondents mentioned that scientific policy should generate not only knowledge, but also wealth, connecting science with technology and economic development.

Respondents recommend the following:

- Transform the specialization profile of the country, making it more knowledge intensive and more open to the opportunities represented by human resources that have received advanced, specialized education abroad.
- Establish priorities in research topics.
- Educate the community, politicians, executives, entrepreneurs, and others on the importance of knowledge in creating competitive advantages.
- Develop human resources that can help bridge science and technology.
- Develop a clear industrial policy.
- Create an infrastructure and a solid program to coordinate, organize, and leverage contributions from the diaspora.
- Revitalize and strengthen public education.
- Develop a scientific and technological program that is coherent, consistent, and sustainable.
- Increase R&D investment as percentage of GNP in order to create new opportunities for progress.
- Take advantage of capacity-building grants offered by foreign organizations to democratize local access to these opportunities.
- Invite the diaspora to contribute to the design of a scientific policy that connects science with technology and opens the possibility of creating a specialization profile with strong demand for highly qualified human resources.

Professionals in the diaspora recommend a specialization profile that differs markedly from the current one, which relies heavily on resource-intensive products and commodities. About 40 percent of respondents recommended focusing on software and biotechnology and 66 percent of the sample recommended focusing on knowledge-intensive activities. Eighty percent of the sample recommended knowledge-intensive sectors, medicine, pharmacy, and basic sciences. The specialization profile recommended for Argentina does not differ substantially from that of the diaspora, suggesting that the knowledge of the diaspora could be of great value.

One respondent proposed establishing joint projects in certain priority areas, coordinated by the government, with the participation of scientists, engineers, entrepreneurs, nongovernmental organizations, and political parties. He envisioned a state program, not just a program of a particular government (with a short life span). Projects would receive subsidies from the state within a public-private partnership. Some of the income generated by projects would be reinvested in order to spur innovation and finance new projects, creating a virtuous cycle. The program would first focus on high-priority areas, as Finland did in focusing on the telecom and wireless sectors before expanding into the biotechnology, pharmacology, and food industries.

Recommended Strategies and Actions

Several possible strategies emerge for leveraging the diaspora to help Argentina develop a knowledge economy. The results of the survey suggest the following strategies for the short to medium term:

- Identify strategic areas in which Argentina could develop a competitive advantage within a few years.
- Identify elements needed to create competitive advantages that will allow Argentina to successfully compete globally in certain niche markets.
- Define and implement a strategy and plan of action.

A model of technology cluster development is needed that strongly leverages the diaspora and its networks. Such a model would increase opportunities for diaspora professionals to participate in the development, education, and training of the local workforce and private sector. It would leverage the interests, experience, networks, and resources of all partners in complementary ways to establish a cost-effective means of increasing the number of transactions in areas of strategic interest. The plan should be implemented in a way that ensures sustainability in the long run, given the demonstrated potential for a profit-driven business model. Within four to five years, the project should be self-sustainable by providing services to the government, corporations, new ventures, and service providers, acting as a catalyst for deal generation.

Stage 1: Designing the Plan and Identifying Key Players

In June 2004, two diaspora organizations in the United States, the Argentinean Center of Students and Graduates Abroad (Centro de Estudiantes y Graduados Argentinos) (http://www.centroargentino.org) and the North American Association of Argentines to Advance Science and Culture (Asociación Argentino-Norteamericana para el Avance de la Ciencia, la Tecnología y la Cultura) (http://www.anacitec.net), in collaboration with the Argentine Embassy in the United States, organized an event to discuss models of collaboration between public and private organizations in Argentina and the United States. This event, the Workshop for Collaboration with the Diaspora (Encuentro de Colaboración Diáspora-Argentina), brought together more than 80 senior and midlevel professionals from industry, academia, and government in Washington, DC. Participants revealed a strong desire to build an organization to cooperate with Argentina, to catalyze business opportunities and research collaboration partnerships, and to develop programs for training and strengthening human resources for the knowledge economy. The Argentinean Center of Students and Graduates Abroad and the North American Association of Argentines to Advance Science and Culture have been coordinating efforts along these lines since then.

In December 2004 a second conference took place at the Ministry of Labor in Buenos Aires and was attended by more than 200 local and diaspora participants from industry, government, and academia. Participants included top officials from the ministries of Education, Labor, Foreign Relations, and the Economy; executives from large multinational companies and local start-ups; and representatives from leading universities and research centers. The agenda included both plans for cooperation and sessions focused on software, biomedicine, and material science and nanotechnology. In

June 2005 a third conference took place, at the Argentine Embassy in London, with a video conference with Buenos Aires, Miami, and Washington, DC.

The North American Association of Argentines to Advance Science and Culture seeks to build a sustainable organization to promote Argentine science, technology, and business opportunities in global markets. It intends to work with both diaspora and local organizations, including universities and multinational corporations, to build partnerships, exploit synergies, and develop joint projects. It also intends to establish a strong partnership with the federal and local governments in Argentina. Relevant government organizations include the Secretariat for Science and Technology and the ministries of Education, Foreign Relations, Economy, and Labor. The Argentinean Center of Students and Graduates Abroad could be viewed as a business development organization in start-up mode. The center is in the process of defining its business model, raising funding, and building its team.

Stage 2: Implementing the Plan

The plan should be sponsored or financed in part by the government and have its strong political support. It is not possible to build a sustainable network linking Argentina with its diaspora without strong economic and political support from the government. Similar efforts by Asian, European, and other countries (including Chile) have been initiated by federal, provincial, and/or local governments. They usually involve collaboration by several ministries or agencies. In most cases, foreign governments have teams or agents in the United States to foster interactions and create bridges between their countries, their diasporas, and the United States or regions within the United States, such as Silicon Valley.

Infrastructure should include a Web portal and online linkage programs in Argentina and the diaspora, including databases, electronic meeting rooms, and online advisory services for local start-ups, as well as working groups for different professional specializations. Several professional diasporas have been using Web portals to link their members to professionals in the home country. To encourage professionals in the diaspora and in Argentina to use the portal, it should include the following:

- access to global networks;
- access to relevant information;
- information on business opportunities, including information on start-up formation and investment and partnership possibilities;
- identification of opportunities for technical and scientific exchanges;
- access to universities, potential customers, suppliers, employees, and employers.

A portal that includes strong search capabilities and a solid database (directory, resources) is critical to involving the diaspora (box 7.4). Access to knowledge and resources facilitates the creation of bridges between local communities and their diasporas, building strong relationships in the mid- to long-term among members with common interests or areas of specialization.

A more advanced phase in the evolution of a network involves the generation of transactions in addition to information. A transaction could involve the commercialization of technology, such as the sale of intellectual property abroad, or more

---

Box 7.4 *Using the Web to Create Links with the Diaspora in Armenia*

In 2002, the Armenian High-Technology Council of America and the Union of Information Technology Enterprises in Armenia launched SiliconArmenia (http://www.siliconarmenia.com), a Web site designed to boost Armenia's burgeoning high-tech sector by increasing its exposure to international companies and investors. The site seeks to foster cooperation and trade among Armenian technology companies and technology professionals in the Armenia diaspora and the global technology community.

The site, which is in Armenian, English, and Russian, includes news and analysis related to the Armenian technology sector; information on business opportunities, tenders, and requests for proposals; a database of Armenian technology companies; success stories of Armenian technology companies and entrepreneurs; and e-learning, online training, and skills development.

The fruit of an extensive public-private effort, SiliconArmenia received support from a number of technology organizations and individuals and from the World Bank. It seeks to build critical mass by encouraging companies and professionals to register to receive SiliconArmenia newsletters; submit company and organizational profiles; post company and organization news; participate in the Web site's forums and exchange opinions and experience with colleagues; and post business opportunities, tender announcements, and requests for proposals.

---

sophisticated operations, such as the raising of venture capital in or the moving of a company's headquarters to the United States, assisted by members of the diaspora. This model has worked for Israel, and other countries, such as Mexico, have adopted it as well.

Stage 3: Showcasing, Evaluating, and Disseminating Results

The project should showcase successful examples of transactions linking diaspora and local organizations. It should evaluate and learn from early experiences and promote and disseminate information about successful cases. The process is iterative, so lessons are applied to improve infrastructure and transaction processes.

Incorporating the Diaspora Into Government Plans and Programs

If a project is to succeed, it must be integrated with national programs in science, technology, and economic development, such as the plans of the Secretariat for Science and Technology and other government organizations. Diaspora contributions are relevant only if there is strong local interest in collaborating and the government and other relevant organizations include the diaspora in their plans and allocate an appropriate budget to create and sustain programs. Project continuity and sustainability despite changes in governments and agencies are critical.

Networks include two types of agents: proactive agents, who put their social and financial capital into network activities (by leading a commercial transaction for example), and organizational agents, who perform the needed work to create, maintain, and expand the network. Both these types of agents are critical if the network is to grow and generate a bidirectional flow of transactions.

A strategic, long-term program should be defined in the form of a document that evolves as it is implemented and as new lessons are absorbed. It should generate a bidirectional flow of transactions (scientific and technological exchanges, business deals, venture capital investments, and so forth) between the local community and the diaspora. The quality of the exchange should be high in global terms in strategic areas in which Argentina could generate global competitive advantages. In the selected strategic areas, it should contribute to the development of a skilled workforce that is not only technologically savvy, but also able to actively engage with the global community and participate in both the supply of and demand for high-tech industry by conducting business transactions, performing R&D for leading global corporations, attracting international capital, generating leading technologies, starting promising new ventures, and so forth.

Annex. Results of the Survey of Argentine Professionals in the Diaspora

Table A7.1 *Importance of Various Channels for Encouraging Participation in Scientific, Technological, or Business Exchanges with Locals*
(percentage of respondents)

Channel	None	Limited	Moderate	High or very high
Support from colleagues and institutions in Argentina	17	17	19	47
Recommendations by colleagues and institutions in Argentina	26	24	13	37
Support from colleagues and institutions from abroad who work with Argentina	37	18	14	31
Incentives from the Argentine government or Argentine nongovernmental organizations	33	22	14	31
Support of government organizations in the country of residence (National Science Foundation and others)	29	24	16	31
Support from international organizations	23	25	22	30
Changes in Argentina (in the education system or the selection of priority areas in innovation and education, for example)	36	24	11	29
Support from the government of the country of residence or other governments	52	27	10	11

Source: Authors' survey.

Table A7.2 *Factors Limiting Argentina's Ability to Generate, Promote, and Sustain Scientific Technological and Economic Development*
(percentage of respondents)

Factor	Not limiting	Low	Moderate	High or very high
Corrupt legal system	28	7	8	57
Capacity of national government	29	8	11	53
Instability of the financial system	32	6	11	51
Capacity of local government	37	7	10	46
Local investment in relevant areas	42	10	11	37
Lack of participation in the global economy	49	10	10	31
Regional instability	47	9	13	31
Physical infrastructure	40	16	15	29
Local actors' grasp of how the global economy works	52	9	10	29
Flexibility to work in poorly structured systems	50	16	9	25
System of innovation for technological development and financing for support of high-tech industry	57	8	13	22
Entrepreneurial spirit	58	14	8	20
Quality of the education system	44	20	17	19
Capacity for teamwork	46	20	16	18
Communication infrastructure	48	21	19	12
Capacity to establish networks	55	19	16	10
Quality of skilled workforce	59	30	8	3
Quality of unskilled workforce	62	29	6	3
Creativity of Argentine professionals	57	37	3	3
Quality of products manufactured in Argentina	92	3	2	3
Quality of natural resources	62	33	3	2

Source: Authors' survey.

References

Albornoz, M., L. Luchilo, G. Arber, R. Barrere, and J. Raffo. 2002. "El talento que se pierde: Aproximación al estudio de la emigración de profesionales, investigadores y tecnólogos argentino." Working Paper 4, Centro de Estudios sobre Ciencia, Desarrollo y Educación Superior, Buenos Aires.

Albornoz, F., D. Milesi, and G. Yoguel. 2002. "New Economy in Old Sectors: Some Issues Coming from Two Production Networks in Argentina." Paper presented at the summer conference of the Danish Research Unit for Industrial Dynamics, "Industrial Dynamics of the New and Old Economy: Who Is Embracing Whom?" Copenhagen and Elsinore, June. http://www.druid.dk/conferencies/summer2002/papers.

Albornoz, M., E. Fernández Polcuch, and C. Alfaraz. 2002. "Hacia una nueva estimación de la fuga de cerebros." *Revista Redes* (Universidad Nacional de Quilmes, Centro de Estudios e Investigaciones, Quilmes, Argentina) 9 (18).

Bisang, R., G. Gutman, C. Roig, and R. Rabetino. 1999a. "La oferta tecnológica de las principales cadenas agroindustriales en el Mercosur ampliado." Serie Resúmenes Ejecutivos 12. Buenos Aires. http://www.procisur.uy/proglobal.htm.

——. 1999b. "Los sistemas nacionales de innovación agropecuaria y agroindustrial del Conosur: transformaciones y desafíos." Serie Resúmenes Ejecutivos 14. Buenos Aires. http://www.procisur.uy/proglobal.htm.

Gereffi, G. 2001. "Beyond the Producer-Driven/Buyer-Driven Dichotomy: The Evolution of Global Value Chains in the Internet Era." *American Behavioral Scientist* 44 (10).

Hirshman A. 1996. "Tendencias autosubversivas." Ensayos, Fondo de Cultura Económica, Mexico.

Holm-Nielsen, L. B., and K. Thorn. 2003. "Higher Education in Latin America: A Regional Overview." World Bank, Washington, D.C.

Novick, M., and A. Gallart. 1997. "Competitividad, redes productivas y competencias laborales." Cinterfor-OIT, RET, Montevideo.

Poma, L. 2000. "La producción de conocimiento: Nuevas dinámicas competitivas para el territorio." In *Territorio, conocimiento y competitividad de las empresas: el rol de las instituciones en el espacio global*, ed. F. Boscherini and L. Poma. Universidad Nacional de General Sarmiento-Centro Antares, Forli, Italy, and Editorial Miño y Dávila, Madrid.

Rullani, E. 2000. "El valor del conocimiento." In *Territorio, conocimiento y competitividad de las empresas: el rol de las instituciones en el espacio global*, ed. F. Boscherini and L. Poma. Universidad Nacional de General Sarmiento-Centro Antares, Forli, Italy, and Editorial Miño y Dávila, Madrid.

World Bank. 2005. *India and the Knowledge Economy: Leveraging Strengths and Opportunities.* Washington, DC: World Bank Institute.

Yoguel, G. 2000. "El tránsito de la sustitución de importaciones a la economía abierta: Los principales cambios en la estructura industrial argentina entre los 70's y los 90's." In *El desempeño industrial argentino. Mas allá de la sustitución de importaciones*, ed. B. Kosacoff. Santiago: Economic Commission for Latin America.

8

South Africa: Evolving Diaspora, Promising Initiatives

Jonathan Marks

South Africa has suffered from extensive skills loss, beginning before the end of apartheid. Current emigration data do not provide an accurate picture. Both the South African Department of Home Affairs and Statistics South Africa acknowledge that they track only emigrants who declare themselves as such (Crush and Williams 2001). The true number of emigrants could be as much as three times official figures. Whatever the actual figure, there is little disagreement that skilled workers continue to leave South Africa. Among workers who could emigrate, more than two-thirds state that they have considered doing so. Despite the perception that emigration is dominated by skilled, white South Africans, research shows that there is no difference across racial groups in the desire to emigrate.

Researchers have begun to rename the brain drain the brain exchange in recognition of the fact that many skilled workers leave for a period of time and then return to their home countries with new skills and abilities. Those that remain in their host country put down roots, but remain connected with their country of birth. This realization has led to a global movement toward diaspora networks: formal and informal networks that comprise expatriates and others concerned about home country development. Members of these networks band together to invest, provide knowledge transfer, or merely remain connected with their homelands.

South Africa has two such diaspora networks. The South African Network of Skills Abroad (SANSA) was developed through collaboration between the University of Cape Town and the Institute for Research and Development, the French development agency. The network has concentrated on linking expatriate and South Africa–based academics, researchers, and practitioners working in science and technology. It is now managed by the National Research Foundation (NRF), a division of the South African Department of Arts, Culture, Science, and Technology.

The South African Diaspora Network was developed by the University of Cape Town's Centre for Innovation & Entrepreneurship with assistance from the World Bank Development Marketplace.[1] This network focuses on developing knowledge and entrepreneurial connections between South African firms and well-connected and strategically placed individuals in the United Kingdom.

---

[1] The Centre for Innovation & Entrepreneurship is jointly supported by the government, the private sector, and international development organizations. It aims to develop South Africa's entrepreneurial capacity through teaching, research, and business development.

These two initiatives are by no means enough. Greater support and involvement is required from the South African government, international development organizations, and the host countries that benefit directly from the migration of skilled South Africans.

The South African Economic Context

With South Africa's movement to democracy in 1994 came greater economic development and the country's re-entry into the global economy. The key economic challenge facing South Africa is spurring growth and increasing foreign demand for South African exports through both foreign investment and local investment. At the same time, the government is faced with pressing socioeconomic issues, including the HIV/AIDS pandemic, continued abject poverty, job losses, unemployment, and the migration of skilled South Africans.

Key to growing the South African economy has been a focus on increasing export-based revenues. A relatively weak rand (relative to the U.S. dollar) has kept South Africa price competitive. Increases in exports have a multiplier effect on the economy, increasing domestic incomes, especially wages, and profits, which leads to overall expansion and increased capital investment. With the strengthening of the rand with respect to all major currencies, especially the U.S. dollar, South Africa has begun to see a decline in export revenues as its export competitiveness has fallen. The U.S. dollar exchange rate has stabilized at about R7.00 to the U.S. dollar after having reached R13.50 to the dollar in December 2001. The strength of the rand had a substantial impact on the South African economy, reducing corporate profits, tax revenues, and public spending.

The Migration of Skilled South Africans

South Africa has long suffered from a migration of skilled people to developed countries. The reasons for this are varied, but tend to fall into three broad categories: political, social, and economic. While the migration of skilled professionals from South Africa has been prompted by certain push factors—including an oppressive political system, limited economic resources and opportunities, social problems such as crime, HIV/AIDS, and declining health care and education standards—a number of factors pull South African professionals to developed countries, particularly Australia, Canada, New Zealand, the United Kingdom, and the United States. These factors are often the opposite of the push factors: a democratic and stable political system, greater demand and reward for skills, better resources and opportunities, and a safer environment. South Africa's re-entry into the international economy and the continued growth of the knowledge economy mean that skills move to where they are most valued or prized (Robinson 2003).

Immigration Versus Emigration

Several studies have compared migration to and from South Africa (Kaplan 1997). They show that immigration outpaced emigration except in 1961, 1977, 1978, 1986, and 1993. These years correspond to political events that may have spurred emigration: the Sharpeville uprising (1961), national unrest following the Soweto uprisings (1976), the declaration of a state of emergency (1985), and the political transition leading to South Africa's first democratic election (1993).

In 2000, 2,439 skilled workers emigrated from South Africa while 331 immigrated to South Africa (Robinson 2003). The government has not made it easy to recruit people with needed skills. The Immigration Bill, passed in May 2002, places a number of barriers in the path of local employers. These include having to adhere to a quota system and having to train local workers to eventually replace foreign skilled workers. The argument has been made that immigrants will take jobs from local skilled workers, but a study by the Southern African Migration Project shows that skilled immigrants are not only needed to help the South African economy grow, they often create new enterprises and jobs, pass on valuable skills and knowledge, and help develop and enhance existing businesses (Robinson 2003).

Obtaining accurate data on the migration of skills out of South Africa is a challenge for researchers. Statistics South Africa, the state-run statistical service, relies on data collected at South Africa's three international airports (Cape Town, Durban, and Johannesburg). These data are often inaccurate, because emigrants may not fully disclose their reasons for leaving the country and South African citizens are not obliged to provide details or reasons for their international travel.

Notwithstanding the lack of accurate migration data, various estimates have been made of the number of skilled South Africans abroad. The Southern Africa Migration Project finds the following (Crush and others 2001):

- The skilled population in South Africa numbers about 1.6 million people within an economically active population of 17 million.
- As a result of the system of reserving skilled jobs based on race under apartheid, 72 percent of skilled workers are white, 18 percent are African, 8 percent are colored, and 3 percent are Indian.
- Of the pool of skilled people, 69 percent say they "have given the idea of emigration some thought." Only 20 percent indicate that it is "very likely" that they will leave South Africa.
- About 2 percent of the population is characterized as having "very high" potential to emigrate (defined as leaving South Africa for two years or more within the next two to five years). People with "high" potential to emigrate account for 10 percent of the population; people with "moderate" potential to emigrate represent another 25 percent.
- If people who have "very high" potential emigrate, South Africa would lose about 32,000 people. If those with "high" potential emigrate as well, it could mean a skills loss of up to 192,000 people.
- The five most often mentioned destinations for skilled migrants from South Africa are the United States (24 percent), Australia (22 percent), the United Kingdom (15 percent), New Zealand (12 percent), and Canada (11 percent).
- More than 60 percent of the skilled population possesses a high school certificate and a tertiary qualification (technical university or academic university degree). Five percent of skilled workers have a master's degree, and 1 percent have doctorates (Robinson 2003). Nine percent graduate with honors degrees.

Given that data collected at ports of exit by the South African Department of Home Affairs do not provide a true or complete representation of the number of skilled workers leaving South Africa, the task of counting the number of skilled individuals in the South African diaspora is a complex and difficult one.

The Southern Africa Migration Project estimated the flow of skills out of South Africa (Crush and Williams 2001). Data were obtained from Statistics South Africa for emigration to each of the five major destinations (table 8.1). These data were then compared with immigration statistics from each receiving country. Immigration categories were deemed comparable, with limited differences in recording methods.

The data reveal consistent underreporting of emigration by Statistics South Africa. The data, while useful inasmuch as they reflect a trend of continued migration, do not shed sufficient light on the migration of skilled people. Calculations by Kaplan (1997) indicate that 41,496 skilled professionals (excluding those in managerial, administrative, and executive positions) left South Africa between 1989 and 1997. The official figure for this same period and category of emigrants was 11,255.

Government Response to Skilled Migration

There has been limited response from the South African government in addressing the migration of skilled South Africans. Government support has been offered to the Homecoming Revolution, a nonprofit organization aimed at encouraging South Africans living abroad to return. The campaign consists largely of advertising and media-based efforts, with no formal structure in place apart from a Web site to promote and publicize South Africa. Efforts are being made to provide knowledge support (passport and visa queries, job opportunities, and so forth) through the Web site (Lundy and Visser 2003).

The South African Department of Health has initiated a special allowance program for some skilled health care professionals in a bid to stem the tide of migration of qualified health care workers. The program has a budget of R 500 million, which will be used as incentives for 33,000 rural health care workers and 62,000 public sector workers classified as having scarce skills. This appears to be a transition by the government from punitive to incentive-based measures to control skills migration (South African Broadcasting Corporation, January 29, 2004).

High-level discussions between South African President Thabo Mbeki and his Nigerian counterpart, Olusegun Obasanjo, have been held to find ways in which the two countries can collaborate in encouraging African scientists, engineers,

Table 8.1 *Flow of Skills Out of South Africa to Five Major Destination Countries, 1987–1997*

	1987		1992		1997		Total	
	RC	SSA	RC	SSA	RC	SSA	RC	SSA
New Zealand	632	411	422	126	2,689	1,157	14,009	5,979
Australia	3,792	3,484	1,021	694	4,281	1,508	28,747	17,650
United Kingdom	6,700	3,817	6,900	1,987	10,988	2,162	90,788	26,169
Canada	1,748	755	1,141	285	1,898	557	18,125	6,354
United States	1,741	543	2,516	314	2,563	832	46,724	5,936
Total	14,613	9,010	12,000	3,406	22,419	216	198,393	62,088

Source: Statistics South Africa and receiving countries' statistical agencies.
Note: RC = receiving country, SSA = Statistics South Africa.

academics, and professionals to return home. There has been no publicized outcome from these discussions. Given the large outflow of skilled South Africans, the
response of the government has been minimal, probably because of more pressing
socioeconomic issues at home (*Mail & Guardian,* January 23, 2004).

Characteristics of the South African Knowledge-Based Diaspora

As the migration of skilled professionals continues, an increase in efforts to maximize expatriate resources will be evident. Given the options open to home
countries—restrictive measures, repatriation, or mobilization—the mobilization of
diaspora communities, especially those comprising skilled professionals, will
become crucial to development planning.

The size of the South African diaspora is not known, but various estimates have
been made. The number of South Africans who left the country as tourists between
1945 and 1994 exceeded the number of returning tourists by more than 500,000,
indicating that the vast majority of those emigrating did so without declaring their
intent (Kaplan 1997). Many left South Africa following the political unrest of the
1960s and 1970s and are well established and settled in their host countries. The
British High Commission estimates that more than 300,000 South Africans live in
the United Kingdom (Robinson 2003). This figure is based on anecdotal evidence.
In addition, about 800,000 South Africans hold British passports. Not included in
this figure are the South Africans who are eligible for work permits in the United
Kingdom based on British ancestry.

In May 2003, a survey was performed by the World Bank in order to gain a
deeper understanding of the characteristics of the South African skilled diaspora
community (Devane 2003). The 39-question survey was designed to investigate
attitudes toward homeland investment and professional contributions by South
Africans living in the United States. Five hundred surveys were mailed to
U.S.–based expatriate alumni of the University of Natal. Forty-five responses were
received, a response rate that is typical of cold call mail surveys.

The results indicate that the average age of respondents was 47 and that their
average tenure in the United States was 12 years; 37 percent of the sample had lived
in the United States for more than 20 years. This mean age is consistent with
research done by the SANSA network, which showed that the average age of
skilled emigrants is increasing, possibly indicating that more South Africans are
completing their studies before migrating (table 8.2).

Table 8.2 *Average Age of Skilled South African Migrants at Migration, 1930–9 to 1990–9*

Period	Average age (years)
1930–9	16.0
1940–9	16.5
1950–9	22.6
1960–9	23.8
1970–9	27.5
1980–9	30.9
1990–9	32.5

Source: Brown 2003.

Relative to the rest of Africa, South African professionals tend to leave when they are older and better qualified. African emigrants from other countries are more likely to enter the United States as students.

The group surveyed is highly educated: all have bachelor's degrees and 73 percent have graduate degrees or professional qualifications. These data are supported by other data, which show that 40 percent of SANSA members hold masters' degrees and 30 percent hold doctorates (Brown 2003). A promising sign for South Africa is that 35 percent of respondents to the World Bank survey indicated that they are independent professionals or small business owners rather than employees. Assuming these individual have some discretion over their activities, they could become valuable members of the diaspora community.

An important aspect of mobilizing a diaspora network is determining the degree of contact and travel that expatriates undertake with the home country. The survey of South African professionals indicates that the majority travel to South Africa every one to two years (Devane 2003). Only 29 percent of respondents indicated that they rarely travel to South Africa. There is no correlation between tenure abroad and frequency of travel, suggesting that the reason for travel is continued family ties and business in South Africa. This is supported by research on 1,500 first-generation Chinese and Indian migrants by Saxenian (1999), who found that 50 percent return to their home countries at least once a year. She found that 74 percent of Indian respondents and 55 percent of Chinese respondents indicated that they hoped to start their own business in their home countries. A survey of high-tech businesses started in Taiwan's (China's) Hschinchu science-based industrial park revealed that 40 percent of the companies were led by returning expatriates (Saxenian 1999).

South African survey respondents maintain contact with their home country through a variety a means. Thirty-one percent stay abreast of events in South Africa through the media, 22 percent have ongoing business contact with the country, 20 percent maintain contact through academic exchanges and relationships, and 7 percent use conferences and other professional activities to stay in touch. These data support the hypothesis that skilled South Africans living in the diaspora wish to remain in contact with their homeland.

South Africans have power and influence in their host countries. One-third of respondents indicate that they have considerable or a lot of influence over the investment decisions of their organizations. Forty percent report that their organizations are engaged in some international and developing market activities, with 35 percent of organizations having business activities in South Africa. Fifty-four percent of respondents work in organizations of 1,000 people or less. Only 13 percent work in organizations with more than 1,000 employees and have considerable influence over their company's investment decisions.

Respondents were asked what the key barriers to doing business in South Africa were. Half listed crime as the main issue. This is supported by research by the Southern Africa Migration Project, which found that the issues that caused the most dissatisfaction among skilled South Africans were the cost of living, current levels of taxation, safety and security, and the standard of public and commercial services (Crush and others 2001). These attitudes do not differ along racial lines, except with respect to standards of education and health services and general economic conditions. The Southern Africa Migration Project research highlights the fact that skilled whites are less satisfied with their lives now than they were five years ago.

The World Bank survey finds that 96 percent of respondents feel that their South African expatriate status and knowledge and experience of the country and its environment gives them an advantage when doing business in South Africa (Devane 2003). Most list ongoing personal relationships and personal knowledge of the country as the reason for this. With respect to participation in general professional and business networks, 53 percent of respondents reported being involved in such networks, with 78 percent reporting that these networks are formal with regular meetings. Half the networks had established contact with or had operations in South Africa. There was a positive response to the suggestion of extending professional network contacts to South Africans.

South Africans are less positive about investing in South Africa. Only 15 percent report any probability of doing business in South Africa within the next two years, a much smaller percentage than in other diaspora communities, such as Armenians (55 percent) and Cubans (82 percent) (Gillespie and others 1999). More than 65 percent of the South African sample indicate that there is little or no probability that they would invest or do business in South Africa. While this may be an indicator of political feelings related to recent emigration, it does not explain the attitude of those who have been away from South Africa for 20 years or more. There is more interest in professional exchanges: 40 percent of respondents report that they might involve themselves in such exchanges and 11 percent indicate that they are already involved in professional exchange relationships.

Respondents cite a number of ways of improving South Africa, such as strengthening the health and education systems, addressing cultural cohesion, and tackling crime. Some expatriates indicate a willingness to contribute to the development of South African knowledge workers by teaching, mentoring, or coaching. What is clear from the survey is that a signal from the South African government that value is placed on the diaspora community would go a long way toward mobilizing the skills that reside outside the country.

South African Diaspora Networks

Research by Meyer and Brown (1999) at the University of Cape Town identifies 41 expatriate knowledge networks around the world. This list is limited to networks that attempt to connect expatriates with one another as well as with the home country. Other diaspora networks not based on knowledge also exist, which lends support to the overall argument in favor of mobilizing expatriates. Only six expatriate knowledge networks are linked to African countries (Brown 2003).

Various initiatives have been undertaken to address the loss of skills from Africa. Following the Regional Conference on Brain Drain and Capacity Building held in Addis Ababa in February 2000, the Ghanaian government initiated the Homecoming Summit, which brought together government officials, local professionals, and expatriate professionals. Only two formal South African diaspora networks are working with skilled South Africans living abroad, SANSA and the South African Diaspora Network.

South African Network of Skills Abroad

Established in 1998, SANSA is a joint initiative of the University of Cape Town's Science and Technology Policy Research Centre and a leading French agency for scientific cooperation, the Institute for Research and Development.[2] SANSA was launched based on the knowledge that South Africa has a large pool of skilled expatriates and that harnessing this resource could allow it to play a meaningful role in South Africa's development.

The goal of SANSA is to connect highly skilled expatriates in the fields of science and technology with their counterparts in South Africa to create an environment for collaboration and skills transfer. The network provides the means for expatriates to play a role in the development of South Africa without having to return home. The network was formed by accessing the alumni networks of all major South African academic universities and technical universities in order to provide the opportunity for local academics, researchers, and scientists to form connections with their counterparts in the diaspora. No charge is levied for listing or accessing the SANSA database.

SANSA developed a Web site as the main point of entry into the network. The site (http://www.sansa.nrf.ac.za) provides information about the network, its objectives, and opportunities for networking with other members, as well as general information about South Africa. The site's questionnaire gathers demographic and biographic information about applicants. Once the form has been completed and submitted, applicants become members of SANSA.

The Web site also contains electronic bulletin boards and discussion groups, which facilitate exchange, networking, and communication among members. There are seven themed discussion groups (the arts; sports and recreation; engineering, technology, and architecture; humanities and social sciences; management and administration; natural sciences; health sciences) and one on general issues. Use of this feature is low. There is greater use of the bulletin board, which includes postings of job offers, cooperative ventures, general announcements, services needed and offered, and seminars and conferences.

SANSA is a nonprofit, independent, apolitical association of highly skilled South Africans that is open to all people concerned with the socioeconomic development of South Africa. Some key attributes are as follows:

- As of March 2002, SANSA had 2,259 members, up from 2,100 in April 2001 (a 7.6 percent increase in one year). Three-quarters of its members are men.
- Members are located in more than 60 different countries. Fifty-eight percent are South African citizens. Other members come from Canada, Germany, the United States, and elsewhere. Forty percent of members live in the United Kingdom and the United States.
- Network members come from a range of professions, including management and administration (24 percent), the humanities and social sciences (23 percent), the natural sciences (18 percent), and engineering and related fields (15 percent). The remaining members work in the health sciences, the arts, and sports and recreation.
- Network members are highly qualified, with 82 percent having at least a bachelor's degree. Forty-seven percent hold masters' degrees, and 29 percent hold doctorates. While 85 percent of members obtained their undergraduate

---

[2]This section draws on Brown (2003).

degree in South Africa, about half obtained their doctorates in their home country.

- The majority of members are 31–55 years old, indicating that the network is professional rather than student based.

The SANSA network project was handed over to the NRF in October 2000. The NRF forms part of the National Department of Arts, Culture, Science, and Technology, which is responsible for advancing South Africa's research capabilities in the humanities, social sciences, and natural sciences. It has taken full responsibility for management, administration, and development of the network.

The handover of SANSA to the NRF met with some concern from network members, who expressed distrust of government institutions managing such an initiative. This does not seem to have hindered the NRF's management of SANSA or the continued involvement of network members. The NRF underwent organizational restructuring that resulted in a lack of direction and guidance for the SANSA network. The problem was addressed by appointing a new director of research and information, as well as a project manager with responsibilities for the management and strategic direction of the network.

A survey of the bulletin board and discussion forum facilities on the SANSA network indicates that there had been limited traffic in 2002 and that most activity and discussion centered on general issues. Recent discussions with the NRF indicate that the network is not being directly managed, but has been added to a broader community of practice areas under the Records and Document Management section (personal communication, Kholane Chauke, National Research Foundation, Co-coordinator, Records and Document Management, Pretoria, February 5, 2004).

The following conclusions can be drawn from the SANSA network:

- The network does not have the ability to track the outcome of exchanges and communications between network members. As a result, no data exist to provide evidence of the success of the network. To date the network has filled an informative function by linking South Africans. Some future version of the SANSA network may include the ability to track and monitor these relationships in order to be able to measure the network's success.
- The average age of the members of the SANSA network appears to be rising. This is consistent with data on skilled migration, which indicate that older, more highly skilled people are emigrating. It is unlikely that these members will return to South Africa, making the continued success of the network of utmost importance, as these individuals will no doubt begin to make more significant contributions over time.
- The number of new members has been diminishing since the network's inception in 1998. This may be due to a number of factors: the initial passion and enthusiasm for the network that was shown by its initiators has waned and has not been replaced by the NRF, the network has been promoted and marketed in a low-key manner, the activities of the network have received only limited media coverage, and a driving force behind the network is lacking.
- The majority of members are located in the United Kingdom and the United States. This may be an unexpected bonus for the continuation of the network's aims to connect academics, researchers, and scientists in the diaspora with those in South Africa. It will also make it easier to connect with

these individuals on a more personalized basis. Organizations such as the South African Business Club could help the SANSA network establish an on-the-ground presence.

- The business sector accounts for 34 percent of SANSA members and the academic sector for 38 percent. This may indicate that the network is becoming balanced between business interests and those of the NRF, namely, science, academia, and research.

The future of the SANSA network is uncertain. The NRF intends to continue managing and developing the network, but the network is not its core business or focus. More direct and active management of this important diaspora asset is needed.

South African Diaspora Network

A second diaspora initiative in South Africa began in 2001 with funding from the World Bank's Development Marketplace.[3] This project, housed at the University of Cape Town's Centre for Innovation & Entrepreneurship, was initiated to develop a diaspora network of South African expatriates and those interested in South Africa's growth and development, particularly with regard to growing entrepreneurial ventures, links, and relationships. This network uses existing expatriate organizations, such as university alumni associations and the South African Business Club, an organization with members in the United Kingdom and the United States.

The key objectives identified for the project were to

- Facilitate networking between respected and influential business people from South Africa in key overseas markets and young, high-potential, South African–based start-up ventures.
- Increase the quality of international market and competitor information available to such ventures.
- Reduce the cost, time, and risks of obtaining reliable information from overseas markets by such ventures.
- Minimize the risk that this process compromises sensitive, proprietary information.

A choice existed at the start of the project between developing a network based on quality or one based on quantity. The decision was made to focus energy and resources on the development of a small network of high quality, which was considered more likely to have an impact.

The project was initiated as a pilot project during 2002–3. It addressed two main groups, local members and overseas members. Local members are South African–based business people who wish to expand into international markets and recognize the need for assistance, guidance, and support in their endeavors to internationalize. They were recruited through extensive media coverage in South Africa. More than 60 South African companies applied to be part of the diaspora project.

---

[3]This section draws on Marks (2003).

Overseas members are well-connected South Africans living in the Greater London Area recruited by means of presentations held at the South African Business Club in London, as well as at a meeting of the University of Cape Town Graduate School of Business Alumni Association held at Old Mutual, Plc. The same presentation was also given to the network of the graduate schools of business of the universities of Cape Town and Stellenbosch. More than 40 well-placed South Africans living abroad expressed a desire to help young South African businesses and entrepreneurs. To provide a broader base for including local and overseas members, contact was made with a number of potential alliance partners and collaborators from both the public and private sectors.

Suitable local members were introduced to overseas members and encouraged and supported in their discussions. An overseas member, the chair of the U.K. chapter of the South African Business Club, visited South Africa and met with a number of the local members (box 8.1). To date no trade has occurred, but a number of parties are in discussions, some at an advanced stage.

The South African Diaspora Network attracted an array of local clients and overseas members. Local clients included technology and software developers and providers, consulting and legal services companies, sports goods manufacturers and producers, and manufacturers of fast-moving consumer goods. All these companies were small or medium enterprises with fewer than 500 employees and annual turnover of less than R50 million.

All overseas members are South Africans, either by birth or naturalization, and all joined the network through the linkage with the South African Business Club. Overseas members come from a broad range of disciplines and backgrounds, including consulting, manufacturing, legal and accounting services, trade, export advisory services, and retail. Some members, particularly those who have retired, come with a wealth of contacts and the desire to contribute and transfer their skills, knowledge, and networks.

The interest shown in the project suggests that there is a need and broadly based support for a project of this nature. There is little or no measurable impact from the

---

Box 8.1 *Benefits of the South African Diaspora Network for South African Businesses*

Based on the initial presentation at the South African Business Club in London, the chair of the club traveled to Cape Town, at his own expense, to meet with six local businesses and provide them with a free assessment of their internationalization strategies. The intention was to identify a high-potential company that could be used as a test case to support the efforts of the South African Diaspora Network. Each of these businesses benefited from the advice they received, and all but one recognized that they lacked the skills and readiness to expand into international markets. A high-potential business was identified and an offer was made to assist it in internationalizing into the European market. The firm had already committed to an export contract in the United States, however, and thus declined the offer of assistance.

All the businesses assessed expressed their eagerness and willingness to participate in the South African Diaspora Network, but most decided to address internal operational issues before expanding internationally. This led to the development of a new strategy for the South African Diaspora Network that links potential local participant firms with an export readiness skills program to ensure a smooth transition from local to offshore markets.

pilot project, but this is probably because emphasis was placed on developing quality relationships rather than building a quantifiable network with a greater focus on volume.

The pilot phase of the South African Diaspora Project yielded the following lessons:

- The network cannot be based purely on a few high-quality local and overseas members, but will need to include more participants in order to have an impact. Better systems to manage larger numbers of participants are needed, perhaps through alliances with groups such as South Africans Worldwide and the South African Business Club.
- A broader geographical base of overseas members will be required to ensure wider acceptance of the project.
- A nominal fee should be levied on local members to access the network. This will need to be supported by a substantially larger network that covers three broad markets (Australia, Europe, and North America).
- Greater support from the public and private sectors, as well as international development organizations, will be needed. The network will need grant, donor, or aid funding to survive, but it could also generate some of its own revenue.
- A number of initiatives assist businesses with the process of internationalization, supporting and developing efforts to make South Africa a strong, export-based economy. The South African Diaspora Network, while offering a unique service, did not have the ability or budget to clearly differentiate and articulate its benefits. Greater emphasis on marketing and promotion will be needed as the project rolls out.
- Collaboration among nonprofit organizations assisting South Africans to export and internationalize is inadequate. The Centre for Innovation & Entrepreneurship, through the Diaspora Project, has a key role to play in this regard and could encourage other nongovernmental organizations to use the Diaspora Project model in their initiatives. This represents an opportunity to expand the South African Diaspora Network to other major economic centers and to empower organizations such as the Centre for Innovation & Entrepreneurship with the skills and contacts to continue the work in their geographical areas.
- Overseas members represent a moving target, as their interest level, availability, and commitment to the project waiver and shift. This problem will be addressed through a larger network of overseas members.
- Local clients often have a short-term view of exporting and internationalizing, and many are not operationally ready to take advantage of export opportunities.
- More sharing, collaboration, and cooperation are required between for-profit and not-for-profit organizations working to increase South Africa's export and internationalization capacity.
- The key lesson from the South African Diaspora Network is that the decision to follow a mentoring model will take time to yield results. A mentoring model provides guidance, support, and encouragement, without any direct intervention in moving potential trade relationships forward. The mentoring model follows a passive path in terms of direct engagement with network members;

there is no onus on members to build relationships or engage in trade. The mentoring model will be slow to show results, but the enthusiasm of participants in the pilot project is a positive indication that it is on the right track.

The South African Diaspora Network pilot project is currently dormant because of lack of funding and personnel. A presence on the Centre for Innovation & Entrepreneurship Web site and contact with key individuals within the South African Business Club in the United Kingdom and the United States have been maintained. There are continued requests for assistance from South African businesses and an ongoing indication of support from South Africans in the diaspora. What is required is a realistic and achievable business plan and sufficient funding to allow for a long-term commitment to a business model.

Recommendations

How can skilled expatriate South Africans be tapped to spur development in South Africa? What policies, strategies, and action plans should be adopted?

Policy Implications

Given the many pressing needs of the South African government, limited resources are available for investment in diaspora projects. These resources should be deployed in a variety of ways.

HIGH-INTENSITY INTERVENTIONS. High-intensity interventions—that is, active and direct action that builds South African institutions that have the capabilities to cooperate with the diaspora community in order to transfer skills and knowledge back to South Africa—include the following:

- direct financial support for privately initiated diaspora networks through the departments of Trade and Industry; Education; and Arts, Culture, Science, and Technology;
- initiation of diaspora hubs within South African trade missions and embassies around the world that would act as infrastructural bases for expatriate diaspora involvement;
- adjustment of policy on the immigration of high-skill workers to begin to address the shortage of skills in South Africa.

OCCASIONAL INTERVENTIONS. Occasional interventions are opportunistic and serendipitous involvement of the diaspora in South Africa's development. They include continued support for the Come Home Campaign and the Homecoming Revolution to make South African expatriates feel welcome and a part of South Africa's development and vocal support for the involvement of skilled expatriates in South Africa's socioeconomic development.

INCENTIVE SCHEMES FOR RETURNING EXPATRIATES. There is insufficient international evidence to support a policy of financial incentives for returning expatriates. Attempts to lure skilled expatriates back to their home countries began in the 1970s. There was little success with these schemes except in a few countries, such as India, the Republic of Korea, and Taiwan (China) (Brown 2000). For expatriates to return home, they need to be offered salaries, standards of living, infrastructure, and support that are similar to those in their host countries. A negative consequence of bringing expatriates back home is that uprooting them breaks many of the links and connections they have made in their host countries.

The role that the government can play with respect to policy adjustment is minimal. At best, it can support private and public sector initiatives. There is undoubtedly a need for financial and political support from the government to build capacity for diaspora projects, but the two diaspora networks illustrate that sufficient creativity and enthusiasm exists outside of government structures to develop and grow these networks.

Future Strategies

Most efforts toward building diaspora networks and harnessing expatriates' skills will be undertaken by the private sector or through public-private partnerships. Future strategies for initiating diaspora networks and activity include the following:

- Provide ongoing, long-term financial support for existing diaspora networks. These networks will take time to bear fruit and often require dedicated human resources to ensure that they run efficiently and consistently.
- Develop a combination of virtual (Internet-based) and relationship-based networks. Virtual networks allow for greater ground to be covered at the lowest cost, while relationship-based networks create a greater bond and sense of belonging.
- Continue to use university alumni associations as the entry point into existing informal overseas networks. Provide better incentives for universities to share their alumni lists.
- Form stronger alliances among all organizations, both pubic and private sector, involved in diaspora activity.
- Form alliances with expatriate business networks, such as the South African Business Club, to increase the number of overseas members and increase the presence of all the diaspora networks.
- Launch an awareness and marketing campaign encouraging South Africans to remain in touch when living abroad to create awareness about how expatriates can contribute to South Africa's development.
- Publicize stories of successful diaspora projects in South Africa in order to increase awareness of what can be done and to create a culture of "nothing is too little," so that all efforts from abroad can be used and valued.
- Gain access to emigrants and knowledge about channels of communication once emigrants arrive in their host countries by working with travel agents, relocation agents, and others involved in helping South Africans emigrate.

Action Plan

The proposed action plan takes a broad view of the strategies and provides achievable and measurable actions that could be taken to bring these various initiatives to life. Representations should be made to the government and to nongovernmental organizations involved in formulating policy recommendations regarding emigration and skills migration. This activity would be best achieved by providing data on skills migration and supporting research on skilled migration.

The South African Diaspora Network could serve as a blueprint for other such networks in South African and around the world. Unlike SANSA, the network has limited government involvement, giving it greater credibility and influence. Given that a pilot project has already been undertaken, what is now required is a detailed and comprehensive business plan that will lay out a strategy for scaling up the network. The document could act as a road map and policy document for practitioners as well as policymakers.

Should additional long-term funding be secured, the following changes should be made:

- *Adopt a new business model.* The existing business model should be changed to include one that generates revenue from a combination of sources. Membership in the network for overseas members would remain free, but local companies would pay for access to information. Various levels of membership could be offered, each providing a different level of information. In addition, a consulting model should be employed that would assess and advise local companies on their export readiness. This could include, for example, development of export marketing plans, operational interventions, or management mentoring and coaching. The intention would be to secure sufficient medium-term grant and donor funding to put a sustainable business model in place. Doing so could take at least two years.

- *Involve local companies.* Bringing local companies on board will require greater collaboration with agencies concerned with export development in South Africa, such as the Department of Trade and Industry and the various industry export councils. A system of online registration will need to be introduced to help identify the best candidates for export assistance. This would help deploy resources more effectively and encourage local companies to assess their suitability. Targeting certain industries would allow the network to build skills in certain disciplines and to grow an overseas member database that is focused. Industries that represent more lucrative short-term opportunities should be targeted initially.

- *Attract more overseas members.* Attracting overseas members will require a combination of an online campaign like that used by SANSA and a face-to-face campaign like that used by the South African Diaspora Network. Together these two methods will allow better deployment of resources and encourage deeper involvement and ownership by overseas members. A broader geographical base, including Australia, Europe, and North America, will need to be covered from the beginning. Consistent communication with overseas members will be required to ensure their continued support and buy-in. This should be done through a combination of online media (newsletters, email, and Web site publication) and presentations and gatherings in host countries.

- *Strengthen the network's infrastructure.* A more substantive infrastructure will be required to achieve the potential of the South African Diaspora Network. This will include a Web site and online database, as well as a system for tracking interactions and transactions. The University of Cape Town's Centre for Innovation & Entrepreneurship remains committed to the South African Diaspora Network, and certain resources can be made available at marginal cost. The greatest resource that will be required will be human resources: someone will have to manage the network and ensure that it grows. The majority of initial funding will be for salary and travel costs.

- *Garner government support.* The development of the network and its national rollout will require support from local governments and the national government. Additional funding will be required, and political and social support for the network will be required to ensure broadly based participation from local companies and overseas members. This can be achieved through test cases that show initial short-term gains. By continuing to invest in the South African Diaspora Network in the Western Cape, a model can be created that will be attractive to other provinces and to the national government.

References

Brown, M. 2000. "Using the Intellectual Diaspora to Reverse the Brain Drain: Some Useful Examples." Paper presented at the Regional Conference on Brain Drain and Capacity Building in Africa, Addis Ababa, February 22–24.

———. 2003. "The South African Network of Skills Abroad (SANSA): The South African Experience of Scientific Diaspora Networks." In *Diaspora Scientifiques*, ed. R. Barre, V. Hernandez, J. B. Meyer, and D. Vinck. Paris: Institute for Research and Development Editions.

Crush, J., D. McDonald, V. Williams, R. Mattes, W. Richmond, C. M. Rogerson, and J. M. Rogerson. 2001. "Losing our Minds: Migration and the Brain Drain from South Africa." Migration Policy Brief 18, Southern African Migration Project, Ontario.

Crush, J., and V. Williams. 2001. "Counting Brains: Measuring Emigration from South Africa." Migration Policy Brief 5, Southern African Migration Project, Ontario.

Devane, R. 2003. "South African Diaspora Survey." World Bank Institute, Knowledge for Development Program, Washington, DC.

Gillespie, K., L. Riddle, E. Sayre, and D. Sturges. 1999. "Diaspora Interest in Homeland Investment." *Journal of International Business Studies* 30 (3): 623–34.

Kaplan, D. 1997. "Reversing the Brain Drain: The Case for Utilizing South Africa's Unique Intellectual Diaspora." *Science, Technology and Society* 2 (2): 1–18

Lundy, G., and W. Visser. 2003. *South Africa: Reasons to Believe!* Cape Town: Aardvark Press.

Marks, J. 2003. "The South African Diaspora Network: Final Project Report." University of Cape Town, Centre for Innovation & Entrepreneurship, Cape Town.

Meyer, J. B., and M. Brown. 1999. "Scientific Diasporas: A New Approach to the Brain Drain." Paper prepared for the United Nations Educational, Scientific, and Cultural Organization and the World Conference on Science, Budapest, June 26–July 1.

Robinson, V. 2003. "Brain Drain to Brain Gain." *Mail & Guardian*, January 22.

Saxenian, A.L. 1999. *Silicon Valley's New Immigrant Entrepreneurs.* San Francisco, CA: Public Policy Institute of California.

9

Promise and Frustration of Diaspora Networks: Lessons from the Network of Colombian Researchers Abroad

Fernando Chaparro, Hernán Jaramillo, and Vladimir Quintero

The Network of Colombian Researchers Abroad (Red Caldas) (was established in 1991 as part of a policy to link Colombian researchers abroad with the Colombian scientific community and with the activities and programs of Colombia's national scientific and technological system. The intent was to strengthen the national research community by benefiting from the participation of Colombian researchers studying and working abroad and to use the scientific diaspora to integrate national research groups into regional and global research- and knowledge-intensive networks. This chapter examines the network's evolution from a single network to a range of specialized research and knowledge networks, an evolution that reflects an important change in the perception of the role scientific diasporas play.

Economic Growth

With 45 million inhabitants, Colombia has the third largest population in Latin America after Brazil and Mexico. Located midway between North and South America, Colombia is the only country in South America with coasts along the Pacific Ocean and the Caribbean Sea and easy access to African, Asian, European, Latin American, and North American markets. Colombia has one of the highest adult literacy rates in Latin America, but the quality of education has suffered in recent years as a result of efforts to extend coverage, and the country faces a major challenge in ensuring the development of the competencies required by the new knowledge-intensive economy.

Colombia has one of the most stable economies in Latin America, with steady economic growth that exceeds the Latin American average. Until the late 1970s, the economy grew at an average rate of 5.0 percent a year. Growth slowed to 3.7 percent a year in the 1980s, still far above the 1.1 percent average for Latin America. Liberalization of the economy in the early 1990s laid the foundation for accelerated economic growth. As a result, between 1993 and 1995, the economy grew at an average rate of 4.7 percent a year. This positive performance was mainly the result of the macroeconomic stability, a longstanding democracy, and a favorable foreign investment policy.

Economic growth declined dramatically in the mid-1990s. Real gross domestic product (GDP) growth fell from 5.2 percent in 1995 to 2.1 percent in 1996 because of a contraction in private sector investment and a slowdown in the growth of private sector consumption. The economy recovered somewhat in 1997, when it grew 3.4 percent.

During 1998, as a result of a sharp increase in domestic interest rates, the effects of poor weather (El Niño) on the agriculture sector, the negative effects of the financial crises in Asia and the Russian Federation, and the significant decline in the international prices of crude oil and other commodities, the Colombian economy suffered a severe slowdown, growing just 0.5 percent. The economy worsened in 1999, contracting 4.5 percent, the deepest recession in Colombian economic history. In 2000, the economy began to rebound, growing 2.9 percent in 2000, 1.5 percent in 2001, 1.8 percent in 2002, 3.9 percent in 2003, and 3.5 percent in 2004. Inflation, as measured by the consumer price index, averaged 17.9 percent a year between 1994 and 1999, falling from 22.6 percent in 1994 to 9.2 percent in 1999 and 6.5 percent in 2003.

Emergence of the Colombian Diaspora

By 1990, 11 million migrants from Latin America and the Caribbean were living outside the region, three-quarters of them in the United States (Pellegrino and Martinez 2001). In some countries, such as Brazil, Colombia, and Peru, almost half of migrants over 25 with some education have tertiary-level training (table 9.1). In other countries such as Mexico, migrants tend to have only a primary or secondary school education.

Colombian migrants to the United States have three more years of schooling than the average Colombian (Gaviria 2004), and their level of education has been increasing. Before 1995, the average migrant had 11.8 years of schooling. That figure rose to 12.6 years in 1996 and 12.8 years in 1998. The average income of the 500,000–700,000 Colombia migrants in the United States is more than twice that of the average resident of Colombia.

The motivations for migrating to the United States have changed in recent decades (Gaviria 2004). From 1965 to 1975, migration was stimulated by the reform of immigration regulations in the United States. From 1975 to 1985, it was fueled by the illicit drug business in Colombia by members of the drug trade moving abroad. From 1985 to 1995, when Colombian migration to the United States stabilized, it was stimulated by a combination of factors, including the growing internal conflict. Since 1995, migration has remained lower than in previous years, and has been fueled by internal conflict and the economic crisis of the second half of the 1990s.

The migration of highly trained people to developed countries because of disparities in job opportunities, research facilities, and income levels poses a serious challenge to developing countries. Some countries consider such migration as a loss of their investment in the emigrants. Others seek to integrate their expatriate

Table 9.1 *Proportion of Migrants from Selected Latin American Countries with Tertiary Education, 2000*

Country	Percentage of migrants with some education who have tertiary-level training
Brazil	54.6
Peru	52.9
Colombia	46.2
Mexico	14.0

Source: Adams 2003.

communities into their scientific and business communities, taking advantage of the expatriates' ability to facilitate access to knowledge through participation in knowledge networks (Pellegrino 2001, 2003; Pellegrino and Martinez 2001; Solimano 2003). An evolution is taking place in which what was once viewed as brain drain is now viewed as an opportunity for brain exchange, brain circulation, and brain gain. This evolution enables scientific and business diasporas to play important roles in the development of their home countries.

Nature, Objectives, and Functions of Red Caldas

Red Caldas was established in 1991 to link young Colombian researchers studying or working in research laboratories abroad into Colombia's scientific community and national research programs. The objective was to strengthen national research capacities and to increase the internationalization of the Colombian scientific community through contacts and collaborative research efforts with research groups in other countries facilitated by Colombian researchers abroad.

The first node was established in Paris. Other nodes rapidly emerged in the main cities of Europe and in North America, where most Colombian researchers work. The Internet and e-mail facilitated interaction between nodes and between nodes and the Colombian Institute for the Development of Science and Technology (COLCIENCIAS), the coordinator of this emerging global network.

The first global symposium of Red Caldas nodes took place in Bogota in 1994. Its purpose was to facilitate interaction between researchers in Colombia and the 874 researchers from the 29 national nodes in 27 countries outside Colombia (table 9.2).

The network was formed at the same time that COLCIENCIAS expanded its graduate training program, greatly increasing the number of Colombian graduate students abroad, especially at the doctoral level (table 9.3). From 1992 to 1997, COLCIENCIAS sent 51–176 graduate students abroad a year, gradually creating a community of almost 850 graduate students at the best universities in the world, most of them at the doctoral level. This community of Colombian graduate students became the backbone of Red Caldas. The years of expansion of this program (1992–97) coincide with the years of strong development of the Red Caldas network.

In 1998, COLCIENCIAS's program almost disappeared and few students were sent abroad until 2002. The national nodes immediately felt the impact of this drastic reduction. The decline in the number of graduate students limited the potential of the few nodes that still exist.

Red Caldas links graduate students and young researchers in the diaspora with the scientific community in Colombia to take advantage of the potential role the

Table 9.2 *Geographical Distribution of National Nodes and Members of Red Caldas, 1994*

Region	Nodes		Members	
	Number	*Percent*	*Number*	*Percent*
Europe	14	48	441	50
Americas	10	35	392	45
Other regions	5	17	4	5
Total	29	100	874	100

Source: Authors.

Table 9.3 Number of Students Sent Abroad by COLCIENCIAS for Graduate Training, 1992–2003

Year	Master's degree	Doctorate	Total
1992	1	54	55
1993	5	84	89
1994	1	50	51
1995	3	118	121
1996	14	112	126
1997	40	136	176
1998	0	0	0
1999	0	0	0
2000	2	6	8
2001	3	6	9
2002	13	125	138
2003	0	73	73
Total	82	764	846

Source: COLCIENCIAS data.

diaspora could play in helping internationalize Colombian science. It includes only a small number of other members of the scientific diaspora, who could play an equally important role.

The main practical objective of the network was to develop collaborative research projects between Colombian research groups and research groups at the universities where Colombian students were studying. The activities of Red Caldas were organized around the following lines of action:

- *Identifying areas of potential scientific cooperation through collaborative research projects between research groups in Colombia and their colleagues abroad.* Collaboration was achieved by organizing workshops or symposiums, either at the general level, such as the first global symposium of national nodes held in 1994, or at the specialized level, such as the 1997 workshop on research on catalytic cracking in oil production, part of a process of formulating a joint research program in this area.
- *Supporting graduate training abroad and facilitating students' return.* Red Caldas complements COLCIENCIAS funds for graduate training, facilitated the return of students and researchers to Colombia, and provided a link between students and researchers who remain abroad and Colombian research groups.
- *Supporting visiting fellows and exchanges of researchers.* Through Red Caldas, COLCIENCIAS supported visits by Colombian researchers abroad or visits by researchers from other countries to Colombia. This exchange of researchers played a strategic role in the development of joint research projects. It also led to collaboration agreements between universities in Colombia and other countries. The exchange of researchers was often cofunded with institutions from those other countries, such as the National Science Foundation in the United States and the German Academic Exchange Service.
- *Engaging in information and dissemination activities.* From the beginning, Red Caldas relied on Internet and e-mail, which were expanding rapidly in the early 1990s. One of the main functions assigned to the network was to

ensure the two-way flow of information (on scientific events, publications, research trends and results, training opportunities, and so forth) between researchers in Colombia and those working abroad. The network developed mailing lists of Colombian researchers abroad. Coordination of this information system was heavily centralized in COLCIENCIAS, one of the main weaknesses of Red Caldas. The true nature of the Internet as a decentralized communication tool was not well understood until the late 1990s, when the evolution toward specialized research networks took place.

- *Tapping into specialized knowledge networks.* Beginning in the late 1990s, Red Caldas recognized that knowledge is increasingly being generated by specialized communities and networks that work in a given area and that access to this knowledge is increasingly dependent on participation in such networks. Red Caldas was placing less emphasis on generating joint research projects, as it had been doing initially, and more emphasis on using the diaspora to access the specialized networks. This requires a much more strategic view of what is happening in science at the global level. It necessitates understanding of main trends, critical advances and breakthroughs and their implications, opportunities being generated for Colombia, and challenges of scientific and technological changes for the Colombian production structure (including their potential negative impacts). This kind of strategic view allows Red Caldas to identify the strategic knowledge networks or communities in which it must participate to be able to harness the potential of science and technology for the development of the country. The first effort to move in this direction was the Hannover 2000 Program, described later.

Organizational Structure

The organizational structure of Red Caldas was simple and flexible. In the first phase (1992–7) it had three components: national nodes, an information and communications system that linked the nodes in a global network, and a central coordinator.

National nodes were created in countries that had a sufficient critical mass of Colombian graduate students and researchers to create a formal or informal association. By 1994, Red Caldas had 29 nodes in 27 countries, with 874 graduate students and researchers affiliated with them (some large countries, such as the United Kingdom and the United States, had more than one node). COLCIENCIAS provided some seed money to support the nodes, allowing them to purchase computers for their secretariats, hire secretaries or assistants, and construct mailing lists of local Colombian researchers. The node secretariats were often located in Colombian embassies. In Brussels, the node included non-Colombian researchers interested in Colombia or in topics related to its development, such as biodiversity and tropical agro-ecosystems. This led other nodes to integrate "Colombianistas" into their activities.

An information and communications system linked the various nodes into a global network, with databases and mailing lists of Colombian researchers facilitating communication. A central coordination group located in COLCIENCIAS managed the information and communications system linking the nodes in the network. It facilitated links with research groups in Colombia, provided information on Colombia, helped organize workshops to formulate collaborative research projects, and provided financial support for projects approved through a peer review system.

This excessive concentration of power in COLCIENCIAS was a major weakness of Red Caldas. Even though the national nodes played an important role, at the global level the network model adopted was too centralized and too heavily based on COLCIENCIAS support and initiatives. At the same time, despite use of the Internet, its nature as a decentralized, Web-based, communication environment was not well understood. The centralized model adopted by Red Caldas proved to be a fatal mistake.

Two important types of networks can be distinguished. The first is the centralized radial network model initially adopted by Red Caldas. The second is the decentralized network model that operated during the second phase, when a gradual shift took place toward specialized research and knowledge networks.

Main Actors

Four main actors played key roles in the development of the Red Caldas: node members, Colombian embassies and consulates, COLCIENCIAS, the National Science and Technology System, and scientific leaders.

Colombian embassies and consulates housed the nodes' secretariats and integrated the network's functions into their responsibilities. For the first time, the Colombian diplomatic service formally adopted science and technology into its regular functions. This laid the basis for the scientific diplomacy program that the Ministry of Foreign Relations and COLCIENCIAS are currently developing.

COLCIENCIAS is the main promoter and funding agency supporting Red Caldas. The researchers and research groups of the National Science and Technology System are the main partners that have developed the collaborative research projects that constitute the lifeblood of Red Caldas, especially during its first phase.

Scientific leaders played an articulating or catalytic (gatekeeper) role. Every initiative and project formulated and developed within the framework of Red Caldas had a key person who played a leading role in establishing contacts, facilitating dialogue among potential partners, organizing project development workshops, and conceiving and orienting the collaborative research project that emerged. When no leader emerged, ideas and possibilities never crystallized into concrete projects or programs. The most successful cases included scientific leaders from both the diaspora and Colombia who worked together.

Main Phases in the Development of Red Caldas

Three phases can be identified in the development of Red Caldas. In the first (1991–7), the national nodes played the central role in developing collaborative research projects. In the second phase (1995–2001), which overlapped with the first, the node structure weakened and specialized research and knowledge networks emerged. During the third phase (2001–4), the network underwent an identity crisis and tried to learn lessons that would help it redirect its efforts.

First Phase, 1991–7

The first phase focused on research partnerships and project development led by the national nodes. In June 1994, COLCIENCIAS organized the first global symposium of national nodes of Red Caldas with the purpose of identifying the main research areas important to Colombia and to research groups in the countries in which the network operated. On the basis of this convergence of interests, working groups were established to formulate joint research projects that brought together researchers in Colombia, Colombian researchers working abroad, and researchers from developed countries interested in the topics. The main results of this symposium were the establishment of a strategic framework for the research program, the formulation of a research agenda, the identification of potential projects to be carried out jointly by researchers in Colombia and abroad, and the identification of specific research groups interested in the topics included in the research agenda.

During the next three years (1994–7), network members formulated and developed projects that could be carried out through research partnerships. Red Caldas did not maintain a registry of such projects, so determining how many projects were successfully formulated and implemented is difficult.

This first phase culminated with the second global symposium of national nodes, organized by COLCIENCIAS in May 1997. That symposium covered three main topics. It reviewed some of the most successful projects implemented between 1994 and 1997, examined the experience of Red Caldas as a new organizational mode that allowed scientific research communities in developing countries to internationalize themselves and to integrate their efforts with global scientific research, and analyzed the factors weakening Red Caldas and eroding its effectiveness. The cases and studies presented at the symposium were published in two books (Charum and Meyer 1998; Meyer and Charum 1998).

Second Phase, 1995–2001

The second phase witnessed a weakening of the node structure and the emergence of the specialized research and knowledge networks. Parallel to the development of Red Caldas, another process was taking place during the 1990s: Colombian researchers and research groups were participating in specialized research and knowledge networks. These networks were being developed in different areas of science and technology with the participation not only of researchers, but also of stakeholders and other end-users of knowledge.

In the second half of the 1990s, two complementary processes took place. The first was a gradual weakening of Red Caldas, which started losing the momentum it had built up in the first half of the decade. The second was the increasing importance of the specialized research and knowledge networks in achieving the objectives that had been established for Red Caldas.

Third Phase, 2001–4

In the third phase, most of the national nodes lost their relevance and started disappearing (exceptions include the nodes in Belgium and Switzerland, which remain active). With the budget constraints COLCIENCIAS confronted in the late 1990s and early 2000s, it discontinued support to the national nodes. Except in Belgium and Switzerland, the nodes had not been "appropriated" by local stakeholders. When support from COLCIENCIAS ended, most of the nodes vanished, because the role they had played and their relevance had not been institutionalized and appropriated by local stakeholders. This is one of the implications of having adopted the centralized radial network model. When a decentralized network model is used, local stakeholders are much more involved because of their greater degree of participation and local ownership.

Equally important was the negative impact of the slashing of the COLCIEN-CIAS graduate training program between 1998 and 2001 (table 9.3). This program started operating again in 2002, albeit at a much lower level of funding. Disruption of the supply of graduate students abroad dealt a heavy blow to Red Caldas, the impact of which was felt two or three years after the program collapsed, when many node leaders started returning to Colombia without being replaced by new graduate students.

Creating Research Partnerships and Tapping Global Knowledge Networks

Red Caldas created partnerships between Colombian scientists in the diaspora and those in Colombia. This section reviews the success of these partnerships during the first two phases of the network's development.

Innovative Research Partnerships Generated by Interaction between National Nodes and Colombian Universities

The first phase of Red Caldas was based on the activities of the national nodes. These nodes were responsible for

- formulating and implementing collaborative research projects,
- promoting collaborative projects between host country universities and Colombian universities to support graduate training programs,
- promoting institutional support projects aimed at strengthening research centers in Colombian universities,
- supporting the exchange of researchers and university professors,
- developing general collaboration agreements between universities and research centers.

Some activities were carried out in research areas considered important to Colombia, identified either at the 1994 symposium or through interaction between Colombian researchers and researchers abroad (boxes 9.1 and 9.2). Chaparro, Jaramillo, and Quintero (2004) analyze other activities developed during the first phase.

Innovative Research Partnerships Generated by Specialized Research and Knowledge Networks

With the gradual weakening of the national nodes in the second half of the 1990s, specialized research networks became much more important. These networks facilitated the internationalization of the Colombian scientific community through research partnerships with advanced research groups in key scientific fields, facilitated access to knowledge in areas related to development challenges in Colombia, assured advanced training, and involved the scientific diaspora in these efforts.

Because food security, rural poverty, and sustainable development feature prominently on the global agenda, agricultural research is one of the most globalized areas

---

Box 9.1 *Finding Solutions to Problems in the Oil Industry: The Catalysis Network*

The Catalysis Network was spearheaded by the Belgian node, together with the French and Spanish nodes, working in collaboration with the Colombian Catalysis Network. The latter network emerged at a 1986 symposium attended by representatives of Colombian universities, the Colombian Oil Research Institute, and the Colombian Oil Company. A Latin American network soon emerged, integrating universities and technological research institutes in Argentina, Brazil, and Mexico. The oil companies were interested in catalysis, because catalytic cracking and hydrotreating can convert heavy crude fractions into light gasoline and fractions that are easier to pump through pipelines.

A group of European universities was working on similar topics with similar applications. National nodes in Europe played a bridge function, putting research groups in Colombia in contact with their counterparts in Europe. These initial contacts led to the Iberoamerican-European Symposium on Catalysis, held in Bogota in 1995, organized by COLCIENCIAS; the Colombian Catalysis Network; and the national nodes of Belgium, France, and Spain. Researchers from the University of Louvain, the Petrochemical Research Institute of Gant, the University of Poitiers, the University of Nottingham, and the Science and Technology for Development Program of Spain participated in the symposium.

The following three main products emerged that provide a good example of the type of program Red Caldas carried out:

- a common research agenda, which served as a unifying platform for the network and was organized around five topics: environmental catalysis, computational catalysis (modeling), catalytic valorization of natural products such as oil palm, catalytic cracking, and hydrotreating of heavy crude fractions;
- a training and exchange program, through which graduate students were sent for advanced training to the University of Louvain in Belgium and the universities of Poitiers and Marseille in France, and an exchange of visiting professors among the participating universities;
- an information system that allowed participants to tap the knowledge of the centers of excellence belonging to the network and in which several Colombian universities participated, including the Industrial University of Santander, the University of Antioquia, the University of Valle, and the National University, as well as Colombian Oil Research Institute and the Colombian Oil Company.

To create a bridge between university research and production requirements, the Colombian Oil Research Institute constructed a pilot plant to scale up and test laboratory results. In addition to various technological results that have been integrated into the oil industries of the participating countries, the network facilitated access to information and knowledge on various topics, not only for researchers, but also for the Colombian Oil Research Institute and the Colombian Oil Company. When specialized knowledge was required for troubleshooting or other problems, the network operated as a source of knowledge and of experts.

---

of scientific research. During the mid-1960s, a network of international research centers was established to carry out research aimed at developing technology for achieving food security, especially for the rural poor, and ensuring sustainable agricultural production systems. This network, which is coordinated by the Consultative Group on International Agricultural Research, is one of the largest undertakings in global science related to development issues. Its first major contribution was the so-called green revolution, which produced new varieties of basic food crops that helped prevent famine in India and other developing countries in the 1960s and

---

Box 9.2 *Monitoring Environmental Quality in Conjunction with Swiss Researchers: The Environmental Impact Analysis Program*

The Environmental Impact Analysis Program emerged from the common research agenda initially developed by a group of Colombian and Swiss institutions. The Swiss node played an important role in facilitating the articulation of this program. The program consisted of seven projects on environmental monitoring and impact assessment, namely:

- monitoring and control of air quality in Sogamoso, Boyacá;
- environmental impact assessment in oil exploration and production;
- measurement and control of atmospheric pollution and the development of impact indicators;
- treatment of toxic contaminants in water used for industry;
- analysis of chemical contaminants in water, air, and soil;
- application of existing technologies for water treatment in small communities;
- use of geographical information systems in environmental impact assessment.

All seven projects were carried out in two regions of Colombia (Boyacá and Huila). Each project combined a common research agenda, implemented through research partnerships with the active participation of local governments and stakeholders; the provision of advanced training in these specialized fields; and an information system to facilitate access to the knowledge and expertise needed to provide support both to the research process and to the environmental management process in local communities. Participants in the program constituted a temporary network, but they also sought to facilitate the participation of program members in other networks related to environmental management and impact assessment, thereby integrating this group into the larger knowledge community working on these topics.

1970s. This was a major technological contribution to addressing the needs of development, but serious questions were raised about the sustainability of the new varieties and of monocrop production systems.

In the 1990s, this global research network was responsible for the main advances in biotechnological research and informatics applied to agricultural production and rural development problems. Its research is carried out through specialized research networks that bring together researchers at international research centers, national agricultural research institutes of developing countries, universities of both developed and developing countries, and stakeholders of agricultural research and production (producers, peasant organizations). Among developing countries, Colombia is the largest investor in this global research network. The Colombian Agricultural Research Corporation and other agricultural research centers in Colombia actively participate in the research networks that have developed in the context of the Consultative Group on International Agricultural Research, such as the Rice Research Network, the Genetic Resources Research Networks, the Agricultural Biotechnology Research Network, and the Participatory Research Network.

In the late 1990s, COLCIENCIAS and the Colombian scientific community led two important initiatives, the establishment of the Regional Fund for Agricultural Research and Technological Development and the Global Forum on Agricultural Research for Development. Both initiatives, one at the regional level and the other at the global level, aim to strengthen both North-South and South-South research partnerships and networks around specific agricultural research and natural resource management problems. These networks bring together agricultural research institutes and universities, as well as nongovernmental organizations and producer organizations (stakeholders), from both developed and developing countries in research partnerships focused on agricultural production and environmental management challenges. Like Red Caldas, they share a common research agenda that constitutes the basic platform that integrates the network, provide advanced training at the graduate and postdoctoral levels, and support an information system closely related to an expert system on specific topics. An additional important characteristic that these specialized networks have is the active participation of stakeholders such as farmers and other end-users of knowledge.

Lessons Learned

Toward the end of the 1990s, Red Caldas lost the momentum it had built up between 1991 and 1997. Many of the national nodes started losing relevance, and most of them disappeared. Although COLCIENCIAS' budget constraints contributed to this process, the following factors also played a role:

- The Internet played a critical role in the development of Red Caldas, but its real nature as a decentralized communications environment was not well understood. The centralized radial network model did not allow effective utilization of the Internet or facilitate dynamic networking. Furthermore, it made the network dependent on the central node's capacity to function properly; when that node was weakened, the system of national nodes collapsed.
- The emphasis of Red Caldas on developing and funding collaborative research projects was both a strength and a weakness. It focused the network on collaborative research, but it also led the network to ignore other important functions the diaspora could play, such as facilitating access to knowledge networks. Little attention was given to innovation networks and industry-based knowledge networks. With few exceptions, most collaborative research projects were university based.
- The opportunity for Red Caldas to become a network of networks, that is, a clearinghouse for the specialized networks, was missed. Taking on this new role could have reinvigorated Red Caldas. In the event, the specialized networks developed largely outside the Red Caldas system.
- The significant cuts in government spending that took place between 1997 and 2000 drastically reduced the capacity of COLENCIAS to support the participation of Colombian research groups in collaborative research projects. Researchers lost interest in Red Caldas once it could not provide funding for their research.

Despite the significant downsizing of Red Caldas, its story offers grounds for cautious optimism. It shows that productive collaboration from within transnational scientific networks is possible, but it also demonstrates the fragility of diaspora scientific networks. Once active leadership ended and the funding of graduate scholarships abroad stopped, the network disintegrated. Thus the story of Red Caldas highlights the tension commonly found between the promising potential of diaspora networks and their constitutional fragility.

References

Adams, R. 2003. "International Migration, Remittances, and the Brain Drain: A Study of 24 Labor Exporting Countries." Policy Research Working Paper 3069, World Bank, Poverty Reduction Group, Washington, DC.

Chaparro, F., H. Jaramillo, and V. Quintero. 2004. "Aprovechamiento de la diáspora e inserción de Colombia en redes globales de conocimiento: El caso de la Red Caldas." World Bank and Universidad del Rosario, Bogota,

Charum, J., and J.-B. Meyer, eds. 1998. *Hacer ciencia en un mundo globalizado: La diáspora científica colombiana en perspectiva.* Bogota: Tercer Mundo Editores and Colombian Institute for the Development of Science and Technology.

Gaviria, A. 2004. "Visa USA: Fortunas y extravíos de los inmigrantes Colombianos en los Estados Unidos." Documento CEDE 2004-17, Universidad de los Andes, Bogota.

Meyer, J.-B., and J. Charum, eds. 1998. *El nuevo nomadismo científico: La perspectiva Latinoamericana.* Bogota: Escuela Superior de Administración Pública.

Pellegrino, A. 2001. "Drenaje o éxodo? Reflexiones sobre la migración calificada." Universidad de la República, Montevideo.

———. 2003. "La migración internacional en América Latina y el Caribe: Tendencias y perfiles de los migrantes." Series on Population and Development 35, Comision Economica para America Latina y Caribe, Santiago.

Pellegrino, A., and J. Martinez. 2001. "Una aproximación al diseño de políticas sobre la migración internacional calificada en América Latina." Series on Population and Development 23, CELADE-FNUA/CEPAL, Santiago.

Solimano, A. 2003. "Globalización y migración internacional: La experiencia latinoamericana." *Revista de la CEPAL* (Santiago) 80.

Part IV
Implications for Policy and Institutional Development

10

A Model Diaspora Network: The Origin and Evolution of Globalscot

Mairi MacRae with Martin Wight

Globalscot is an international business network of Scots and people with an affinity for Scotland, all of whom responded to an invitation from Scotland's first minister (equivalent to prime minister) to contribute to and share in Scotland's economic success. The network is financed and managed by Scottish Enterprise, Scotland's economic development agency, which is accountable to the Scottish Executive (the devolved government for Scotland), from which it receives an annual budget of about £450 million.[1]

The development of globalscot was approved in March 2001 as a response to the challenges set out in Scotland's economic development strategy: *A Smart, Successful Scotland* (Scottish Executive 2001). In early 2005, less than three years after its launch in March 2002, it had developed into a powerful national resource of more than 800 influential businesspeople.

Before globalscot was created, Scotland's diaspora, which includes some of the world's most highly educated and motivated business professionals, was underutilized as a resource for economic development. Globalscot seeks to harness Scottish expertise in leading businesses around the globe and to mobilize that expertise to improve economic conditions in Scotland. In an effort to increase business activity in Scotland, globalscot members offer their time, experience, contacts, knowledge, and skills to businesses and other domestic beneficiaries.

Engaging Diasporas as a Knowledge-Based, Economic Intervention

As one of the first economies to industrialize, Scotland sits firmly within the developed world. Per capita gross domestic product (GDP) is more than $26,000, and more than 80 percent of employment is in the service sector (Scottish Executive 2004b). Scotland nevertheless faces significant development challenges as it seeks to compete with much of the developed and developing world, particularly China and India, in the knowledge-intensive sectors of the world economy. At the heart of the active development of Scotland's diaspora network is the desire to more effectively tap in to the global knowledge flows that will determine Scotland's future competitiveness within targeted sectors.

The political environment provides further context for Scotland's efforts to engage with its diaspora. In 1997, Scotland secured a devolution settlement within

---

[1]Scottish Enterprise has a budget of about £450 million. The annual budget for globalscot is about £300,000.

the United Kingdom that gave Scotland its own parliament for the first time in almost 300 years. Scotland's re-emergence as a distinct political entity has raised its international profile, fueled its desire to inform the world about what it has to offer, and increased its interest in changing both its own and external perceptions of Scotland. Issues of confidence and ambition—for both individuals and the nation—are central to the new government's vision for Scotland. If Scotland's diaspora can be convinced that things have changed and be invited to contribute substantively to further development, who better to communicate this change to the rest of the world.

Repositioning Scotland as a Knowledge Economy

Scotland is a relatively prosperous northern European country of about 5 million people. Like the rest of the United Kingdom, it is currently enjoying a low level of both unemployment and inflation that is unprecedented in the past 30 years. However, Scotland faces a number of significant challenges to its longer-term competitiveness that are set out in its economic development strategy, *A Smart, Successful Scotland.* The strategy focuses on developing an economy that can compete successfully in knowledge-intensive, higher-value activities.

Scotland has key assets in the knowledge economy. About 27 percent of the workforce is qualified to degree level or above (Hepworth and Pickarvance 2004). About 35 percent of employment is in knowledge-intensive sectors, where at least 40 percent of employees are qualified to degree level or above (Hepworth and Pickarvance 2004). The research output of Scotland's universities has global influence: Scotland leads the world in terms of academic papers per capita, with 47 citations per 1,000 population (Universities Scotland 2004).

A Smart, Successful Scotland highlights the major challenges as follows:

- *Raising productivity.* Along with the rest of the United Kingdom, Scotland has a significant and longstanding productivity gap with leading competitor nations. In 2002, GDP per hour worked in Scotland was 76 percent of the U.S. level and only 58 percent of the level enjoyed by the best performer, Norway. Scotland's labor productivity places it in the third quartile of the Organisation for Economic Co-operation and Development (OECD) (Scottish Executive 2004b). Scotland has developed a framework to assess its progress against other OECD economies with the target of joining the top quartile of OECD economies.

- *Spurring entrepreneurship and innovation.* Scotland has relatively low levels of new firm formation. In 2002, about 28 new firms were established per 10,000 adults, far fewer than the 38 established in the United Kingdom as a whole. Moreover, only a small number of Scottish firms become businesses of scale: in 2003, just 5 of *Business Week*'s top 1,000 companies were Scottish. Business growth is hampered by low levels of innovation, with business investment in research and development markedly lower than in other developed economies. In 2001, Scottish businesses spent just 0.65 percent of GDP on research and development, or about a quarter of the spending of countries in the top quartile of the OECD, where spending averaged 2.47 percent (Scottish Executive 2004b). The lack of spending on research and development is surprising given the strength of academic research in Scotland.

- *Increasing labor participation.* Scotland has a well-qualified work force and low levels of unemployment. On measures of adaptability, such as skill development while employed, Scotland also performs well: with 20 percent of employees having received training in the past four weeks, Scotland ranks at the top end of European economies (Scottish Executive 2004b). However, while unemployment is low, a significant number of Scottish adults of working age are economically inactive. In Scotland's largest city, Glasgow, 30 percent of the working-age population does not work (Scottish Executive 2004a). As a result of this pattern and of demographic trends, which project an aging and declining population, the size of the working-age population in Scotland is projected to fall 8 percent by 2028 (Government Relations Office Scotland 2004).

One of Scotland's key strengths is the openness of its economy. The country has a strong track record of attracting investment, and measures of openness such as export sales per employee ($32,450) place Scotland among the top quartile of OECD countries (Scottish Executive 2004b). Harnessing and intensifying this openness is one of the central strategic mechanisms for addressing Scotland's development challenges.

A Smart, Successful Scotland is based on three themes: growing businesses, enhancing learning and skills, and developing and strengthening global connections. The ministerial foreword to the substrategy on global connections notes the importance Scotland places on increasing openness to international influence (Scottish Executive 2001):

> If Scotland is to thrive rather than simply survive in the rapidly evolving, knowledge-driven, global economy, we need to be more fully integrated within it: to be well connected physically, digitally and intellectually with the rest of the world. We need to tell the world about Scotland and tell Scotland about the world. This will enable us to learn from abroad and earn abroad. In improving the flow of products, technologies and ideas in and out of Scotland, the measure of our achievement will be how globally connected we are as a people and as an economy.

The further internationalization of Scotland's business remains a priority. Since the launch of *A Smart, Successful Scotland,* the country has made significant strides in enhancing its physical and digital connections to the world. Between 1999 and 2003, the number of international destinations served by direct air services grew 69 percent. By July 2004, 81 percent of Scottish households had access to broadband. Broadband costs for businesses fell 49 percent between October 2000 and August 2003 (although they remain higher than in competitor countries) (Scottish Executive 2004b).

To move up the economic value chain, Scotland is focusing on attracting knowledge from overseas and helping Scottish knowledge generate value for Scotland abroad. Traditionally, Scotland's focus was on attracting knowledge through inward investment and on generating value abroad through trade. Recently, it has focused on more intensive engagement between Scottish and foreign entities. Scottish companies have built alliances and joint ventures with overseas companies and Scottish universities have partnered with overseas companies on leading-edge research, tapping into the global market for venture capital or technology foresight.

The diaspora is already proving to be a potent asset in building this type of engagement. Moreover, a network is particularly appropriate when the goal is securing insights and connections rather than just leads for foreign direct investment projects or export opportunities.

Another avenue of knowledge transfer being actively pursued by Scotland is the movement of people. The government has launched the high-profile Fresh Talent Initiative, declaring Scotland open to skilled migration. While driven partly by concerns about Scotland's demographic trends, the Fresh Talent Initiative is also responding to the need for new thinking and ideas. As Jack McConnell, Scotland's first minister, put it (Scottish Executive 2004c):

> An economy that attracts and retains its key resource, its human capital, is a healthy economy. It is symptomatic of dynamism and creates a powerful image across the world. Scots leaving to work and study elsewhere and then returning home bring with them experiences, knowledge and skills that ratchet up the strength of the labor market. Likewise, exposure to international ideas and different peoples can have a creative impact on both the economy and local communities.
>
> But I believe that flows of people, particularly skilled and talented people, will be an increasingly important factor in a nation's international competitiveness. Partly for the skills they hold, but most of all for the contribution they can make in building a Scottish culture of ambition.

Although out-migration and in-migration are now in balance, the Scottish psyche still fears brain drain. However, as McConnell's comments suggest, the issue is not the level of brain drain or brain gain, it is about ensuring that Scotland is an integral part of global brain circulation. Scotland's diaspora network may play a part in convincing some Scots in the diaspora that their next move should be back to Scotland, but regardless of their location, their primary value to Scotland is their ability to increase the quantity and quality of global knowledge circulating through Scotland.

Development of Globalscot

The globalscot initiative set out to establish a global network of influential individuals who have an affiliation with Scotland and who can contribute to and share in Scotland's economic success. Work to establish the network began in July 2001, following a six-month research exercise to assess the possibility of creating a Scottish diaspora model focused on the development of Scotland's economy. The following core development objectives were agreed on for an initial three-year development period:

- Build an international network that can contribute to Scotland's economic success.
- Mobilize members to undertake roles that will benefit Scottish Enterprise activity and the economy.
- Maximize opportunities produced by network relationships, knowledge, and expertise.

Globalscot was created as part of a long-term approach to addressing market failures, such as risk aversion and information deficiencies, reflected in low levels of entrepreneurship and confidence. It was designed to address these market failures at the following three levels:

- *Infrastructure.* globalscot provides a means of harnessing untapped expertise and knowledge to create capacity and increase connectedness. It accelerates the processes of creating and implementing solutions by increasing resources and offering vast potential for forging valuable relationships.
- *Operations.* globalscot enables its members to respond to specific and immediate demands from customers. A wide range of businesses and organizations has already benefited from member contributions that allow better exploitation of knowledge, international experience, and global connections.
- *Aspirations.* globalscot represents a bold effort to engage with a global knowledge economy and to invite wide participation in these efforts. It plays an important role in stimulating a networking aptitude, which is critical to establishing ongoing connectivity, lowering risk aversion, and increasing confidence and ambition. Culture changes of this nature take time, yet there are signs that globalscot is increasing the propensity to network globally.

Understanding the distinct levels at which a diaspora-based intervention like globalscot can contribute to a country in economic development terms is important. Perhaps more important is an appreciation that the configuration of these levels is what is most potent in relation to long-term development. globalscot and other diaspora- and network-based interventions represent the explicit development of powerful social capital, a complex of relationships that can accelerate the processes of creating and implementing solutions. Appreciating globalscot as a form of social capital is key.

From the outset, the development of the globalscot network focused on creating value by generating effective relationships with members and other key stakeholders. Broadly speaking, the first two years focused on the supply side by developing an infrastructure to support and engage members. The third and fourth years witnessed continued member engagement with an increasing demand-side focus on enabling Scottish Enterprise teams and customers to take advantage of the globalscot resource.

Each year the emphasis was set against an evolving understanding of the processes of network development, a process in which, over time, the value of individual and collective network relationships increases. The process is not a linear one: individual relationships develop at differing rates and members give and receive value depending on their ability, opportunity, and appetite to engage. Developing a network depends on a combination of infrastructure and activity that supports a diverse membership at different stages (figure 10.1).

Early Lessons

A number of key lessons were learned in the early stages of development of the network that had a significant role in shaping its future development.

Acceptance Rate

The acceptance rate for globalscot invitations has consistently been around 75 percent, an unusually high percentage and, certainly in the early stages of development, much higher than anticipated. As globalscot grows, gaining momentum and credibility, a

Figure 10.1 *The Life Cycle for Developing the Globalscot Infrastructure*

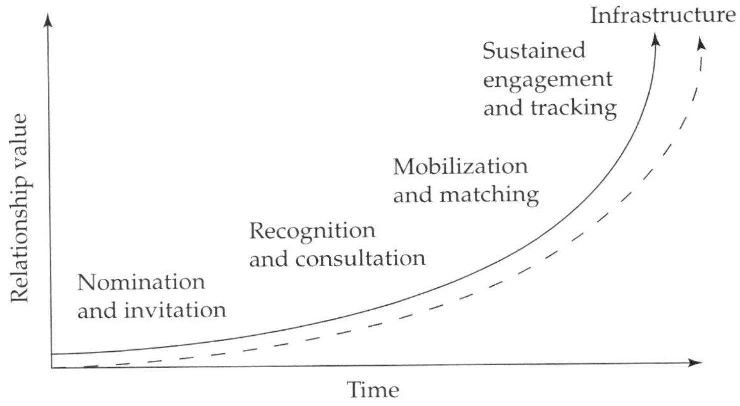

Source: Author.

high acceptance rate is less surprising. However at launch, when an initial group of 300 founding members signed up within three months of invitations being sent to 450 people, there was genuine disbelief at the speed and strength of positive responses.

This can be attributed to a couple of factors. First, the clarity of the proposition to support Scotland's economic development, set against the backdrop of the significant political changes heralded by devolution and Scotland's new parliament, provided a compelling call to action at a time of genuine transformation. Second, invitations coming directly from the first minister gave additional potency to the call to action. Subsequent research on globalscot's development suggests that the recognition of a member's ability to support and shape Scotland's development implicit in the invitation process is itself a status symbol and a significant factor in encouraging a positive response.

Engagement Levels and Expectation Management

The research that fed the design phase of globalscot was clear that the model deployed would be based specifically on Scotland's ambitions to be a knowledge-based economy by making and facilitating inward and outward connections and empowering members and beneficiaries to run with ideas and solutions once connections had been made. The role of Scottish Enterprise as home agency was to make such a model possible through facilitating, connecting, and informing member interactions with the institutional strength and associated investment and infrastructure afforded by Scottish Enterprise.

A critical part of this infrastructure is the system of member support managers (MSMs), local Scottish Development International senior staff, housed in Scottish Enterprise's overseas offices worldwide, who are assigned responsibility for managing relationships with members.[2] MSMs consult with new members, usually

---

[2]Scottish Development International is the international arm and overseas brand of Scottish Enterprise.

face-to-face, to provide an overview of Scotland's current economic situation, challenges, and development priorities. This exercise, which was particularly intensive
during the initial recruitment phase, also allows members to offer their views on
how they might contribute and the extent to which they wish to be engaged.

This process gave rise to the second main lesson. Whereas a brokering model was
strategically anticipated, what was not anticipated was the level of engagement that
the globalscot invitation prompted. The initial design was based on only 10-15 percent of the membership being interested in engaging in tangible projects to support
Scotland's efforts. The majority was assumed to want either to engage infrequently
within sectoral or geographic communities or to play a largely dormant role as recipients of information and occasional connections. Instead most members indicated
that they expected to actively engage, clearly a success story in and of itself, but one
that required Scottish Enterprise to swiftly deliver and scale up the brokering model.

Stimulating Demand and Maintaining Supply

Once a founding membership base of willing "supply" was clearly in place, the key
ingredient for active brokering became a steady stock of requests, and at this point
the process of selling the resource in Scotland began. It became apparent, however,
that whereas members' expectations of being called on were higher than anticipated, "demand" was harder to stimulate.

A number of reasons can be suggested for this. First, the very market failures the
project is designed to address relate in part to low levels of confidence and ambition. These market failures are arguably manifested by a lack of willingness to
engage with an international networking initiative.

Second, data protection legislation and other regulatory concerns required that,
certainly in the early stages, access to the membership was carefully guarded, with
requests channeled through a five-person globalscot team, the MSMs, and a limited
Web infrastructure. Reconfiguring the brokering model to widen access and disin-
termediate in a managed way took time, planning, and—with hindsight—more
caution than was necessary.

Third, a brokering service guarantees only connections that may elicit results.
Gathering and packaging these results in the form of success stories to stimulate
further demand is an important part of ongoing marketing efforts, but is also
resource intensive.

Finally, and somewhat paradoxically, where a strong institutional presence can
ensure the investment and infrastructure to establish a model like globalscot, attract
the membership, and garner momentum, it may also inhibit take-up among beneficiaries if the network is seen as belonging to the agency. Engendering ownership
among members and beneficiaries appears to be critical to the sustainability and
success of a network-based initiative like globalscot, therefore close attention must
be paid to the point and nature of intervention as the network evolves.

Nomination and Invitation: Targeted Membership and a Clear Value Proposition

At the time of writing, globalscot had more than 800 members worldwide, all of
them senior people with strong connections to Scotland and relevant sector skills

in more than 40 countries. The broad specification for membership requires members to

- be influential and active in a key sector, that is, a sector agreed to be a priority for Scotland's economic development;
- have a strong affinity with Scotland;[3]
- be based in a target location, that is, predominantly one in which Scottish Development International has a presence;
- be motivated and able to participate.

As noted earlier, the invitation is issued by the first minister and sets out a clear value proposition for the network, focused on the country's economic development. In line with *A Smart Successful Scotland*, members are nominated (typically by Scottish Development International field staff or existing members) because they are active and influential in sectors central to Scotland's continuing success, such as biotechnology and life sciences, financial services, electronics and new technology, creative industries, and energy. At 48 percent, North America accounts for almost half the members; 25 percent are based in Europe; 12 percent are based in the Asia and Pacific region; and 15 percent are based in Scotland, providing a local link for the internationally-based membership.

Members hold senior positions within organizations, run their own companies, or are in academia. All have international experience at senior levels in business and government and, if effectively engaged, are in a strong position to help drive Scotland forward. Members include

- a general manager for Royal Dutch Shell in the Netherlands,
- the financial director of a software company based in Ireland,
- the chief executive officer of a national bank in Australia,
- an executive director of a major pharmaceutical company based in Tokyo,
- a KPMG partner for China,
- a chief operating officer of venture capitalists developing business in Asia,
- a vice president of Hewlett Packard based in California and Texas,
- the president of a food consulting business in the United States.

Recognition and Consultation: Infrastructure and Serviced Relationships

Upon registration, members are sent a recognition e-mail that provides details of the members' Web site and their MSMs. Both the Web technology and the MSM function are key components of the globalscot "infrastructure," a notion that has been central to the evolution of globalscot.

The Web site (http://www.globalscot.com) provides a central point of information and contact for the network and its members. Online services include diary and calendar facilities, listings of international events, discussion forums, and a

---

[3]Globalscot is not an ethnic network as such; members may have studied or worked in Scotland, thereby developing an affinity and willingness to help. The majority of members are, however, members of the Scottish diaspora.

range of resources pertaining to developments in Scotland. The site also offers a profile center, which provides up-to-date biographies of all globalscots and the ability to develop a range of specialist communities that reflect priorities for members, users, and Scotland. The profile center also allows members to determine their own level of exposure and availability.

Globalscot has a central support team of five staff based in Scottish Enterprise's headquarters in Glasgow, which provides strategic and infrastructural development and is responsible for overall management of the network. From the outset, the core team has worked closely with and depended on its senior overseas colleagues to jointly design and deliver the engagement with members through their role as MSMs. Each globalscot member has a dedicated MSM to work with him or her on the development of mutually valuable relationships. There are approximately 30 MSMs worldwide.

A key part of the MSM function is early consultation with new members to permit the management of mutual expectations in the context of the particular member, the sector, and the location. During the consultation stage, members are strongly encouraged to visit the profile center and provide comprehensive information about their expertise, background, connections, and interests. This information has proved critical to the successful mobilization of members and to matching requests for support with appropriate members.

Moblization and Matching: Facilitated Engagement and Brokered Connections

The network organizes international gatherings and events that allow members to meet and to develop their involvement in different initiatives. The events focus on specific business issues that are relevant to Scotland's development and provide members with opportunities to meet representatives of Scottish companies. The events play an important part in the globalscot agenda, providing a fertile environment for ideas to be developed and an opportunity for members to build on existing business connections or to forge new ones. Feedback from members suggests that events play a critical role in the development of the network and in the ongoing engagement of members.

Events typically support field activities in particular markets and locations. Holding globalscot events as part of the itinerary for field visits by ministers and other senior government officials is now commonplace. Globalscot events also form a central part of outward trade and development activity, as well as being an important forum for shaping and testing the developing propositions that Scotland wishes to offer the global economy with respect to key sectors, for example, life sciences.

The key message from members is "use us—we signed up to help." Events provide an important forum to enable this, provided that they are purposeful and allow members to engage at an appropriate level. More generally, the promotion of requests to globalscot members from Scottish businesses and other beneficiaries has proven the most critical and complex aspect of the mobilization of members. Brokering the supply of member expertise with well-matched requests has demonstrated the current and long-term potential of investing in the development of a diaspora-based network focused on economic development. At the same time, developing globalscot to effectively stimulate demand and facilitate the connections on offer remains the central challenge.

Simple advertising proved ineffective in generating customers at the outset. Thus the core team developed a more proactive program of tailored presentations for Scottish Enterprise teams and their respective beneficiary audiences to generate demand within particular customer groups, for instance, a particular sector or company size. Concurrently, a number of early roles were piloted with the membership by inviting members to sign up to, for example, mentor a company, advise on a sector strategy, or adopt a school. This activity generated a small number of early success stories (box 10.1) that were used to generate further demand; scale up particular roles; and learn important, early lessons about successful matching, for example, the critical importance of having member profiles available for searching, the need for well-crafted requests that ask specific questions, and the necessity for managing expectations appropriately.

Early matching also demonstrated the importance of ownership and the need for disintermediation to allow colleagues across the Scottish Enterprise network to access the globalscot resource and manage requests for member engagement on behalf of their particular customers. In late 2003, the Access Partner Program was unveiled to approximately 90 participants, initially internal Scottish Enterprise staff. This program, which opened up the globalscot infrastructure to allow a wider range of staff and partners to search for and contact members to support their own activities and agendas, now has almost 200 partners.

More than 200 requests for globalscot support were registered in fiscal 2003/4, with almost two-thirds of these seeking assistance for Scottish Enterprise customers (mostly Scottish businesses). Requests typically come from access partners through the central globalscot team and are directed, using a bespoke request system built into the Web infrastructure, to those members and MSMs thought to be the most appropriate. Figure 10.2 shows the distribution of fiscal 2003/4 requests by type.

Sustained Engagement and Tracking: Managing and Measuring Contributions

The engagement and use of globalscot members generates a range of benefits for Scotland, whether for Scottish Enterprise or for others. These benefits are currently tracked as member contributions either direct to customers, where members provide support directly to a business, school, or other organization in Scotland, or in support of Scottish Enterprise's agenda, where the contribution is to Scottish Enterprise as the economic development body.

Contributions are classified as follows:

- supporting business (box 10.2)
  - targeted identification of overseas opportunities
  - advice on market entry and assistance with negotiations
  - access to business contacts, introductions, and knowledge
  - guidance on business strategy
  - advice on business start-up and product and project development
  - mentoring support and advice on company and management development

Box 10.1 *Early Successes*

The following are a few examples of early success stories.

- An investment project was identified through one of the first founding members to respond to the invitation. It has now brought an Internet licensing company to Glasgow, initially employing eight people, which, according to the founder, will quickly become a multimillion pound business.
- An electronic engineering company that designs, tests, and manufactures innovative condition monitoring systems received, within a day of requesting it, a full day's advice on obtaining a license to deal with a large, U.S., blue chip company at a crucial stage of negotiations.
- A specialist training provider to the international oil and gas industry looking for an entry point into the Gulf of Mexico was connected to a globalscot member (the former president of Enterprise Oil in the Gulf of Mexico), who introduced the provider to a number of oil and gas companies in the region, leading to business with several of the companies and a firm foothold in the market.
- A company specializing in the creation of virtual characters for gaming software was able to make valuable connections with a number of globalscots during a trip to California for an exhibition. A nonexecutive director at the company described the contacts as "an absolute bullseye target for the type of business advice needed . . . people you would never dream of trying to reach as there would usually be about a dozen gatekeepers between you" (personal communication with the author).
- A globalscot member who is vice president of production procurement at IBM donated one day a month to working with Scottish Enterprise's electronics team, providing insight into the global electronics sector by advising on new product developments, growing and shrinking markets, and new opportunities.
- A University of Strathclyde spinoff company developing innovative three-dimensional display technology for use in medical imaging and the oil industry requested access to U.S.-based globalscots who could advise on the commercial development of imaging technology. Thirty-two members in the medical imaging sector responded immediately, resulting in valuable relationships that avoided initial consultancy fees and opened doors to commercial entities that would otherwise have been inaccessible.
- A globalscot member who is chief scientist and vice president for research and development for a U.S. biotechnology company located on the West Coast undertook a two-day tour of the Scottish biotechnology sector that directly influenced Scottish Executive's biotechnology strategy. Back in California, he involved other members in the life sciences in an initiative that resulted in a program to develop internships for Scottish life science students in Californian firms.
- A £450-million, 10-year project, Intermediary Technology Institutes Scotland, is intended to encourage and support precompetitive research in key market areas with strong economic and business development potential. Globalscot members were actively involved in the initial consultation process, ensuring that final proposals were specifically targeted to address the particular strengths of the Scottish economy. One member, the president of the University of Maryland's Biotechnology Institute, also delivered a virtual address at the launch of Intermediary Technology Institutes Scotland, observing that "extremely innovative, cross-cutting research is already under way."

Figure 10.2 *Distribution of Requests by Type, Fiscal 2003–2004*

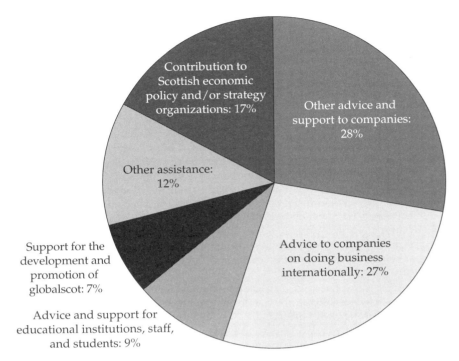

Source: Globalscot records.

- leveraging contacts and expertise (box 10.3)
    - advice on economic development opportunities and strategies
    - intelligence on new global trends, technologies, products, and practices
    - opportunities for Scottish businesses on trade missions and learning journeys to provide a competitive advantage
- raising aspirations (box 10.4)
    - support in schools for enterprise mentoring
    - guidance on improving employability skills
    - provision of placements and employment for Scottish students
    - lecturing at Scottish universities

Some 440 contributions from globalscot members were recorded in fiscal 2003/4, evenly split between internal assistance (furthering Scottish Enterprise's economic agenda) and external assistance (direct to Scottish Enterprise customers). A recent exercise indicated that 60 percent of members had been contacted with a request and that 42 percent had responded. Clearly a minority— was especially active, responding to several requests. Most requests securing responses achieved more than one contribution (several stimulating 10 or more). On average, a request generated 3.8 contributions, with members in the United States averaging 4.8 contributions.

Of the contributions recorded for fiscal 2003/4, 52 percent were in the leveraging contacts and expertise category, 40 percent were in the supporting business category, and 8 percent were in the raising aspirations category. More than 500 contributions were recorded in fiscal 2004/5.

Box 10.2 *Supporting Business*

Members' expertise lends itself naturally to helping companies access new markets and build partnerships in areas critical to their success.

Assisting High-Growth Start-Ups

Several globalscot members are working with Scottish Enterprise's High-Growth Start-Up Unit by providing hands-on support to major start-up projects across Scotland. Nick Price, nonexecutive director of the High-Growth Start-Up Unit company Purple Patch Wireless, requested mentoring and advice on business plans from a number of globalscot members. Purple Patch is the creator of the world's first dual-technology hotspots, enabling fast access to the Internet or to a corporate intranet from a variety of mobile devices without wires. Scottish Enterprise identified a selected group of members for Price to approach, with one helping Purple Patch to negotiate a financing package and introducing the company to a major hotel group to present its product. Thanks to Price's connections, Purple Patch won the right to two pilot deals with the hotel chain and the member became a nonexecutive director of the company, resulting in additional investor interest and investment.

Facilitating Access to Markets

Globalscot members are ideally positioned to help Scottish companies research overseas markets and take their products and services to new international audiences. A&I Accessory is a company specializing in the repair and overhaul of accessory components associated with aerospace, industrial, and marine gas turbines. It needed help reaching potential client companies in the United States. Globalscot facilitated an introduction to David Speirs, then senior vice president of customer support for BAE Systems, Regional Aircraft, Inc. Components and repairs in this sector require Federal Aviation Administration approval. With Speirs' support, A&I Accessory has secured contacts in North America and is being sponsored for accreditation to carry out work for the Federal Aviation Administration. "Getting US accreditation opens your markets dramatically and allows you much more competitive power" (personal communication with the author).

Facilitating Trade Missions and Learning Journeys

Members help facilitate personal introductions to potential business partners, overseas buyers, and agents or distributors for Scottish companies on trade missions to their locations. To date, the globalscot network has assisted trade missions to California, Texas, and Russia. During a recent mission to Houston, 30 members attended a networking dinner for 12 participating Scottish companies. Each member was asked to bring a business colleague who could assist the visiting companies through further introductions.

Future Development: The Role of the Home Organization

Scottish Enterprise, the home organization, has been central to the development and management of the globalscot network and will continue to play a critical role as globalscot evolves. What is as clear as the centrality of Scottish Enterprise's role in the establishment of globalscot is the requirement for that role to evolve with globalscot, adapting to provide more sophisticated infrastructure as the network, and its capacity to support Scotland's development, grows.

The remainder of this chapter concentrates on the main learning points from globalscot's initial development phase and how this learning is shaping the future development of globalscot and the evolving role of Scottish Enterprise as the home organization.

Box 10.3 *Leveraging Contacts and Expertise*

Members are helping drive Scotland's economic development by engaging in consultations, sharing knowledge, and providing leading-edge market intelligence for Scottish Enterprise's industrial and sectoral strategies.

Some of the best examples of globalscot expertise enriching the knowledge base available to Scotland can be found in the contributions of members invited to join Scottish Enterprise's International Advisory Board. The board acts as a strategic forum to help direct Scottish Enterprise's economic growth policies by analyzing Scotland's global development strategies and providing advice to Scottish Enterprise on its landmark projects and initiatives. The caliber of the board members and their proven commitment to Scotland is impressive. They make an important contribution to the thinking of the executive team at Scottish Enterprise and bring a genuine commercial edge to the economic growth policies being developed for Scottish businesses.

Commenting on recent gatherings, Scottish Enterprise's Chief Executive Officer Jack Perry described the International Advisory Board as "quite simply one of the most 'high octane' groups I have had the privilege to sit down with—ever. They take a large chunk out of their working week to come here from all over the world because they believe in giving something back to Scotland" (personal communication with the author). The board now meets every six months, with agendas covering a wide range of topics from the role of higher education in Scotland's economic development to the impact of global market trends on foreign investment. Board members also supply direct strategic and operational assistance to promising Scottish businesses by holding sessions to diagnose problems pertaining to specific companies. Some of the 13 board members include Crawford Beveridge, executive vice president, People and Places, and chief human resources officer, Sun Microsystems, Inc.; Christopher Forbes, Forbes, Inc.; Dennis Gillings, founder and chair, Quintiles Transnational Corporation; Hugh Grant, president and chief executive officer, Monsanto Company; Gordon Hewitt, distinguished professor, International Business and Corporate Strategy, University of Michigan Business School; Robert L. McDowell, corporate vice president, Business Critical Solutions, Microsoft Corporation; Helen Sayles, senior vice president, Human Resources and Administration, Liberty Mutual Group; and Kevin Sneader, principal, McKinsey & Company.

Reviewing Key Learning and Current Challenges

Much of the research on networks and other forms of collaboration highlights difficulties pertaining to development and sustainability that greatly intensify the likelihood of failure or underperformance. Therefore, while the diaspora foundation on which the globalscot network is built provides a strong basis for early engagement of members, appealing to the Scottish diaspora as a unique audience does not, in and of itself, provide the means of engagement. The challenge of supporting the development of one's home country provides a clear and compelling call to action, but without robust infrastructure and an appreciation of the reciprocity required in developing relationships, cannot assume results.

The experience of globalscot has highlighted that effective engagement of members is both the essential challenge and opportunity and requires ongoing attention to be paid to the following:

- The centrality of the relationships with members. This is important for harnessing their expertise and maintaining their interest. The globalscot "resource" can never be assumed and depends on members' ongoing interest in contributing and ability to do so.

> **Box 10.4** *Raising Aspirations*
>
> The globalscot network aims to promote entrepreneurial confidence among Scots of all ages, and many globalscot members are providing Scotland's young learners with some of their insight and experience.
>
> **Support to Schools**
> One initiative works within Scottish secondary schools by connecting globalscot members with Scotland's young learners. Through the program, globalscot members provide pupils with an entrepreneurial role model through a host of activities, including, e-mail mentoring, site visits and guest lectures in schools during trips to Scotland, staff development and management consultancy for principals, and videoconferencing and Web streaming on selected topics. The initiative is driven by globalscot members who want to provide Scotland's young learners with a degree of enterprise mentoring that perhaps is not available to them otherwise. Currently 35 members are serving the program as so-called entrepreneurs in residence.
>
> **Student Placements**
> A group of globalscot members in the East Coast of the United States coordinated student placements for a group of 11 Glasgow University students. The next group will be looking to set up 100 placements. The globalscot team has also received a request for a similar life sciences program in California and will be looking to enlist the support of local members. In addition, some members have organized placements for individual students within their companies.

- The importance of ongoing reciprocity. Ultimately, the network system must create an environment and opportunities that can respond to the motivations and expectations of many diverse players rather than placing the network at the service of one partner, namely, the home organization or whomever is funding and managing the network.
- The ongoing development of a supporting infrastructure (people, process, and technology) that shapes the protocol; enables communications; and guides membership, operations, and decision taking.
- The spreading of ownership. Members who feel a sense of ownership will engage proactively and in doing so will develop the capacity of the network. Similarly, other stakeholders and "users" (staff of Scottish Enterprise and Scottish Development International and of companies and beneficiaries across Scotland) who see globalscot as their resource are the ones who make it work.

These learning points raise three critical issues that are now central to the globalscot network's development strategy:

- how to reorganize to expand ownership in order to realize greater potential and alleviate various frustrations pertaining to not being engaged or used effectively,
- how to increase the flow of business into the network,
- how to track the network's benefits and in so doing direct investment in terms of infrastructure development and the point of intervention.

Reorganizing for Wider Ownership

Figure 10.3 provides a simple view of the ownership challenge that the globalscot network needs to address. It extends the development cycle of globalscot through the

Figure 10.3 *Widening Ownership of the Globalscot Resource*

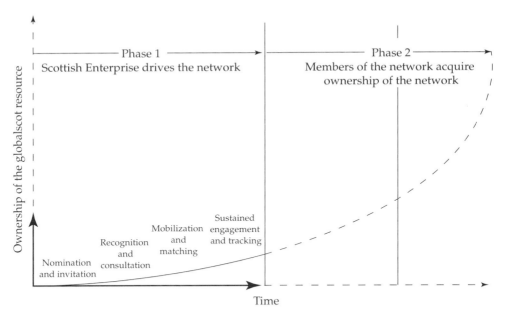

Source: Author.

recognized stages (figure 10.1) to show exponential growth for phase two premised on greater ownership by both members and the wider Scottish community.

The design of globalscot rested on the belief that the network would add value for Scotland by generating value for all participants. This implied that all the players—members, customers, management, and wider stakeholders—would derive benefit from the network's operation and that as its capacity developed over time, the network would deliver a progressively richer variety of benefits. Much of the initial success of globalscot can be attributed to its ability to leverage the wider Scottish Enterprise infrastructure to establish and grow the network. However, as globalscot develops, increasing demands—from Scottish beneficiaries for access to the resource and from members to be more usefully engaged—challenge aspects of Scottish Enterprise's intervention that were initially, and appropriately, deployed to facilitate the setup and early use of the network.

Moving into phase two of development, Scottish Enterprise's focus is on facilitating wider awareness, access, and ownership to ensure that all parties and potential parties can choose to engage with and seek value—as they define it themselves—from the globalscot experience. Overall that implies a different level of partnership where the emphasis shifts from awareness of globalscot as a Scottish Enterprise initiative to wider appreciation of globalscot as a resource for Scotland.

Increasing the Flow of Business into the Network

Managing for deeper and wider ownership is premised on one key issue, namely, demand; that is, the availability of appropriate projects for members to engage with and the access of Scottish beneficiaries to prompt and promote requests for support.

Lack of demand surfaced as a significant issue in the early stages of development of globalscot and has been a consistent complaint over the past two years. It is not, however, a complaint that is as straightforward to deal with as may seem. Mobilizing and matching demand is a complex process that has been exacerbated to some extent, by the very infrastructural elements that have also allowed for the success of the initiative to date.

The MSM role, for example, was essential in the early engagement and mobilization of members, generating and uncovering a high degree of enthusiasm among members. It was this process that established that a willing supply of members were indeed at the disposal of the Scottish development agenda. The process of feeding that supply base with requests for support has not, however, been straightforward and has led to some members' expectations not being met. Having all member engagement delivered through the MSM function is neither feasible nor desirable. Widening the pool of opportunities for members to engage with requires that much demand be the product of more direct engagement with a wider pool of beneficiaries in Scotland, which calls for further disintermediation strategies.

Similarly, the specific agenda (with related targets) that Scottish Enterprise is tasked with delivering provides a comprehensive and clear agenda around which momentum has developed. Much of the successful engagement to date has been around Scottish Enterprise's priority projects and sectors, and more could be done to engage members in Scottish Enterprise's agenda. For example, Scottish Enterprise could enable more proactive member engagement models where members themselves research and manage projects to support investment flows into Scotland, for example. However, much could also be done to widen the globalscot resource to companies and development projects that, while not priority areas for Scottish Enterprise, could benefit from (and in so doing support) globalscot through extension of the existing infrastructure at little or no cost.

The mobilization of demand is therefore inextricably linked with the ownership agenda. Future development in this regard requires paying due attention to development strategies that increase demand by widening ownership and develop the infrastructure to enable interaction between all stakeholders and across different perspectives, as outlined in model 3 (figure 10.4).

Appreciating the Nature of the Intervention and Appropriate Measurement

Networks call for new ways of working and, particularly when employed as economic development tools, new ways of understanding the appropriate point of intervention, ongoing investment, and measurement. In many respects this is the central challenge for Scottish Enterprise's evolving role. As a public agency, Scottish Enterprise faces accountability and transparency challenges and—after the grace period following the setup phase—calls for an accounting of the outputs and the return on investment that globalscot provides.

Here lies the challenge: globalscot was shaped and launched as a working network to create the possibility of opportunities and connections that could be conceived of, but not necessarily expected or assumed. By their nature, networks deliver capacity that in turn delivers outputs. However, a development and measurement focus on output rather than capacity restricts the serendipitous dynamics and knowledge flow that are the lifeblood of a healthy network.

Figure 10.4 *Strategies for Developing the Globalscot Network*

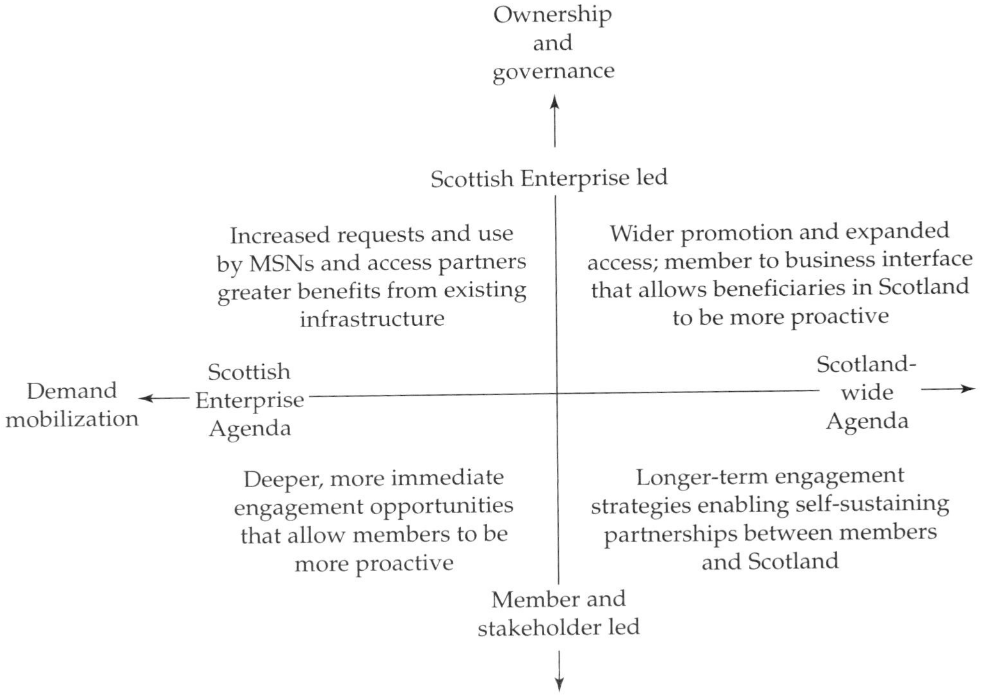

Ownership
and
governance

↑

Scottish Enterprise led

| Increased requests and use by MSNs and access partners greater benefits from existing infrastructure | Wider promotion and expanded access; member to business interface that allows beneficiaries in Scotland to be more proactive |

Demand ←— Scottish Enterprise Agenda ————————— Scotland-wide Agenda —→
mobilization

| Deeper, more immediate engagement opportunities that allow members to be more proactive | Longer-term engagement strategies enabling self-sustaining partnerships between members and Scotland |

Member and
stakeholder led

↓

Source: Author.

Globalscot is a high-value, network of individuals whose motivation to contribute is based on a shared strategic intent, namely, to contribute to the economic betterment of Scotland. Success in this regard offers significant rewards for Scottish Enterprise, but there are also risks. Building globalscot's capacity creates an independent network that will (and as previously noted should) tend to serve an increasingly wide range of stakeholders that extend beyond Scottish Enterprise's agenda. This presents difficulties in monitoring, tracking, and measuring the inputs; the processes; and the outputs of globalscot activity. The more active and effective the network becomes, the less control Scottish Enterprise has and the more difficult detailed measurement becomes.

However, here also lies an opportunity, albeit a complex one. Fundamentally, globalscot seeks to develop Scotland's social capital by strengthening the global network infrastructure that is positively disposed to engage with Scotland's current and future development. A focus on these aspirational and infrastructural dimensions provides a means to put in context the measurement of outcomes while simultaneously introducing notions of engagement levels and creation of social capital as central to understanding the system that allows globalscot to generate and sustain value for Scotland.

Model 4 (figure 10.5) introduces Scottish Enterprise's current thinking on a future performance framework for globalscot where

- members' contributions that enable improved outcomes and add to the capacity of Scottish organizations are recognized as being possible due to an engagement infrastructure;
- infrastructure is accepted as the factor that attracts and facilitates further engagement by enabling members, clients, and other stakeholders to expand the capacity of the network and its outcomes;
- sustainability of the entire "system" is seen to be premised on the generation of social capital.

The premise is that all globalscot transactions, whether they succeed or fail to produce their intended benefits, generate some form of relationship value through norms of trust and reciprocity that may be available for use at a later date. The measurement focus is therefore released from an overemphasis on activity and outcome measures that is in danger of both misrepresenting the nature of the intervention and misguiding further investment. Instead, appreciation and measurement of engagement levels and relationship value (as agreed with and defined by members and other stakeholders) provide context and complement the measurement of

Figure 10.5 *Developing a Measurement Framework for Globalscot*

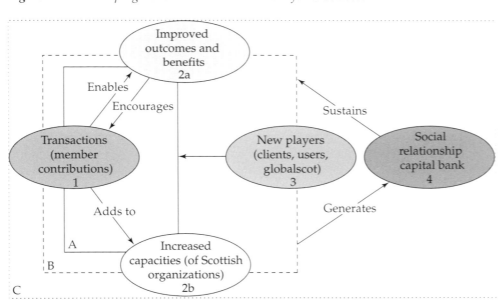

Source: Author.

activity (member contributions) and outcomes, thereby providing a more comprehensive picture of success.

Conclusions

Networks and networking are well documented and recognized as the central means of operation of the knowledge economy. When coupled with the strength of a call to action provided by a diaspora-based value proposition, the opportunity on offer to Scotland through the globalscot network is vast.

The challenge moving forward is to fully embrace the potential of the globalscot network and the inherent implications for the appropriate point of intervention. This will require close attention to the provision of forward infrastructure to ensure that the institutional strength offered by Scottish Enterprise as the home organization remains so, releasing rather than constraining potential activity by working to widen ownership and increase the flow of business.

A strong institutional presence in the form of a home organization has been, in Scotland's experience, a critical factor in the establishment and ongoing development of its diaspora network. Note, however, that institutional strength may become a weakness if the intervention is not carefully reviewed and developed to heighten the opportunities on offer for all stakeholders as effectively as possible.

Scotland's experience can offer two main observations in relation to the development of diaspora-based economic development interventions. First, a clear and credible value proposition built on a country's defined strategy provides a crucial focus that not only enhances the sense of the personal call—what is unique to the ambitions (and history) of the homeland—but also the likelihood of a development model that is suitable for the purpose. Form follows function, and a clear idea of what is being asked of (and promised to) the diaspora, along with an appreciation of the institutional challenge and available resources, is critical to effective functionality.

Second, while specifics of the value proposition and model may vary greatly from country to country, an inevitability of any explicit diaspora-based intervention is that success and sustainability will depend on the development of effective, mutually beneficial relationships and a willingness to see relationships as central from a measurement as well as a management perspective.

References

Government Relations Office Scotland. 2004. *Projected Population of Scotland.* Edinburgh.

Hepworth, Mark, and Lee Pickarvance. 2004. *The Geography of the Scottish Knowledge Economy.* London: Local Futures Group.

Scottish Executive. 2001. *A Smart, Successful Scotland.* Updated in 2004.

———. 2004a. *Annual Scottish Labour Force Survey 2003/04.*

———. 2004b. *Measuring Scotland's Progress Towards a Smart, Successful Scotland.*

———. 2004c. *New Scots: Attracting Fresh Talent to Meet the Challenge of Growth.*

Universities Scotland. 2004. *Top of the Class: Benchmarking Scottish Higher Education.*

11

Leveraging Diasporas of Talent: Toward a New Policy Agenda

Yevgeny Kuznetsov

Members of expatriate communities have three resources that position them to make a unique contribution to the development of their home countries: unusually high motivation to have a significant influence on the course of events in spite of and against all odds; knowledge and expertise of both global opportunities and local particulars; and, frequently, financial resources to act on new opportunities. When these resources combine, usually as a matter of pure luck, the contributions of diasporas can be spectacular, as the experiences of China and India indicate.

In practice, the stakes are even higher. Diasporas can also help establish robust institutions, including key state institutions, as they did in 19th century Palestine. Zionists from Europe wanted to change their "home" country in Palestine. Edmond James de Rothschild, a French Jew, provided these exceptional individuals with funding on humanitarian grounds. This money helped set up a government in exile and initiate gradual colonization and development of Palestine.

The promise of diaspora involvement, as shown throughout this book, is high, and so is the frustration. For every success story from China, India, and Scotland, there are many more stories—from Argentina, Armenia, and Colombia—of diaspora members who have tried to contribute to their home countries but encountered major problems in doing so. Elsewhere diaspora networks have failed to emerge despite the large number of high-skilled migrants who do not even try to get involved with their home countries, for example, those from the Russian Federation and Ukraine. This chapter provides an analytical perspective of policy interventions to help realize the high potential of diasporas and avoid disappointment and failure.

Successful diaspora networks combine the following three main features:

- Networks bring together people with strong intrinsic motivation.
- Members play both direct roles (implementing projects in the home country) and indirect roles (serving as bridges and antennae for the development of projects in the home country).[1]
- Successful initiatives move from discussions on how to get involved with the home country to transactions (tangible outcomes).

Talent and Motivation as Key Resources of a Knowledge-Based Economy

The defining characteristic of a network of expatriate professionals is that it deals with talent: technical, managerial, or creative. Talent is an elusive but powerful

---

[1]By antennae I mean a capability for sensing new windows of opportunity (global technology trends, new projects) and the ability to fit them into local circumstances.

asset. A working definition used in this book is talent as individuals of high impact. That impact can be in science and technology, business, culture, and politics.

Talent is about creativity and new ways of doing things. Hence innovation (not necessarily technical innovation) is at the root of talent. Talent is impossible to measure, but can be seen in unusual personal trajectories. These personal trajectories are all the more unusual when one considers the international migration of talent. Leaving the home country is an act of risk taking, a leap of faith that is impossible to measure objectively.

Innovation—technological and institutional—is at the root of successful development. Expatriate talent could be a key resource for home country development precisely because of its inherent creativity and inventiveness, but something else is involved: motivation. Talented people tend to be characterized not just by high motivation, but, more important, by intrinsic motivation. The ability to achieve results despite many obstacles and against all odds is due to intrinsic motivation. An intrinsically motivated activity is one carried out for its own sake. The activity is an end in itself, not a means to some other end. The factors that motivate a person to pursue an activity for its own sake are usually based on self-identity.[2] When asked why she abandoned the comfort and security of her home to come to a newly formed Israel, Golda Meir responded, paradoxically, that the task was so challenging and huge that "I must be a part of it. Just pure selfishness, I suppose" (Meir quoted in Hirschman 1982). This is a classic example of intrinsic motivation.

Talent and intrinsic motivation are two key factors in the creation of knowledge. To capitalize on talent, knowledge-based economies are designing new organizational forms to make talent the driving force of business enterprises and create conditions to enhance individuals' intrinsic motivation to advance knowledge. Diaspora networks of expatriate talent are one such new organizational form of the emerging global, knowledge-based economy.

However, intrinsic motivation is not the only factor, often not even a central factor, in spurring people to become involved with their home countries. The more traditional external motivation of professional advancement is also crucial. High-profile members of the Indian diaspora took the risk of convincing their U.S. bosses to establish research operations in India because doing so was a smart career move (chapter 4). In general, in the early stage of personal development of expatriate talent, the motivation of professional advancement predominates; this overarching motivation makes a migrant forget where he or she came from. Migrants are usually concerned with getting ahead individually and are not concerned with collective diaspora identity, and those personal ambitions drive the nature of the projects they sponsor at home, which are often limited to unpublicized sporadic and individual efforts. This embryonic stage of diaspora involvement is apparent in many postsocialist countries, such as the Russian Federation and Ukraine.

As migrants advance from lower-paid and lower-skilled jobs, they acquire the confidence needed to think about contributing to the communities of their home countries. Thin search networks for simple job searches evolve first into thick search networks for professional advancement, mentoring, and learning and then into diaspora networks. Whether simple job search, professional advancement, and engagement to

[2]Engagement with diaspora organizations, including involvement with activities to support the home country, can be seen as a tool for preserving national identity. Thus, for instance, pride in Israel after the 1967 war helped shape U.S. Jewish organizations (Freidman 1990)

Table 11.1 *Evolution of Diaspora Engagement with the Home Country*

				Examples	
Stage	*Motivation*	*Type of engagement*	*Organizational structure of diaspora*	*General*	*High-skilled professionals*
Embryonic	Individual success; belonging to the diaspora viewed as a disadvantage	Sporadic, unpublicized involvement; purely commercial projects driven by quick profit motives	Mostly informal and small networks	All countries of the former Soviet Union except Armenia; most African countries	All countries of the former Soviet Union except Armenia; most African countries
Developing	National pride, desire to engage with the home country	Diaspora organizations and the government provide general support but little specific involvement; relatively small start-up costs of engagement	Large and diverse informal networks assisted by a variety of professional diaspora organizations	Pakistan, most Latin American economies	Argentina, Armenia, Chile, India, Republic of Korea, Mexico, South Africa

Source: Author.

contribute to home countries are stages of the process or its functions is an open question. Tentative evidence from Armenian, Indian, and Mexican diaspora networks suggests that skipping stages is difficult and that thinking of a succession of stages is more accurate. The sequencing shown in table 11.1 does not mean, however, that an association of, say, Argentine professionals in the United States should wait decades before designing a meaningful agenda of giving back home or that it should mimic the evolution of other professional associations, such as the Indus Entrepreneurs.

To the extent that motivation to engage with the home country is intrinsic, that is, it comes from inside rather than in response to a set of incentives, insights from psychology can be useful. Maslow's hierarchy of needs argues that people need to satisfy their basic needs before indulging in the luxury of self-actualization (Maslow 1971). Frankl (1962) provides a no less compelling personal account of how self-actualization became a precondition for mere survival. To the extent that diasporas are called upon during critical times of crisis and transition (Israel in the 1940s and 1950s, Armenia in the 1990s, Afghanistan and Iraq today), these issues of commitment and motivation are central to a rapidly growing literature on how to elicit participation by diaspora members. They are rarely discussed, however.

Two Roles of Diasporas: Search Versus Direct Involvement

This volume documents the critical role expatriates have played in accelerating technology exchange and foreign direct investment in China, India, and Israel. Expatriates frequently took on the role of pioneer investors at a time when major capital markets regarded these economies as too risky. Some of these investors were prompted to undertake early-stage participation because of nonfinancial intrinsic motivation and some had access to effective mechanisms for risk mitigation that were not available to other investors.

Today many countries that are also regarded as too risky for mainstream investors have successful expatriate communities. Other countries—in Latin America and the expanded European Union—enjoy significant foreign direct investment, but face the challenge of moving to more knowledge-intensive development. Expatriates from both groups of countries can serve as an entry point into new markets.

Three paradoxes about diaspora networks can be noted. First, when the role of diasporas is most useful, it is most difficult to define (box 11.1).

Second, while the strength and magnitude of the talent abroad is important, the capacity of home country institutions to use talent abroad is critical. Thus Chile, Korea, and Scotland (chapter 10)—countries with strong institutions—use their diasporas well, whereas Argentina and Armenia (chapters 6 and 7) fail to take advantage of their talent despite many programs. A third set of countries (Bosnia and Herzegovina, the Russian Federation, Ukraine) does not yet recognize expatriate talent abroad as an opportunity.

Third, although successful cases of diaspora engagement are relatively rare, when they do occur, it is not usually due to deliberate intervention. In most cases, diasporas and expatriate networks emerge spontaneously. Serendipity seems to be much more important than government interventions.

In explaining these paradoxes, distinguishing between direct contributions, or the engagement of diaspora members in well-defined roles such as investors, consultants, lawyers, philanthropists, or business angels, and indirect contributions, that is,

---

Box 11.1 *Using the Diaspora to Obtain Cutting-Edge Technology in Korea*

The diaspora played a critical role in Korea in the late 1990s, when *chaebols* (highly diversified private sector firms) such as Samsung found themselves unable to obtain key technologies from U.S. multinationals through licensing as they had done for decades. U.S. firms viewed these *chaebols* as too advanced and the technologies too critical to warrant licensing. The Korean government put together an expensive precompetitive-stage consortium to deal with the problem. It largely failed because the *chaebols* did not trust each other and had little experience of working together.

Where a high-intensity government program failed, a light-touch diaspora intervention succeeded. A small network of Koreans working for cutting-edge firms in the United States proved critical in identifying binding constraints and designing ways to obtain and transfer the necessary knowledge. Some of these expatriates returned to Korea to work for the *chaebols,* while others remained in the United States as antennae for expertise, creating a transnational search network. The contribution of these expatriates was neither reverse engineering nor industrial espionage. They helped identify critical constraints, ways to get around them, and relevant technical knowledge in the United States. These expatriates formed a search network. Other institutions—the Korean *chaebols,* the government, and small firms (often spin-offs of the *chaebols*)—acted based on their leads.

---

the search role of the diaspora and its function as bridge, translator, and midwife, is important. In a search role, expatriates open doors and make connections, but someone else still has to do the work. This is why the government and private sector of the home country are so crucial because they, not diaspora members, need to do the work. Diasporas may be crucial in helping formulate innovative projects, but it is up to home country organizations to implement them. However, because those organizations are often weak and rudimentary, diasporas are sometimes expected to compensate for this weakness by substituting for the underdeveloped institutions. This is an understandable expectation, but it is wrong. Diaspora members can complement the activities of home country organizations, and can be instrumental in strengthening home country organizations, but cannot substitute for them.

Diasporas' direct role can include financial contributions, both commercial and noncommercial, and contributions in terms of knowledge transfer (table 11.2). In contrast to diasporas' direct contributions, their indirect role—as members of search networks—is more difficult to define, in part because the variety of possible roles is so extensive. This indirect role is illustrated by globalscot, a successful Scottish search network, and two diaspora networks in the making, one in Chile and one in Mexico.

Globalscot is a highly innovative and successful network of about 850 high-powered Scots from all over the world who use their expertise and influence as antennae, bridges, and springboards to generate projects in Scotland (chapter 10). Taking inspiration from globalscot, Chile is in the process of designing a program called ChileGlobal. The program is housed in Foundation Chile, a premier and highly idiosyncratic organization that designs and finances business innovation projects. As of February 2006, ChileGlobal included about 70 influential Chileans living in Canada, the United States, and Europe. The program is a natural extension of the core business of Foundation Chile, an incubator of search networks. The foundation's management and board of directors see ChileGlobal as yet another search

Table 11.2 *Types of Direct Contributions by Expatriates*

Type of support	*Form of involvement*	*Examples*
Noncommercial financial	Private transfers	Direct remittances to family (Comoros, Somalia); collective remittances to community groups to support development projects (El Salvador, Mexico)
	Philanthropic contributions	Contributions to specific projects (support to universities in Somalia, construction of family houses in Albania and Bangladesh)
Commercial financial	Investment in commercial enterprises	Investments in information technology in India, in communications in Somalia
Provision of critical skills	Provision of political leadership	China (Sun Yat Sen), Baltic countries
	Filling of public sector positions	Actively recruited in Afghanistan; Web sites covering both opportunities and available diaspora members to link supply and demand (Nigeria)
	Filling of private sector positions	Major impact on the information technology sector in India
	General	Ethiopian diaspora skills bank
Knowledge transfer	Documentation of knowledge and experience, especially in the home country language	Publication of books; support for universities, distance learning (Thailand, Turkey)

Source: Adapted by the author from personal communication with David Potten (World Bank).

network, albeit a special one, special because unlike other search networks that the foundation creates it is not linked to any particular project. Rather, ChileGlobal is a means for developing and implementing new technology projects (see chapter 10 for details of how globalscot performs this project development function).

Search networks' ability to help uncover partial solutions that are working is illustrated by the case of Mexico. About 1 million Mexicans with a tertiary education live in the United States, about 400,000 of them in managerial positions. To benefit from the talents of these expatriates, the Mexican Ministry of Science and Technology, with advisory assistance from the World Bank, established the Mexico Talent Abroad Network, a search network similar to globalscot and ChileGlobal.

The project got off to a rocky start. By their nature, search networks are interdisciplinary and interorganizational: they bridge boundaries, identifying new projects by finding previously unnoticed similarities and affinities. Bridge organizations, such as Foundation Chile and Scottish Enterprise, are critical, because they serve as incubators of search networks. Mexico lacks both such an institution and a tradition of meaningful interorganizational communication and joint action. It has no dearth of interministerial councils to coordinate issues, but they tend to be cartels of established interests, that is, arenas in which each agency protects its turf. Moreover, every action in Mexico is mandated from the top, and breakdowns of the corporatist system result in governance paralysis at the federal level.

To proceed, the Mexico Talent Abroad Network required creative day-to-day collaboration between different agencies, which is sometimes difficult in a bureaucratic government setting in which agency pursues its own agenda. A solution to provoke the free flow of ideas found by a high-ranking official of the Ministry of Science and Technology was simple, yet brilliant. He instituted a series of meetings of relevant agencies that were held on Saturdays. The fact that the meetings took place outside the normal work week and, by implication, outside established routines helped initiate meaningful discussion and define a new agenda of concerted action. Management of the program is handled by the Mexican Enterprise Accelerator in San Jose, California, established by the Ministry of Economy. The accelerator also identifies activities to which Mexican talent abroad could contribute. These initiatives show promise of evolving into a Mexican bridge institution similar to Foundation Chile. A humble and small (in terms of its cost to the government) diaspora program is an important organizational innovation that is leading to the development of a postcorporatist governance structure for the country.

Turning Diaspora Networks Into Search Networks: Triggering "Guided" Serendipity

A variety of light-touch interventions can help trigger the creation of diaspora networks and transform them into sophisticated search networks.

Turning "Discussions" into "Transactions": Producing Tangible Outcomes

Diaspora members can be useful to their home countries in two broadly defined modes of involvement: discussions and transactions. Discussions include Web sites, conferences, workshops, online communications, and other activities that help diaspora members get to know one another, connect, and define how they can contribute to the development of their home countries. Transactions involve actions that usually require a time commitment. They can, although they do not have to, also involve monetary contributions.

Diaspora activities are easy to initiate, but difficult to sustain. Enthusiasm about getting involved is enormous and manifests itself in diaspora Web sites, conferences, and other meetings—activities that do not require major commitments of time or money. But initial enthusiasm tends to evaporate as easily as it emerges: people get tired of meetings and discussions alone. The most common mistake in trying to harness a diaspora is to be carried away by discussions without turning them into tangible outcomes. People like to see tangible outcomes, such as the initiation of joint research projects with home country scientists and the provision of assistance to a start-up in the home country so it can find new markets. These tangible activities can be referred to as transactions or projects. Thus a project is a set of discrete activities and outcomes that can be measured. A project can be as small as the visit of a professor to a home country, but does require active commitment in terms of time and money.

Diaspora programs need to elicit commitments from diaspora members. The commitment can come in terms of the time associated with developing a project or the money needed to finance it. A project can be commercial or philanthropic.

Most diaspora initiatives run out of steam, and thus eventually fail, because they fail to transform discussions into projects. Many diaspora initiatives naively assume that initial enthusiasm will spontaneously result in something tangible and that the early enthusiasm will last forever. Too often results are expected quickly; an understandable desire, because demonstrable outcomes are what keeps the process going. Thus a central issue is the long gestation period from initial discussions to commitments, particularly when large commitments are involved. A recommendation is to start with small commitments and small projects, increasing the scale and scope of projects gradually with the accumulation of trust and experience, thereby winning over skeptics who may have had unsatisfactory experiences in the past. Commitments may start with occasional lectures at a home country university or the supervision of a talented student's project and eventually move on to a large research or business project.

Trust and experience build credibility, which must be earned by all participants. Diaspora members may have been involved in activities that started with good intentions, but failed because a key actor (usually the government) was unable to keep its commitments. Once small projects have achieved tangible outcomes, these outcomes can serve as demonstrations that can be celebrated at meetings, conferences, and workshops. Thus the proposed sequence is from small discussions to small transactions and only then to large discussions convened to generate larger transactions. This differs from the usual sequence, which begins with large discussions that gradually devolve into small discussions because of the absence of transactions to focus the participants' energy and maintain the momentum of the process.

Developing diaspora networks is a long process during which the network gradually earns credibility within the diaspora and at home. As the network's credibility strengthens, diaspora members move from negligible contributions ("feel good" engagement) to exploration mode and then to large-scale engagement (table 11.3).

Initiating and Sustaining the Process: The Role of Individual Champions and Institutions

Before the credibility of the network is developed, individual champions initiate the process by investing their own social capital, bringing people together for a cause. One cannot overestimate the role of individuals in mobilizing the diaspora. When little else is available or can be trusted, they are the key institutions. Individual champions make connections, allay skepticism, and propose project ideas. They move the process forward against all odds. Such champions usually combine their commitment as individuals with a high position in a formal hierarchy, using resources and organizational "weight" to initiate the process.

Many diaspora initiatives were unsuccessful because they failed to identify such champions or to ensure that they stayed involved for a sufficiently long time. In the absence of individuals with high personal credibility, little can lend credibility to an insipient diaspora process, particularly because governments begin with little credibility.

While individuals are crucial to initiate the process, home country organizations are what sustain it. The quality of home country organizations appears to be the single most important determinant of diaspora initiatives. Even where diasporas are massive, rich, entrepreneurial, and enthusiastic about getting involved—as in the case of Armenia—they often run up against the binding constraint of home country organizations. This is why Chile and Scotland, with their effective home

Table 11.3 *Synergy between Project Development and Project Implementation in Diaspora Engagement*

Commitment	Level of engagement		
	Negligible	*Relatively small*	*Relatively large*
Low: seed money	"Feel good" philanthropy: small, occasional donations, private transfers	"Let's try it" engagement Self-financed visits to the home country Self-financed participation in diaspora conferences Activism in diaspora organizations Consistent investment of time to develop useful projects Investment in community infrastructure and development of small and medium enterprises through projects based on collective remittances	Development of major projects Mobilization of resources for major research projects Engagement with start-up firms in the home country to help firms enter foreign markets
Large: investments and donations	"Showcase" philanthropy: large and highly visible projects (such as sponsoring local orphanages and schools), private transfers, painting churches	Venture philanthropy and venture investments First-mover projects: development and financing of new types of projects, such as organizing distance learning events to bring cutting-edge knowledge to the home country Venture investments: developing and local financing projects (venture capital networks in China and the Republic of Korea)	Establishment of cutting-edge educational institutions in the home country (business school in India, university in Turkey) Collective diaspora investments (setting up a bank or business incubator in the home country) Return migration of talent (teaching at a local university, setting up a modern hospital)

Source: Author.

country organizations, have had much more success in interactions with their diasporas, even though their diasporas are small and less wealthy than the diasporas of Argentina and Armenia.

Huge variation in the quality and diversity of home country organizations creates a tremendous number of organizational paths for generating credible commitments of diaspora members. In induced development, the government program serves as a trigger; the evolution is from individuals to government organizations to nongovernmental organizations. In spontaneous development, the evolution runs from key individuals outside the government to professional diaspora associations to government organizations, which gradually assume a larger role. Spontaneous development tends to be sufficient in large countries with large diasporas (China and India are two examples), while a more proactive effort is necessary for small countries with small diasporas.

Where home country institutions are weak, donors, who are already engaged with the country despite its institutional weaknesses, can play an important role in mobilizing the diaspora. Using the diaspora as a partner for development provides donors with an additional tool and can be a cost-effective channel through which to provide development assistance, with a considerable upside gain if things turn out well.

Three Generations of Diaspora Debate

The focus of this chapter—the interaction of expatriate talent with countries of origin—has been treated at some length in the literature. The literature on policy interventions to turn brain drain into brain gain for countries of origin has evolved in three distinct generations. The first generation is illustrated by the 1968 debate between Harry Johnson and Don Patinkin in one of the first anthologies on the brain drain (Adams 1968). Both Johnson and Patinkin focused on the physical movement of people; the policy preoccupation was the physical return of migrants to their home countries (for more details, see chapter 2 of this volume and also Bhagwati and Partington 1976). By the 1980s, the debate about brain drain had dissipated and did not receive renewed attention until the 1990s. The sharp increase in skilled emigration from developing countries revived the brain drain debate.

The second generation of literature focuses on networks of professionals organized in diasporas and other forms of brain circulation networks (Brown 2000; Kapur 2001; Saxenian 2000). Partly because the return of expatriate professionals has proved unrealistic, the literature has emphasized leveraging the expertise and capital of expatriate professionals. It is insightful in outlining the potential of expatriate professionals as sources of capital and knowledge, yet in this literature, skilled diasporas tend to fall like manna from heaven. Diasporas and brain circulation networks appear suddenly as a magical solution, allowing home countries to benefit by leveraging the experience of their expatriates. The literature recognizes that much more understanding is needed to uncover the intricacies of the evolution of diaspora networks and their endogenous dynamics. However, because little systematic information on the internal diversity of diasporas is usually available, this subject does not receive proper examination. A hallmark of second-generation programs is the direct role of expatriates as investors, consultants, scientists, and doctors rather than as bridges, mentors, and antennae. This volume's chapters on

Argentina, Colombia, and South Africa describe various attempts to trigger these types of diaspora programs.

A focus on the indirect role of diaspora networks is a hallmark of a third generation of literature that is just emerging and to which this book is expected to contribute. Programs such as globalscot remain as exceptions, but their demonstrated success shows the high potential of this approach. The simultaneous evolution of home country institutions and diasporas is a central thrust of this emerging approach (Saxenian 2005).

Diaspora networks can usefully be compared with alumni networks (personal communication with Lev Freinkman and Richard Devane, September 2003). Both types of networks connect alumni, of a country in one case, of a university in the other; both are institutionalized search networks; and well-run alumni programs generate substantial contributions. As in venture capital networks, financial contributions are important, but they are not all-important: defining a promising project is as important as financing it. Private universities, particularly elite universities in the United States, have perfected the craft of nurturing dispersed alumni. Successful alumni programs at elite institutions can bring in contributions worth 12 times the cost of running a particular program.

The alumni model has considerable relevance for developing countries and the organizations that support them. While all alumni are asked for support, actual support is highly concentrated. For 1 percent of the alumni base, which often includes 100,000 or more members, to provide 90 percent of contributed resources is not unusual. The universities are highly skilled at identifying this group of alumni and maintaining contacts with it through individually crafted programs.

Universities are careful in selecting and cultivating a small core of alumni who form a group of intellectual leaders for the entire alumni community and who can be critically important in successfully mobilizing alumni. This leadership group consists of an exclusive community of the institution's most valuable supporters. Members of the core group, and the alumni as a whole, must have high regard for the alumni leaders' professional achievements. Intensive personal interaction among group members leads to major synergies: through group discussions, members gain better understanding of the needs of their universities. This helps them produce better development proposals and ultimately become more generous in their financial support. Internal competition within the group often increases the average size of members' contributions.

Formation of alumni leadership groups according to these principles could be difficult for many diaspora communities. The leaders of many expatriate associations are volunteers, often political appointees, whose status and resources do not qualify them to be major development partners for governments in the home countries. Most diaspora organizations were created to support the local needs of expatriate communities in their new countries, not to support development of the homeland. Even though their current leaders are not well prepared for such a new agenda, they nevertheless feel entitled to participate in, and dominate, forums about their home country.

The alumni model suggests that governments in home countries should be proactive in creating more selective diaspora leadership groups with more strategic views of home country development. It also suggests that some way must be found to isolate the traditional type of diaspora leaders from leadership meetings without entirely discouraging them. Such upgrading of the diaspora leadership was critical to the formation of the successful Indus Entrepreneurs organization (chapter 4). Charter members of this group had to bring status to, not obtain status from, the group.

Managing an alumni leadership program requires translating benevolence into productive action. Rather than simply hitting alumni up for money, university fund-raisers usually ask them to participate in a vision-building exercise, such as the design of a new direction for the university. In the course of discussing the existing problem and its possible solutions, alumni come to understand the institution's development priorities and to become personally committed to implementing the recommendations that were set up with their participation. Once they become part of the design team, they support the agreed upon recommendations with their resources and influence. Such a participatory process also helps convince major contributors to refrain from pushing individual vanity projects.

Few governments or nongovernmental organizations adopt this approach to diaspora mobilization: expatriate leaders are rarely invited to help design national development programs or support the formation of new strategic partnerships between the government and diaspora leaders. Instead, suboptimal forms of cooperation between home country governments and diasporas dominate. These include traditional, broad, and unfocused government pleas for support, usually for humanitarian relief; intensive political consultations between governments and traditional political leaders of the diasporas; and sporadic attempts by diasporas to rearrange themselves and establish new organizations with a stronger focus on home country developments that usually do not receive adequate support from the government.

The third generation of diaspora programs, in which diaspora networks are viewed as transnational search networks, can be compared with venture capital networks. Diaspora networks are light-touch and informal global equivalents of venture capital networks whose role is to provide seed support for innovation in their home countries. Innovation can be technological, as it has been in India, but institutional innovation is even more important. Venture capital networks combine three ingredients: high-powered motivation, expertise on how to put together and run a project, and access to financing (in the form of equity stakes in a project). A modern view of venture capital downplays its project financing role (to view venture capital as a pool of money is to miss the crucial point that venture capital is first and foremost a search network) while emphasizing its project development role: the pooling of diverse expertise to transform a vague idea into a project that investors can take a gamble on (Avnimelech and Teubal 2004).

Both diaspora and venture capital networks are search networks: both help their members look for new solutions and formalize them in projects. However, the nature of monitoring (the need to stay engaged in the day-to-day management of a project) implies that venture capital networks are neighborhood networks: to stay engaged, they need to be geographically close. By definition, diaspora networks span continents. Members may come from the same neighborhood, but they now probably live on different continents.

Alumni networks of major U.S. universities, venture capital networks, and transnational diaspora networks share many similarities, and all can be referred to as venture search networks. They combine a venture capital perspective on the development and financing of projects with a search network perspective of bridging boundaries, serving as antennae, and mentoring by network members. The following features are common to these networks:

- Members have an equity stake in success or failure. Like venture capitalists, alumni and some diaspora network members provide financial capital. They may also put their reputations and credibility at risk, as in the case of the indirect bridging involvement of the Indian diaspora (chapter 4).
- Nonfinancial tools to develop a project are as important as financial support. Search networks allow a member working on a problem to rapidly identify people or institutions involved in solving a similar or related one.
- Support—financial capital, members' reputations, connections, and knowledge—is provided to meet a well-defined, catalytic objective. It is not provided indefinitely. The objective of support is explicitly catalytic, not to support business as usual.
- Members' intrinsic motivation is enhanced by participation in the network. Networks select individuals who can make projects happen, obstacles and problems notwithstanding.
- Members' extrinsic motivation is enhanced by participation in the network. Members stand to gain from its success.

A tantalizing observation, to be explored in further research, is that venture capital networks, vibrant alumni networks, and transnational diaspora networks seems to be emerging in a given location at a broadly similar pace. The contrast between all three types of networks in the United States and in Europe is striking: the United States pioneered alumni networks, which remain all but nonexistent in Europe; it invented venture capital networks, which remain weak in Europe; and all the third-generation networks of expatriates from China, India, Taiwan (China), and Scotland are led by people residing in the United States.

International Migration of Skills: A Taxonomy of Emerging Policy Agendas

A meaningful analytical model requires understanding the dynamic relationship between country conditions (unfavorable, moderately favorable, and favorable) and the size and sophistication of diasporas of the highly skilled (relatively large and sophisticated versus relatively small and dispersed). Juxtaposing these two classifications yields six analytical cases of diaspora engagement (table 11.4). These categories are, of course, a highly stylized description of reality; in many cases a country's classification is subject to dispute. The main concern is to outline different dynamic trajectories of the interaction of country conditions and diaspora networks. In the best case—favorable growth conditions and large diasporas of talent—a virtuous interaction between country conditions and diaspora networks occurs. In the worst case—unfavorable conditions and weak or dispersed diasporas—such a virtuous cycle of co-evolution is in its infancy or has not yet begun.

Unfavorable Country Conditions, Sophisticated Diaspora: Establish Demonstration Projects

Armenia (chapters 1 and 6) has unfavorable country conditions and a sophisticated diaspora. This is a case where the diaspora holds the most promise and where working with the diaspora results in the most frustration. The promise comes from the wealth and success of the diaspora and its desire to help. The frustration comes from

Table 11.4 *Level of Diaspora Engagement Based on Country Conditions and Characteristics of the Diaspora*

Characteristics of the diaspora	Country conditions		
	Unfavorable	Moderately favorable	Favorable
Relatively large, mature, and well organized (sophisticated diaspora networks)			
Role of expatriates	Antennae and role models	Launching pad to move to knowledge-intensive value chains	Key resource in transition to knowledge-based economies
Activities	Engage diaspora in dialogue about reform and engineer visible demonstration projects	Form brain circulation networks; encourage return migration	Encourage return migration; form sophisticated brain circulation networks
Country examples	Armenia, Bangladesh, Sri Lanka	El Salvador, India, Vietnam	China, Korea, Rep. of, Taiwan (China)
Relatively disengaged (emerging diaspora networks)			
Role of expatriates	Antennae and role models	Gradual engagement	Entry point to knowledge-intensive growth
Activities	Engage diaspora in dialogue about reform and engineer visible demonstration projects	Create expatriate networks; initiate activities to encourage return of talent	Establish brain circulation networks; encourage return migration
Country examples	Colombia, Comoros, Nigeria, Russian Federation, Ukraine	Brazil, Mexico, and other Latin American countries; Pakistan; South Africa; some transition economies	Croatia, Chile, Hungary, Slovenia, smaller Asian tigers (Malaysia, Thailand)

Source: Author.

unfavorable country conditions: Armenia's weak investment climate and protective government preclude quick results and create conditions for disappointment.

A recommendation in this case is to make the diaspora a search network first and only later engage its members in a direct role as investors, philanthropists, and providers of knowledge and expertise. The commitment of time and financial resources is relatively small. The search network role involves designing realistic projects that country stakeholders and diaspora members can implement together, and successful projects can serve as demonstration cases. Unfavorable country conditions mean that demonstration cases are exceptions from the general rule, which is what makes such projects so valuable. For instance, diaspora members in the United States spent much time to attract the Marriot Corporation, the first and only international chain hotel in Armenia. While Marriott's investment in Armenia was relatively small, it was an important signal that a company can do business in the country.

Unfavorable Country Conditions, Dispersed Diaspora: Focus on Individuals and Engagement in Broad Policy Dialogue

Many countries (most African countries, the former Soviet republics, and smaller Latin American countries) have both unfavorable country conditions and dispersed diasporas. All the recommendations for the previous case apply, but the focus needs to be on individuals, because organized networks are generally nonexistent. Expatriates from new diasporas often focus more on individual advancement than on re-engaging with their home countries. Rather than focusing on diaspora organizations, efforts should therefore center on individuals who have already achieved professional success and are interested in sharing their status and credibility with their home countries. Such individuals can then be engaged in discussions of policy reform and vision-building exercises in their home countries and serve as advisers to top government officials.

Moderately Favorable Country Conditions, Sophisticated Diaspora: Use the Diaspora as a Launching Pad to Move to Knowledge-Intensive Value Chains

In countries with moderately favorable conditions, growth is under way, but serious binding constraints remain. In these situations, the impact of the diaspora is greatest. Expatriates do not start projects from scratch, but rather connect emerging domestic success stories with relevant niches in the global economy. The software and knowledge-process outsourcing story in India (chapter 4) is the best-documented case of this kind of impact. Other countries in this category, such as El Salvador and Vietnam, can learn much from India's experience.

Moderately Favorable Country Conditions, Dispersed Diaspora: Engage Gradually

The potential impact of the diaspora is great in countries with moderately favorable conditions, such as Argentina (chapter 7), Brazil, Mexico, and South Africa (chapter 8), but realizing that potential has been a source of frustration. The best strategy is to focus on diaspora networks as search networks and on engineering success stories to generate credibility. In these countries, the return of expatriate talent is also on the agenda, although it is clearly an exception rather than the rule. One hypothesis for this put forward for Brazil (De Ferranti 2003) is that these countries experienced too little brain drain. Brazil's innovation system is too self-contained, thus the international exchange of graduate students and engineers is insufficient. To reduce the relative isolation of its national innovation system, Brazil would benefit from greater mobility of its professionals, scientists, and engineers. Broader and deeper human capital mobility needs to be accompanied by the creation of agile brain circulation networks. In this category of countries, Mexico presents a special case, because its diaspora of professionals is growing rapidly as a result of the North American Free Trade Agreement.

Favorable Country Conditions, Sophisticated Diaspora: Use Diaspora Networks as a Key Resource for Transition to a Knowledge-Based Economy

This ideal case—exemplified by China, Ireland, Israel, Korea, Taiwan (China), and the United Kingdom—is characterized by vibrant brain circulation networks and a massive return of talent. This is the case in which country conditions and diasporas are co-evolving in a virtuous cycle. This virtuous cycle is characterized by a synergy between the search role of diasporas and their direct involvement in home countries: project development and project implementation appear to be two sides of the same coin. Scotland's globalscot program (chapter 10) is a model program for leveraging diasporas of highly skilled professionals. This volume also touches on China and Israel (chapters 1 and 3).

Favorable Country Conditions, Dispersed Diaspora: Employ the Diaspora as an Entry Point to Knowledge-Intensive Growth

Countries in this category are growing and prospering, but many are in transition from reliance on natural resources (Chile) or labor-intensive foreign direct investment (Hungary) to more knowledge-based growth. Expatriates can become important antennae and entry points into knowledge-intensive ventures and initiatives. The main policy message in this category is that leveraging diaspora networks is not a numbers game. Small diaspora networks can have a large impact by bringing new agendas to home countries (see the Ramón García story in chapter 1). Strong institutions in countries like Chile allow policy makers to take concerted action to mobilize and effectively leverage influential expatriates abroad.

Conclusions

The policy agenda summarized in this chapter and discussed throughout the book is both ambitious and humble. It is ambitiously optimistic, because it suggests an opportunity, at least for middle-income economies, for a win-win situation: an evolving virtuous cycle of co-development of migrant human capital and home country institutions. It is humble, however, in recognizing the intricacies of policy solutions that could make this happen. As noted earlier, the creation of a robust diaspora network as a search network requires a substantial amount of time, patience, and institutional capabilities. Above all, good expatriate networks—like any search networks—tend to generate opportunities and projects, but someone else has to act on those opportunities and finance the projects. The capabilities of government and private sector stakeholders remain the key: diaspora networks are no panacea.

On an ambitious note, this volume contributes to a discussion on so-called new industrial policy, a set of interventions that is distinct from the "old" functional and horizontal industrial policy of the 1980s and 1990s, yet is capable of avoiding familiar pitfalls of picking winners and is becoming a subject of policy debate and experimentation. As the example of Mexico highlighted, well-designed diaspora programs can contribute both to the creation of new public sector and new industrial policy. Their significance therefore extends beyond the narrowly defined issues of international mobility of talent.

References

Adams, Walter, ed. 1968. *The Brain Drain.* New York: Macmillan.

Avnimelech, G., and M. Teubal. 2004. "From Direct Government Support of Innovative SMEs to Targeting Venture Capital, Private Equity, and Innovation Clusters." Hebrew University, Jerusalem.

Bhagwati, J., and M. Partington. 1976. *Taxing the Brain Drain: A Proposal.* Amsterdam: North Holland.

Brown, Mercy. 2000. "Using the Intellectual Diaspora to Reverse the Brain Drain: Some Useful Examples." University of Cape Town, Cape Town, South Africa. http://sansa.nrf.ac.za/interface/Publications.htm.

De Ferranti, David. 2003. "Closing the Gap in Education and Technology." World Bank, Latin American Region, Washington, DC.

Frankl, Viktor. 1962. *Man's Search for Meaning: An Introduction to Logotherapy.* Boston: Beacon Press.

Friedman, T. 1990. *From Beirut to Jerusalem.* New York: Anchor Books.

Hirschman, Albert. 1982. Shifting *Involvements: Private Interest and Public Action.* Princeton, NJ: Princeton University Press.

Kapur, Devesh. 2001. "Diasporas and Technology Transfer." *Journal of Human Development* 2 (2): 265–86.

Maslow, A. H. 1971. *The Farther Reaches of Human Nature.* New York: Penguin Compass.

Saxenian, Anna Lee. 2000. "The Bangalore Boom: From Brain Drain to Brain Circulation?" In *Bridging the Digital Divide: Lessons from India,* ed. K. Kennistan and D. Kumar. Bangalore, India: National Institute of Advanced Study.

———. 2005. "The International Mobility of Entrepreneurs and Regional Upgrading in India and China." Paper prepared for the Economic Commission for Latin America and the Caribbean and World Institute for Development Economics Research project on international mobility of talent, Santiago.